The Magazine Maze

The Magazine Maze

A PREJUDICED PERSPECTIVE BY

Herbert R. Mayes

DOUBLEDAY & COMPANY, INC.

Garden City, New York : 1980

Library of Congress Catalog Card Number: 79-8028
ISBN: 0-385-15322-8
Copyright © 1980 by Herbert R. Mayes
All Rights Reserved
Printed in the United States of America
First Edition

For the family

1

There wasn't any uncertainty about it, I never wanted to be anything but an editor. From the time, that is, when I thought of being anything at all, which is a fair way back.

Originally, of course, I wasn't thinking in terms of magazines, weekly or monthly, kind or character. Just being an editor, reading a lot, talking with people who wrote stories, seemed a nice prospect. Cozy, with fireplaces to sit by, and babbling brooks. In the appropriate seasons, naturally.

The day came—it had to come or there wouldn't be much of anything to set down here—when I found myself an editor. Of magazines. The first skimpy, flat-chested; the last very fat, with revenue and circulation way up there in the millions. My mother, seeking to impress friends with her son's success, could prove it. "He got me a pass," she boasted, "to the Radio City Music Hall." In the good old Roxy days.

In time, trying to sound nonchalant, I could mention that Willa Cather and Rebecca West were among my friends, along with Glenway Wescott, Vincent Sheean, and William Faulkner; and I could claim I published Somerset Maugham, John Marquand, and Sinclair Lewis. It goes without saying that every other editor in the field could make the same claim, and has already done so. Now it's my turn.

Some of us are born with a card sense, or a sense of style. Some are natural-born athletes, or mathematical geniuses or politicians. I was—no contrary suspicion entered my mind—a natural-born editor.

Whatever should be inherited to make one, there was none of it in the family background. My parents were native New Yorkers of average and unvarying normality. Until the ninth decade of her life, when blindness came on, my mother's preoccupation was with books. She was as indifferent a cook as housekeeper, couldn't sew a straight seam and didn't care. Such hopes and longings as she had were satisfied by the printed word, and it made no difference which books she read, or about what. She was simply an omnivorous reader (she pronounced it *ob-nivorous*), seemed to remember little, and wasn't bothered. Reading passed time and was more pleasurable than knitting, or darning socks. Though she declared novels by F. Marion Crawford and Robert W. Chambers her favorites, she would persevere with something like *The Light That Failed* that might happen to be at hand, sure that Maisie would learn to love Dick Heldar as he loved Maisie. According to her, every book ought to have a happy ending. My father was quoted as saying that if he transferred her bookmark from one volume to another she might be puzzled for a moment, then go right on, undisturbed that characters had changed names, manner of speech, sometimes color, and that sometimes they were suddenly in Paris instead of Constantinople (it *was* Constantinople once upon a time), where they had been in another book. Once, when she burrowed through *Joseph in Egypt,* I asked her opinion of it. "It's all about Joseph in Egypt," she shrugged. Ever so much later, when I relayed her comment to Thomas Mann, assuming he would be amused, he said drily, "It is." It is, indeed. So is *Alice in Wonderland* all about Alice. In Wonderland. Somehow, from Mann, I expected more.

My father in his small life was proprietor of haberdashery shops, all failures. His ambition had been to be an artist, but he could neither draw nor paint well. But somewhere out of the genealogical background came a legend, apocryphal, never confirmed, that a somewhat esteemed German artist named Paul Meyerheim had been my father's second, third, or even more distant cousin, and that Rosa Bonheur was my mother's great-aunt. Rosa Bonheur's father's first name was Raymond, which is my middle name, but that's not much on which I could lay claim to an inherited talent for editing. Nevertheless, I have always looked at "The Horse Fair" in the Metropolitan Museum with the feeling that it and I were just a little bit related.

2

Editors are immortal. Only authors are immortal for a shorter time. I remember when I believed the name of Hendrik Willem van Loon would be known to readers far beyond the twentieth century. Van Loon was a man who could talk of the triangular plateau of Deccan below the Ganges Valley and describe the types of vegetables there as though he personally had grown them for you; who could reveal the size and shape and furnishings of the Painters' Guild of Delft as though he had been a painter there himself, when Vermeer was. When I went into a Madison Avenue bookshop recently to buy for a friend a copy of van Loon's *Rembrandt,* the young clerk said, "I think we have Kenneth Clark's—but van Loon? Is it something new, do you have the name right?"

No matter what van Loon said, true or false, or wrote, true or false (he improvised a bit as he went along), he had one's attention. "Excess modesty is becoming only in a person with nothing to be immodest about," he would say. I wasn't sure—was often unsure—whether what he was saying was original or a quote from Emerson, Montaigne, or perhaps the Pentateuch. "Man is a manimal," he said. Mammal? No, it was three syllables, distinctly enunciated: manimal. He could be deliberately inaccurate. He was always entertaining. I thought, obviously wrongly, that his books would last. They're around, but not much called for. Once he was one of the most popular authors in America.

He was a raconteur. Perfect host, perfect guest. Constantly performing. A man of parts; so many that he ended up being physically big; so broad he could sport a vest with a pocket large enough to hold pens and brushes and a small box of paints. He was forever sketching little pictures —he did them well—of people and buildings and objects around him.

He fancied himself a chef. One night in his Greenwich Village apartment he kept preparing dinner while we talked of a feature—"The Story of Food"—we'd had in mind. I was impatient for it to be done, had tried more than once to elicit a deadline. "Don't worry, you'll get it in time," he said now. Well, how much time? Perhaps three months, he said, after thinking it over and sampling a sauce, and I said it sounded like an eternity. I moved away from the kitchen door. He followed, and brought a spoonful of the sauce for Jimmie, his wife, to taste. "Too much salt," she said. "Not enough," he said, and turned back to me. "How would you describe eternity?" he asked, as though I'd had some experience with it. Jimmie gave me a look that said don't pay any attention or we'll never get anything to eat. But I walked back to the kitchen, and out of some half-remembered and totally wrong reference, I began, "Add all the particles of sand in the sea, and all the drops of rain that have ever fallen—" "You're not even close," my host interrupted, "but in any case there's a good definition in the *Story of Mankind*. I drew you a picture of a tortoise." It was not in that book, I explained, but in the *Geography* he had sent me. "Well, I'll make amends," van Loon said, and did, though I had long before already acquired a copy for myself. I quote from memory the words of the opening paragraph:

High up in the North, in the land called Svithjod, there stands a rock. It is a hundred miles high and a hundred miles wide. Once every thousand years a little bird comes to the rock to sharpen its beak.

When the rock shall thus have been worn away, one
day of eternity will have gone by.

That's the kind of mind and imagination the man had.

Out of perverseness I once asked van Loon what kind
of bird came to the rock—maybe a vulture? He was an-
noyed. "A *little* bird," he said, "a sparrow. A house sparrow, from Asia."

I knew he was faking, but later I looked it up. There *is*
a house sparrow native to Asia.

Why he found books easy to write, van Loon said,
was because he outlined his chapters in advance, great detail included, everything in chronological order. "The
trick," he said, "is to stick to chronology."

It may be a good trick, but not for here. I came along
hand in hand with the last year of the nineteenth century,
when William McKinley was President. If I stuck with
chronology this book wouldn't be finished until the century
bowed itself out. I don't think anybody can wait that long.

So in a very few minutes I'll be finished with childhood.
The first one.

When I was four, the family moved from New York,
where I'd been born, to Poughkeepsie, called the Queen
City of the Hudson, though nobody could figure out why.
The rooms we lived in probably were adequate, though
there was no indoor facility, as people used to call it. There
were white porcelain receptacles under the beds for night
emergencies. I remember them well, with no affection.

Kindergarten, begun in the red-brick schoolhouse (was
there any other kind?) on Cannon Street, wasn't much. We
made pinwheels. I'd made them before. Everybody had.
We were given crayons to smear ourselves with; and strips
of paper and sticky white paste for making paper chains.
Baby stuff, boring, for *infants*. Miss Dennison, the teacher,
once escorted the class to a blacksmith shop where the
smith hammered horseshoe nails into rings for us. Not very

thrilling. On Arbor Day schools closed early and all the children trudged to Eastman Park to plant trees, which meant we stood around and watched the park attendants plant trees. Each year in June there was a regatta on the Hudson. Everyone went to the river to cheer the crews. I have no idea why, but I always wanted Syracuse to win. More than twenty years later I was in Syracuse for a week, including the day Sacco and Vanzetti were executed in Charlestown, Massachusetts. I had wanted *them* to win.

In Poughkeepsie was the factory that made Smith Brothers cough drops from a concoction resembling tar and licorice. The cough drops emerged a nasty grayish black and were packaged in a white box with pictures on it of the two black-bearded Smith brothers, who were known as Trade and Mark because that was what was printed under their pictures.

After three years, because my father became ill, we returned to New York. My Alma Mater was PS 5. Following three months of Townsend Harris High, I had to go to work. My father had died. It was my first traumatic experience; not my father's death, but having to leave school. Leaving school meant I might never be an editor. How could one get to be, without adequate education?

Is possible.

A play is easier to follow if the program lists the cast of characters. This book may require a cast of magazines. I mean those in whose life I played some part. I should first mention *Good Housekeeping* because with it I served my longest stretch. After that, *McCall's*. For a shorter, earlier period, *Pictorial Review*. In between, on and off, *Town & Country, Cosmopolitan,* sometimes several of them simultaneously. And trade papers. One way or another I suppose they will fall into place.

3

Like other editors who for an extended period have survived the perils of the magazine trade, I have been recipient of a fair share of awards—medals, plaques, parchments, statuettes—from publishing organizations, universities, associations. Any editor around long enough would have to lock himself away in order to avoid having medals pinned on him. One might be surprised to learn how many medals go begging, how deep organizations have to dig sometimes to come up with a name to give a medal *to*.

There never has been an award for making the most horrendous editorial mistake of all time; if available—no contest; I would have won it hands down. In 1935, while I was editor of *Pictorial Review*, an associate—Welmer Pessels—described with trembling voice and dancing eyes the virtues of a novel she had just finished reading. The manuscript, of which she had a purloined copy, was not being offered for magazine serialization, she explained, but through a close friend of hers in the Macmillan Company knew it could be acquired if we made the decision within a week. I had to read it immediately, she said, I would love it, I would insist on having it. It was, she went on, swift-flowing narration, a story teeming with memorable characters and unforgettable action.

I had other things to do at the moment. "Write me a nice synopsis," I said.

"A period novel!" I derided later. "About the Civil

War! Who needs the Civil War now—who *cares?*" So, as things turned out, whether I cared or not didn't bother Margaret Mitchell at all. She won everybody's heart. She sold a zillion copies. She made a billion dollars. She got the Pulitzer Prize.

Not for me to worry, however, because whenever I brooded about it I remembered that Hemingway's "Fifty Grand" had been turned down by half a dozen magazines before being accepted by the *Atlantic Monthly*. It is true, hundreds of literary gems have gone not merely unsung originally but in fact were originally rejected. Hundreds? Can I name a couple offhand? Well, Max Beerbohm's *Zuleika Dobson*. Fitzgerald's *This Side of Paradise*.

All editors have a blind spot now and then. But how could one who calls himself a born editor not have recognized the appeal of *Gone With the Wind?* How often have I said to myself, *How?* The remarkable thing, I suppose, is that it happens infrequently. But in my case there was no reason it should have happened at all. I hadn't read the manuscript, but the synopsis was more than adequate.

Miss Pessels was cool to me after that. She left me and got another job.

In one sense, mention of *Pictorial Review* should come last. I stayed longer with *McCall's*. Very much longer with *Good Housekeeping*. I have been an editor for more than half a century. More than thirty of the years in the Hearst organization.

Van Loon to the contrary notwithstanding, I am not likely to proceed in a straight line from here to there and on to the end of the line. So far I haven't even gotten to the beginning! In this recording of a personal meandering, not all people and events can be expected to be in their apposite places. They will be showing up sporadically, as they come back to me. Haphazardly.

The name of Margaret Cousins could appear here, this instant. It could appear at any time, on any page, and never be out of place. In 1936, at my invitation, Miss Cousins came from her home in Texas to join me in magazine work. Then, wherever I went, she went. Of all the associates I ever had, she was my closest. For twenty-five years I had in her at my side the staunchest ally, adjutant, colleague, teammate, and comforter. Where I needed strength, she advanced it. When I was attacked from any source and for any reason, she was ready to claw, chew up, and rend limb from limb for me. When I was downcast, she substituted her spirit for my lack of it. She was my right arm, and my left. There was no understudy for her. There couldn't be. She was irreplaceable.

Editorially, there was nothing Miss Cousins couldn't and didn't do. She could have been editor-in-chief of any magazine. When I had the opportunity to make her one, I didn't, convinced the political stresses she despised would depress her. She should have had the chance. I disappointed her. And, in the end, myself also.

We were an ideal combination, the perfect partnership. "I can no more get along without you than I could live without oxygen," Maggie once wrote. "You have given me courage, confidence, challenge, love, freedom, and the enduring sense of never being alone. I have always been grateful to have been born in your time."

After she had gone, Maggie Cousins wrote another note: "The day will never come as long as I am alive when I won't come running if you need me."

I have always needed her.

I needed a special man in my life, too: Norton Simon, who was born in Portland, Oregon, in 1907. Fifty years were to pass before I met him. He was worth waiting for. Together, sort of overnight, we made a kind of publishing history.

4

There's not likely to be any mistake about it—my line is editing. I took to it with what could be called fanaticism. Being an editor, it seemed to me, separated the men from the boys, made one very special, invested one with power—maybe only a wisp of it, maybe transient, but usable. With it came opportunity to do some good. It could be made to matter that one had been born.

To be in charge of *American Shipper, Hardware Retailer, Appraisal Journal,* of *Foreign Affairs* or *Scientific American*—in whatever field, the editor has authority and influence. I think other people are special, too—this to show I am not narrow-minded—like doctors, lawyers, explorers, businessmen. All of them have authority and influence, many of them more authority and influence than an editor.

What the editor has more of than the others is the availability of the printed page. He has identity. Regular weekly or monthly identity. His name at the top of the masthead tells who he is.

At the top of the masthead. About that, admittedly, I have been paranoiac. It is where the editor's name belongs because the editor is the most meaningful person on a magazine.

In no small part, that's what this book is about.

Editors, in my early fanciful image of them, were serious of mien, stately in bearing, and wore beards. From available photographs I guessed that Lytton Strachey, Walt

Whitman, and Robert E. Lee would have made really fine editors, along with Charles Evans Hughes and Brahms, and either one of the cough-drop Smith brothers.

When I grew up a bit and got around a little and had a closer view, it occurred to me that to whatever manner born, and at least for a little while, almost any dolt could be a magazine editor. Which of us, indeed, has not been cited? However, I did come to know for sure that when magazines go bust, as practically all of them eventually do, it is no more because of the incompetence of the editors than the incompetence of the management executives who preside over the exchequers.

Editors, not publishers, give magazines their stature. In taking a roll call of this century's distinguished editors such names would come to mind as *The Saturday Evening Post*'s George Horace Lorimer, Time-Life's Henry Luce, *Reader's Digest*'s Lila and DeWitt Wallace, *Esquire*'s Arnold Gingrich, *The New Yorker*'s Harold Ross, *Vanity Fair*'s Frank Crowninshield, *McClure*'s S. S. McClure, *The Atlantic*'s Ellery Sedgwick. They were sovereigns of the magazines in their care. To a person concerned with publishing, their names are remembered and respected. It is an interesting fact, and indisputable, that few individuals, even those long and deeply immersed in the world of magazines, can name the person who was publisher or general manager or president of even one of them.

I had a personal favorite among editors: Henry Luce. I thought him the most stimulating, individualistic, the best of the lot, and in the lot were a lot of good ones. Among other things, in a charming address to the Magazine Publishers' Association, Luce once said, "I am a good example of how many mistakes one can make in this very chancy business and still come out ahead—provided one has enough colleagues with whom one can share the blame."

Various titles are given to such colleagues on a magazine staff: executive editor, managing editor, administrative editor, supervising editor, senior editor—and still others. In a large book-publishing house there are specialty editors, looking after departments that have to do with religion, gardening, science, juveniles. But the title in magazine or book house, the one unambiguous title, is that of editor, or sometimes editor-in-chief. He has the credit for what comes out right, if possessed of any sense of decency shares that credit with his staff. For what goes wrong, the onus is his, all his, and he asks no one to share it with him.

During the early summer of 1948 I asked John J. O'Connell—an associate on *Cosmopolitan*—to call on Myra Kingsley, then the country's most popular astrologer, and suggest she cast the horoscope of Thomas E. Dewey, in the polls at that time an overwhelming favorite to defeat Harry Truman in the race for the presidency. When Miss Kingsley's piece was submitted, I read with utter disbelief her prediction that Dewey would lose. "Tell Miss Kingsley," I said to O'Connell, "that she must change this drivel—she's got to elect Dewey because he's as good as in. Truman again as President! Does she think I'm going to let her make fools of us?"

O'Connell conveyed the message. No whit perturbed, and wanting her fee promptly, Miss Kingsley shifted the conjunction of the planets, recast the horoscope, gave the presidency to Dewey. "Thus the years 1948–49 are destiny-laden for Thomas E. Dewey," the most popular astrologer wrote finally, "and replete with happy portents. They are valuable enough to make him a popular President and will smooth out any difficulties with Congress or among members of his Cabinet."

That's how the feature appeared in the October issue of *Cosmopolitan*, a few weeks before the election. I arranged it. Did it all by myself.

Suren Ermoyan, whom I had appointed art director of *Town & Country*, brought over a painting he intended to use on the magazine's cover. He stood in front of me and held it up for inspection. I declared it an abomination. "But it's by Braque," Ermoyan exploded. I said I didn't care if it was by Michelangelo, or even Howard Chandler Christy, it still made no sense to me. Ermoyan came around to my side of the desk to point out the picture's virtues. "Cripes," he said, "it's upside down." It was, and I didn't know the difference, hadn't even noticed the position of the artist's signature. Ermoyan turned it right side up. "I still think it's terrible," I said, but relented and agreed it could be used to illustrate the issue's essay about Braque. I hated it. Everybody else loved it. I'm not a Braque man.

A monthly column—"If You Ask Me"—was being written for *McCall's* by Mrs. Eleanor Roosevelt, who had been appointed a contributor by my *McCall's* predecessor, Otis Wiese. To balance Mrs. Roosevelt's liberal views, I induced Clare Boothe Luce to write a monthly column which, because of her former ambassadorship to Italy, she felicitously called "Without Portfolio." Mrs. Luce was the best-known woman Republican of the time, as Mrs. Roosevelt was the best-known woman Democrat, and I looked forward to having them as side-by-side contributors; thought I was pretty damned smart about having arranged it. Mrs. Luce was dainty, beautiful, the most feminine of creatures, but when she spoke or wrote it was said it was like being dynamited by an angel cake. It was my belief that Mrs. Luce held Mrs. Roosevelt in low esteem, to say nothing of vice versa. I anticipated widespread publicity for the magazine because of the verbal assaults each woman would make on the other. As a courtesy and with some trepidation I visited with Mrs. Roosevelt to inform her of our new associate. "Dear Clare," Mrs. Roosevelt exclaimed, causing me to blink, "I'm so fond of her. I'm happy she's going to join us." Which was sufficiently discouraging, but in Mrs. Luce's very first column she recommended there always should be two Vice-Presidents of the United States, one of them always a woman. Then she named Mrs. Roosevelt as particularly qualified.

Those are samples of the way I did my guessing.

I recall a letter the writer Bill Adler showed me. It was

from a ten-year-old boy, addressed to the White House. "Dear Mr. Kennedy," it read, "how are you? What are you doing in Washington? Your Pal, Harry Slocum." Many a Harry Slocum might have written to ask what I was doing in an editor's chair. "Learn from the mistakes of others, you can't live long enough to make them all yourself," is a hollow maxim. I have made them all myself.

I don't want to make the mistake of forgetting to mention that no columnist was prompter than Mrs. Roosevelt about turning in copy. She wrote her own, had no ghost writers. (And I'd better add, neither had Mrs. Luce, or I'll have my knuckles cracked.) A gracious lady, Mrs. Roosevelt. No pretense. After luncheon one day in her New York City home she asked the several of us in attendance to have coffee in the drawing room. She grasped the handle of the hot coffee pot, pulled her hand away quickly. "Why don't you use this?" I said, handing her my fresh and neatly folded handkerchief. Several days later, through the mail, in a franked envelope, I received the handkerchief, unlaundered, "all crusheled," as my children said.

Late one afternoon we were having tea in the midtown apartment of Nannine Joseph, her literary agent at the time. As we left and reached the lobby of the building there was a drenching rain. "No point to both of us getting soaked," I said. "It's going-home hour and getting a taxi won't be easy. But if you'll be patient and stay here, sooner or later I'll turn up with one."

"Oh, no," she said, "I don't mind getting a little wet. Let's both go out and stand on the curb and pretty soon somebody will come along in a car and recognize me and offer us a lift." The instant we reached the curb a man ground his car to a halt, asked if he could be of help. "Yes, thank you," Mrs. Roosevelt said, smiling, "you can take us both home."

Once in a while her son Elliott interfered in her affairs and made attempts to serve as her literary agent. When he promised *Cosmopolitan* an article to be entitled "What I

Would Do If I Were a Republican" and the deadline for it arrived, we called Mrs. Roosevelt, who as it turned out had not been advised of the commitment. "It's a ridiculous idea," she said, "and I'd prefer not to do it. But if Elliott made the promise, of course I'll have to honor it." And she did.

While Mrs. Roosevelt was writing *I Remember Hyde Park,* I asked if we might publish it. She agreed, but on condition that it not appear until after her death. "I must confess," she wrote on the opening page, "that despite all my memories of life at Hyde Park, in one sense this memoir could well be titled 'I Remember My Mother-in-Law's Hyde Park.' It was indeed her home, and she made every decision concerning it. For over forty years I was only a visitor there." It was a confession of the bitterness of her personal life. While she lived, it was not for the public to notice.

Patient, generous, an extraordinary woman. Regardless of stress or strain, she retained her dignity. She was often ridiculed, but a rude remark addressed to her she would pretend not to hear, or would counter with a smile. "Nobody can insult me," she said once, "without my cooperation."

Mrs. Roosevelt had to keep busy. Making speeches, advancing causes, writing. "If you had only one thing to do," I asked her once, "is there something on which you'd like to concentrate?" She thought for a while, seemed ready to answer, stopped, finally said, "I think I'd like to be editor of a country newspaper."

It has seemed to me that some time or other everybody wants to be an editor.

When Norman Cousins was associated with the McCall Corporation there was a weekly luncheon to each of which we invited some person of prominence. The gatherings were informal and ended always with a question that as part of the proceedings I was expected to ask of the guest:

Assuming no problems involving family, income, geographical location, etc., what one job would you choose to have more than any other? George Moore, then president of the First National City Bank, promptly specified editorship of a small-town newspaper. U Thant said he would want to be editor of *Saturday Review*. Among the guests were authors, statesmen, generals, industrialists. They included David Sarnoff, Isaiah Berlin, Hubert Humphrey, Richard Nixon, John Lindsay, E. P. Snow, Adlai Stevenson, Constantinos Doxiadis, Lucius Clay. What astonished us was how many of the guests would choose to be editor of a magazine or newspaper.

Does an editor have more power or prestige? Most of our guests had a surfeit of both. It couldn't be money—most of the guests had plenty of it. I don't know who can be sure, but the answer may lie in the pervading sense of being free to think in all directions, establish rapport with a receptive audience, be concerned with people, ideas, things, events, and best of all not have to curry favor with politicians or an electorate.

The responsibilities of a consumer periodical editor are no less than those that beleaguer the principal in any endeavor, nor is there less artifice demanded in coping with competition. The hours an editor must keep are all the hours in the day. He must be endlessly curious. There's little surcease. When Mr. Dooley was explaining to his friend Hennessy all that an editor must do—advise the President of the United States, steer him away from ill-advised foreign entanglements, hold the governor and mayor accountable for their appointments, ensure that the police attend to their sworn duties—when all that an editor must do was explained to Hennessy, he said dolefully, "I shud think the wurk would kill him." "It does," Mr. Dooley said, "many gr-reat editors is dead."

The editor's job does not kill but it is killing. Everything he sees and hears becomes part of his mental harvest. At any time and whatever time of day or night, ideas must be germinating and taking shape. However insignificant the fact, he asks the why and wherefore. *The American's* John Siddall wanted to know why the Bank of England was called the Old Lady of Threadneedle Street, had his secretary write to the bank, which replied, "If you will look in your own Webster's dictionary you will see it is because we are located on Threadneedle Street." *Collier's* William Chenery had to be sure he was right in saying John is the most common name in the world, was flabbergasted to be told it was Mohammed. When DeWitt Wallace landed in Japan for the first time, what he wanted to know first of all was why Japanese babies are reputed never to cry (I am disgraced to admit I have forgotten the reason).

To most of us no other work gives such satisfaction as editing. Some exigencies may seem impossible to put up with, but we survive them. Editing is a joy. I can say it who has known as much as anybody else the accompanying disappointments and heartaches. In the end, the crucial word is "fulfillment."

5

Most of my boyhood friends lapped up the Burt
Standish stories in which Frank Merriwell brought glory
to Fardale by pitching seventy-four successive hitless,
scoreless innings in his senior year and then going on to
Yale, where his furious plunges to touchdowns season after
season were the despair of Harvard. As somebody pointed
out—could be the sportswriter Grantland Rice—Merriwell
played so constantly in so many games he seemed to
achieve the miracle of receiving his B.A. from Old Eli without ever having attended a single class.

It isn't that I wasn't interested in Frank Merriwell, or
his brother Dick for that matter, or the Rover Boys and the
Motor Boys, but I had other concerns and was still in ele-
mentary school when I came across *From a College Window*, a collection of essays by Arthur Christopher Benson
that aroused my curiosity about what life might be like on
campus—the professorial life, lofty thoughts, late-afternoon
heart-to-heart chats with brilliant undergraduates, midnight tea and crumpet tête-à-têtes with contemporary
headmasters or deans. Could be neat, and there was the
thought that one might be editor and professor at the same
time. Right then, however, the academic life was somewhat
remote. *Goodbye, Mr. Chips* had not yet been written or
somehow, I became so enamored of Mr. Chipping, I might
have tried to bluff my way into it.

A good many years later in a book about Benson I

learned he had been born in a schoolhouse, was the son of a schoolmaster and himself a master at Cambridge. His students worshipped him. He had known all of England's men of letters. I marveled that anyone should have such great good fortune. That kind of fortune was not likely to be mine, however, and there was anyway, at age fifteen, the pressing problem of finding gainful employment. Getting a job. Where? On a periodical—no university degree required. As what? Editor-in-chief, naturally.

It didn't happen all that fast, reaching the upper literary echelons. There was the unglamorous beginning part.

For almost five years, getting nowhere, I tried for place, space, spot—anything—on newspaper, magazine, with book publisher. Instead, in grubby mercantile establishments, I was errand boy, office boy, messenger, packing clerk, shipping clerk. Stultifying tasks for an editor-in-chief, natural-born. But out of youthful despair came an idea, not just good but terrific: I would start a newspaper syndicate. My own. By making a few inquiries it was easy to discover which features were most popular with the public. All one had to do was imitate them and sell them cheaper! To compete with O. O. McIntyre's "New York Day By Day" I did "Sights, Sins and Secrets of a Great City." (If "Oscar Odd," as he was called, could do his column without leaving his rooms at the Ritz-Carlton Hotel, why shouldn't I do as well?) But I also had an advice-to-the-lovelorn column, an intelligence test, a word quiz, and eleven other features; planned to write them all myself every week and present the full supply to one newspaper in a town for the introductory price of ten dollars. For that modest sum a paper could use all the features or only a couple and still, it seemed, be getting an irresistible bargain. If Henry Ford could dominate the automobile business with his cheap Model T's, who could stop me from being the Henry Ford of the syndicate world? Editor, writer, syndicator—all in one. Cute?

A slightly older friend* who traveled a lot, selling things to drugstores, offered to stop in at newspaper offices on his trips and explain the unprecedented benefit to be had from my Pioneer Syndicate Company. On his first approach he made arrangements with the Brooklyn *Eagle*, then a prosperous newspaper, whereby in exchange for the features the paper would provide me with several hundred mats. It hadn't occurred to me I'd *need* mats. The second success, for full price, cash, was with the Hartford *Courant*, and I knew with such a distinguished client I was going to be in clover. In no time at all my friend had signed up several other papers; and in that same time, because there was no money available for hiring help and I had to continue to write and type out all fifteen of the features, I ran out of advice to the lovelorn—in three columns had exhausted my store of knowledge—was over my head and overwhelmed; simply couldn't produce the material fast enough. I was originator of the shortest-lived syndicate in newspaper history.

Already, obviously, I had learned to type. Now I bought an Isaac Pitman shorthand manual. Shorthand came easily, I was quite good at it, it got me a job as secretary to an executive in the Merchants' Refrigerating Corporation, which was a step up from the sweeping of floors for the office manager of the Schulte Cigar Stores. At nineteen, adding two years to my age to be eligible to take a civil service examination, I got high marks and became for a year official stenographer in the Children's Court in Brooklyn. The hours were short—from nine to one. The rest of the day was my own. Could be spent, and was, in the local library.

It has surprised some friends to hear there are books printed in shorthand and that I got a little of my reading background from them. *The Vicar of Wakefield* was my first. Then *A Christmas Carol*. Parts of the New Testament.

* Marvin Small, subsequently an author, and originator, among other products, of Arrid, the first antiperspirant, and Rise, the instant shave cream.

Shorthand has been an indispensable convenience. It should be Gregg or Pitman, not a half-baked kind of system, a so-called speedwriting kind of thing. Today, still, I write everything first in shorthand. This book is being written in shorthand.

Of all stenographic appointments, that in a children's court is dreariest and poorest paid. One morning, reading my newspaper on the subway to take my place beneath the bench of Judge Wilkerson, I noticed an advertisement: Editor Wanted. That afternoon I went to the office of the Haire Publishing Company, asked for and glanced through several issues of the magazine mentioned—*The Inland Merchant,* a thirteen-thousand-circulation trade paper for small-town general stores, sellers of everything from groceries to dry goods.

Out of what I guessed a small-town merchant had to do, I wrote titles and blurbs for articles, roughed layouts, that night put together my first magazine dummy. It may come to notice later that I am no shrinking violet. But making that first dummy didn't strike me as any world-shattering accomplishment. Anybody who can pin or clip some pages of paper together has the start of a dummy. Anybody who can block out some article titles and blurbs on the pages *has* a dummy.

When Alphonse Haire granted the requested interview and asked if I had made the dummy myself—he seemed to think it rather smart and I suppose it was—or had the help of someone else, I volunteered, if he gave me a few hours in his office then and there, to prepare an altogether new one. He was satisfied I could do it and did not ask me to do it. He gave me the job.

Other magazines in the company had, I thought, gruesome titles, *Corset & Underwear Review* being one of them. Each magazine had two employees—an editor and an advertising space salesman. No secretary, no budget, no art department; the editor wrote every word, made his own layouts, borrowed linecuts and halftones from advertisers.

Crude? Amateurish? Not so. It was the best learning experience a beginner could have asked for.

For firsthand knowledge of *Inland Merchant* subscribers I went by train, I seem to remember via Galesburg, to Naperville, Illinois, population then four thousand. I recall the sign at the depot there: "This is the smallest town in the United States to have a YMCA." What I hoped to find was the magazine's typical reader. Not then, not ever, did I find a typical reader of any magazine.

So that was it. There it was. No more need to dream of being an editor. I had become one. Knew I was destined to be, would never care to be anything else. Was willing to labor day and night, weekends, forgo any holiday. In time, for people on any magazine staff, I would be willing and ready to shed blood. Real blood. Including some of my own.

From the outset I assumed an editor must run a magazine his own way and learned almost immediately that it might be possible. Alphonse Haire objected to an article prepared for my second issue. "It's no good," he said. With the impertinence of inexperience I said I liked it very much. Mr. Haire glared at me. "You think you know better than I do?" he asked. I said I wasn't saying that, only that I thought the article fine. That wonderful little man leaned back in his chair and roared with laughter. "What a hell of a nerve you have," he said. Then, "All right, I'm only the boss around here, but you're the editor, so I'm not going to argue with you—go ahead and run it."

What happened in that place was patently impossible—before long I was promoted and I resigned. Mr. Haire had asked me to add editorship of the *Corset & Underwear Review* to my duties.

Corsets. Petticoats. Chemises. Women's *drawers!*

Who—*me?* Not on your life.

I heard the Western Newspaper Union had in mind starting a magazine for people in the business of selling cosmetics. I got the job of editing it. Having said which, it is impossible to get away with not mentioning its title: *Good Looks Merchandising.*

For the first issue I wrote the lead article myself; gave it the title "How to Be Ugly!" and used with it a photograph of Lon Chaney as he was made up to play the monstrous Quasimodo in *The Hunchback of Notre Dame.* Through the movie company's publicity department I was able to use Chaney's name as author of the article.

How to be ugly. For a beauty magazine. Clever? That must have been almost sixty years ago, and it seemed clever then. It doesn't seem so bad even now.

6

In no sense except by ourselves declaring it to be so is editing a profession. It is a trade, or craft, we learn it by working at it, as a farmer learns farming in the field. There is no school for training editors. About editing all is empirical. Like a gardener with a green thumb, being a natural-born editor is akin to being able to play piano by ear. Even with that talent, however, one can hit a wrong note.

For a group of youngsters who coveted editorship I once presumed to outline a program of must-haves and must-dos. In my file is a copy of the program, unfortunately. The good editor hears as well as listens, I said portentously; understands the difference between what is serious and what is solemn; gets more out of people than they think they have; must make them better than they think they are. He challenges, I went on, and drives, squeezing the last ounce of creative effort out of himself as of others. He possesses the capacity to surprise—his readers, his staff, and once in a while himself.* He is not merely confident, he exudes confidence. (*Exudes* it? That's what I said!)

Modest reflection and what comes out is gobbledygook, as applicable to the effusions of the scoutmaster of a Cub troop or the manager of a stable of Golden Gloves hope-

* I wish our language was without gender differentiation. Because it isn't, I ask the indulgence of my women friends who are editors and writers. The "he," "him," and "his" references are to be regarded only as grammatical convention.

fuls. I did include a sentence I'd still stand up for: With or without any other qualification, the editor must know how to be boss. There is a proverb—French or German—that says one bad general in command of an army is better than two good ones. George Horace Lorimer put it in different words: "No magazine can survive the mistakes of more than one editor." Which brings to mind the time when members of the Time-Life organization were strongly in favor of supporting Adlai Stevenson for the presidency and Mr. Luce had decided to support Eisenhower. Calling his associates together, Luce is reputed to have said, and it has been reported often enough to have become a cliché, "For the benefit of those of you who do not know who I am, my name is Henry Luce. I am the boss around here. I make the final decisions. I have the right to hire and fire. Any questions?" Somewhat reminiscent of Frederick the Great's "My people and I have come to an agreement that satisfies us both. They are to say what they please, and I am to do what I please."

About the time the presidential election was coming up in 1964, which was about when Mr. Luce announced he was relinquishing his title of editor-in-chief, he came to the office for luncheon with a few of my associates. "Do you really mean," I asked, "that you are no longer going to make the final editorial decisions?" "I do mean it," Luce said. "Well," I continued, "if the new editor of *Life* decides to support candidate A this year, and you personally are for candidate B, which candidate will the magazine support?" "That's simple," Luce replied instantly, "the magazine will support candidate B," proving nothing more than that Mr. Luce was still the largest single stockholder.

A magazine may be blessed with editorial talent; have on staff one, two, or three individuals more capable than the editor. Right or wrong, however, there can be only one head. One person has to be in charge. A group—a committee—can't be. It *cannot*. That's my dictum. Let City Hall fight it.

Quite likely the attitude had its origin in arrogance, but I have no tolerance for committees and little faith in committee decisions. The instance is merely indicative of what I want to establish, but in 1946 the greatly gifted author, critic, and anthologist Clifton Fadiman and popular novelist Laura Z. Hobson were leaders of a group determined to publish its own magazine, on a cooperative basis. Everything in and for the new magazine was to be voted on by members of the staff, with majority vote, I think, being decisive, a procedure contrary to the more tenable maxim that votes should be weighed, not counted. The project was to be called '47: *The Magazine of the Year*. Each succeeding year the title was to be changed, to '48, '49, '50, etc.

In March of 1947 the debut issue carried a Statement of Intention: " '47 is the only national magazine owned and controlled by people who write, paint, and photograph professionally. Its stockholders include many talented men and women whose names you know well. Now, for the first time, they have their own magazine." Hundreds of writers and artists joined up. It would have been cowardly not to seem to want to be part of such a well-intentioned enterprise. Of course, such a magazine was not going to forfeit its dignity by condescending to accept advertising. But in less than a year the magazine made an amazing discovery: printing and all other costs have the disconcerting habit of going up. So the magazine took the unavoidable step: it accepted advertising. Which didn't help. It folded before the end of 1948. One reason it folded is that the talented men and women who became stockholders found little point in submitting to '47 what they could sell to other national magazines for prices five times higher.

Mr. Fadiman has been preeminent in his undertakings. One could say he has been the popular literary conscience of the country and that '47 was a forgivable misadventure. In any case, there is nothing fair about citing only a self-serving example, so I reach into the recesses of memory, recalling the Seneca Civics Club, to which in my middle teens I belonged. A domineering Mr. Louis Fisher had organized it for boys in the neighborhood and during a dispute over an interpretation of the club's constitution he interrupted by announcing peremptorily, "*I* am the constitution." A motion was made and passed to appoint a committee to determine Mr. Fisher's fitness to *be* the constitution. The committee voted unanimously to depose the gentleman. *That* was a *good* committee. Unfortunately it reached the wrong decision. With the elimination of Mr. Fisher, the club went out of business.

"To hear as well as listen." I did prefer an early-morning breakfast with a single associate in a quiet hotel dining room, or orange juice and coffee at the office desk with a fiction editor, or an after-hours hour with an articles editor, where conversation was comfortable if not always amicable. No telephone jangling, no secretary bobbing in and out. Pure peace; or, depending on the subject under discussion, an approximation thereof. To the counsel of one person at a time it is uncircumspect to be averse; so long, however, as counsel is not command. That doesn't just sound nasty. It is. I happen, however, to believe it.

When the endearing Max Wilkinson came to the *Good Housekeeping* staff as an associate editor it was with an excellent reputation well earned in other publishing quarters. "Look," Wilkinson said in the office one day, "I honestly believe I am at least as good an editor as you are. Why is it that you are the head person around here and I am only an assistant? Why don't I ever get your kind of job?"

He had no intention of being insolent, was expressing what must be in the minds of most second-echelon editors. To have told Wilkinson he was too kind, too much inclined to be swerved by the opinions of others even when his instinct was against them, too prone to compromise, not always adamant in resisting the pressures of management, not tough enough—altogether too much of a gentleman—would have served no purpose. "Some other time, Max," I

said, "but right now I'm going to the publisher's office—
there's somebody there I must strangle."

On an occasion when it was necessary to choose
a new editor for *Redbook,* I scouted and interviewed endlessly, with the staff increasingly restless because it was
rooting for Sey Chassler, the managing editor, to have the
job. The staff knew him well. So did I. But he was *there,*
and—there is no sensible reason for it—that can be a disadvantage. The person who is there, and it doesn't matter
what the business, often gets the short end of the stick.
He's doing fine in his particular job, so why upset the ap-
plecart? It isn't that familiarity breeds contempt, it's that
many of us get the notion that somebody somewhere else
has something better to offer and we pass over talent right
under our nose, which means that subeditors like Wilkinson
wait and pray for the chance that rarely comes. When it
does come—when the editor reaches retirement age or for
another reason his tenure is up—as often as not he is replaced by somebody commandeered from the outside.
Come then the mutterings. "Elizabeth Gordon—they're not
going to make *her* editor of *House Beautiful,* are they? For
God's sake, she's never been in anything but fashion promotion." Or: "Ed Thompson—our *Smithsonian* is being
turned over to *him?* Doesn't the front office know he's nothing but an old *Life* has-been?" Or: "Helen Gurley Brown,
that ad agency copywriter—the Hearst morons think *she*
can save *Cosmopolitan?* Well, we can say goodbye to good
old *Cosmo.*"

In the end I appointed Chassler, which was lucky. He
proved to be the ablest editor *Redbook* ever had. So one
never knows, really. The Gordon-Thompson-Brown trio, as
it happened, performed miracles. All of which may suggest
that management, which makes the appointments, is not always inept. Only sometimes.

I can offer even more testimony and should not be included out. I have been editor; and, alas, I have also been
management.

7

One doesn't often get into the practice of medicine or law, or become an architect or engineer or even a chiropodist, simply by hanging up a shingle. Some advance training is demanded before diplomas and working papers are handed out. With editors it's different. An editor can be somebody who when a magazine needs one happens to be on hand.

Reading about what editors have done in the past and examining the magazines they produced makes it possible for anybody to acquire a historical background of publishing and what an editor is and does, or is supposed to be and do. The most comprehensive source of information is Frank Luther Mott's *History of American Magazines,* in five volumes, though Theodore Peterson's one-volume *Magazines in the Twentieth Century* will give almost anybody all he wants to know. Some young journalism students who only glance through the Mott books will forsake journalism then and there. In any business with so many failures, the effort to make the grade doesn't seem worthwhile. I should state that even the exhaustive Mott research didn't uncover the names of hundreds of magazines that have disappeared.

In this technological age magazines haven't much visual similarity to those current when the country was younger, printing presses slow, and circulation sparse. Illustrations were tinted by hand, Sarah Josepha Hale,* the editor of *Godey's Lady's Book,* employing a hundred and fifty women, as I learned, for the purpose. Early advertisements were in the form of "reading notices" that subscribers were supposed to believe represented genuine editorial content. The advertising of valueless patent medicines was rampant, ethics in short supply. Advertisements were vulgar, and some still are. Magazines and newspapers accepted—ardently solicited—advertising for love philtres, abortion recipes, quick cures for cancer, tuberculosis, lost manhood, aching backs and creaking joints. "Electric belts" were advertised that would cure paralysis, fever and ague, malaria, and seminal weakness, "all for the price of $3.00, $4.00, or $5.00, according to quality." What man would not select the best-quality belt for curing seminal weakness? Bernarr Macfadden must have had one. He married—again—when he was eighty, may have been thinking of Socrates, who found time when he was an old man to learn music and dancing. Macfadden took up singing lessons at eighty-two, and lived for still another five years. He never smoked or touched liquor or he might have reached a hundred. Of the magazines he owned his most successful was *True Story,* his favorite *Physical Culture,* with the slogan "Weakness is a crime—don't be a criminal." He had his virtues: opened dozens of Physical Culture Restaurants where patrons could dine well for nine cents a meal.

Most of the quack remedies, like Teddy Ponderevo's "The Secret of Vigour" in H. G. Wells's novel *Tono-Bungay,* contained just enough alcohol or morphine to give the quick satisfaction inevitably promised. "Throw that truss away" was a phrase as commonly encountered as "Publick Occurrences" and could be immediately adjacent. A spittoon was not merely a living-room convenience but could be warranted sanitary; not the spit, just the receptacle. The *Farm Journal* in 1880 was the first magazine to assure sub-

* Famous for the poem "Mary Had a Little Lamb."

scribers they could depend on the truth of advertising in its pages, "would make good losses sustained by readers who find advertisers to be deliberate swindlers," though anybody who tried to pin down a deliberate swindler would get positively nowhere. That could *be* promised.

As so much earlier in England, where they appeared in what were called Agony Columns, "Personals" began to show up in American periodicals: disclaimers of debts incurred by errant wives, rewards for apprentices who vanished before finishing out their indentures, rewards for runaway slaves. James Gordon Bennett in his New York *Herald* ran ads paid for by brothel keepers, and by prostitutes themselves, with their addresses clearly printed. Bennett stopped at nothing to attract advertisers and readers. "Send somebody out to kill somebody," he once directed his city editor, "we must have news."

Authors once sold dedications in their books, which as a patron one paid for with favors—money, title, position— resulting in some novel or history or volume of verse carrying the name of the patron as dedicatee. Authors paid for the advertising of their own books, quite shameless panegyrics. Boswell wrote his own fulsome announcement† for his *Life of Johnson*.

As the country converted from an agrarian and barter society to an industrial economy, as standardized parts began rolling off assembly lines, as bulk merchandise— crackers in barrels, butter and lard in tubs—gave way to packaged goods, manufacturers were dazzled to find how very heavily purchases could be influenced by advertising. Their big problem was to guess if the circulation they thought they were buying was actually being delivered. Most of the time it wasn't. A magazine would decide on what rate it could dare charge for a page, then declare a circulation that would seem to justify it. It was easy to grow fast and get rich by picking a number out of a hat. For several years the Woolworth stores offered customers

† See Appendix.

their choice of the Tower Magazines—one devoted to detective stories, another to love stories, about five or six in all, each priced at ten cents. Advertisers discovered that circulation claims were distorted, trial and conviction of the owner (not the Woolworth stores) followed. From all of which comes to mind an ancient story that may be worth recording once again. I will swear only that I read it, not that it is true: "The editor was dying, and when the doctor placed his ear to the patient's heart and murmured, 'Ah, too bad, the poor fellow's circulation is almost gone,' the editor raised himself in bed and gasped, ' 'Tis false! We have the greatest circulation in the country.' Then he sank back and died, consistent to the end, lying about his circulation."

Before the latter part of the last century few magazines reached beyond the areas in which they were printed. A *North American Review* might have a national distribution of sorts but the total was insignificant. When Congress reduced second-class mail rates to a cent a pound in 1885 and then a little later when the Rural Free Delivery system was inaugurated, magazines began their upward spiral. When sworn statements were issued by the better magazines, unprincipled rivals had no hesitation in swearing to greater circulation. There were no lie detectors then. Not until the Audit Bureau of Circulations was formed in 1914 did publishers, not always enthusiastically, become members and submit their circulation claims for official audit.

In cities and villages everywhere there must be people who can remember having their doorbells rung by young mugs selling subscriptions in order, so they said, to work their way through college; most would have found it hard to work their way through sixth grade. Senior citizens can remember when a subscription to a magazine, or a renewal, would bring a prize in the form of a bicycle, a Maxfield Parrish print, a sewing machine. Actually a piano if a subscriber would only be willing to round up another one or two dozen subscriptions from relatives, neighbors, friends, or for that matter even enemies. A housewife pitying a huckster hobbling to her door on crutches would sign a form that, at first unknown to her, represented an order to purchase *Beadle's Weekly, New Eclectic, Forney's Progress,* and twelve other magazines for all the remaining days of her life; after which the character would limp away and, out of sight, swing the crutches under his arm and scamper off to the home of the next victim. Once a subscriber was signed up, even for a single year, she could be under obligation interminably; publishers wouldn't cease their dunning unless she wrote and specifically demanded her subscription not be renewed. Short of that, magazines would continue to be sent to her, her debt accumulating until every last penny was paid. For the good part of a century the subscription business was in the hands of unsavory individuals. Some of it still is.

There were three or four companies that didn't object to having a few honest rules and trying to live up to them. But they too could enlarge subscription lists primarily through the use of premiums; there wasn't much in the way of alternative. Nevertheless, college scholarships promised by them were usually honored, cash prizes to church and charity organizations usually paid. When Ebenezer Butterick invented the tissue-paper dress pattern and then in 1893 founded *The Delineator,* he arranged to have a pattern given free with each copy. The devices for building circulation were varied and ingenius, some so ingenius that the men who thought them up ended up in jail. Yet most of the time—let's be honest, some of the time—subscribers received their magazines regularly and had them to read when libraries were scarce and the nation expanding and people thirsting for entertainment and knowledge.

Because volume of circulation usually is the determining factor in the sale of advertising space, and because newsstand sales always have been erratic, publishers depended, as most of them still do depend, on subscriptions to meet their circulation commitments. Cutting subscription rates was standard practice; with few exceptions it still is.

A year's subscription to a magazine with a 25-cent cover price would be offered for $1.00, giving rise to the common come-on, "Subscribe now, save $2.00 on the next 12 issues." Even though *Life* in its heyday could boast "2 million copies bought at the newsstands last week," it too discovered that subscriptions were more likely to keep circulation high enough to provide advertisers with a guaranteed total. As costs of paper, printing, and distribution skyrocketed it became necessary for publishers to raise their prices. Magazines that began with a 5-cent or 10-cent cover price went to 10 and 15 cents, to 25, to 50. Some of them up to $1.25. Today a few at the newsstands cost $2.50. Inflation with concomitant higher personal income made a larger portion of the population able to afford the new prices. Whereas advertisements formerly were expected to make up losses incurred by publishers because of virtually nonexistent net income from the sale of copies, more and more magazines found single-copy sales could be made to pay their way and occasionally show a profit; people also were prepared to pay higher subscription rates. All of which may seem to portend a more stabilized industry, but none of which, because of the never lessening pressures of competition and the endless profusion of "sweepstakes" offers, means that the same proportion of magazines won't continue to fold, with new ones arising to take their place. Before long it may be found that newsstand and subscription rates are higher than the public is willing to pay. Managements that keep pushing the price up won't change when circulation goes down, but the editors will be fired. When there's any kind of trouble, usually it's the editors who get fired.

8

A magazine editor plays less of a part in the development of fiction than nonfiction—*I* think so—but for me it was the more enjoyable part of my work. Rewarding sometimes, frequently frustrating, but at no time dull. How to deal with a given writer was determined by what the writer thought he was writing. Most of what we published in magazines could be described in no two words other than "average fare." That doesn't mean the writers thought their fare was average. Sometimes they confused the ability to put together an acceptable story with an evocation of genius. Writers of best sellers are for the most part people who slap together, usually very dexterously, the necessary components of sex, sentimentality, money, and violence. That doesn't make them writers, it only makes them people who write.

If I had been more an admirer of Henry James's later books, I would have had little contentment in my work. I wasn't on the lookout, nor was it my job to be, for a *Salammbô*. I could not have managed to sustain a peaceful relationship with, let us say, a Mary Roberts Rinehart. "Yes," Mrs. Rinehart would say, "I agree this chapter sags a bit, but it's for a deliberate reason." I'd listen as intently as though she *were* a female Flaubert. For half an hour. Had no choice. Would want to sign my mail and get the hell home before my wife called to say guests had arrived and dinner was getting cold. But I'd pay attention, with another fifteen minutes lost. I'd want to say, "Look, old girl, you could be right but you're a jackass for not recognizing . . ." Instead, knowing the author to be sensitive to criticism, I'd say, "By all means, Mrs. Rinehart, I understand your point, and if you insist—"

By the time I had reached my ninth birthday Mrs. Rinehart already had written *The Circular Staircase** and *The Man in Lower Ten*. In popular literature she was already a *force*. After such original successes what chance had I, in her opinion a novice editor, of getting her to change a story? One of the most sought-after writers, she lived extravagantly, worked incessantly for the money necessary to sustain her way of life, hardly ever engaged in conversation without going off at a tangent to complain about the income taxes she had to pay. Asked about her writing habits, she said succinctly, "I write at the point of my pen." At one period in her career she had been asked to succeed Edward Bok as editor of *Ladies' Home Journal*, but declined. It was George Horace Lorimer's idea. It was Mr. Lorimer who gave Mrs. Rinehart most advice and encouragement, who purchased most of her stories. But when Mrs. Rinehart wrote her autobiography—*My Story*—she preferred to have it appear—for no reason that I know of—in *Good House-keeping*. Lorimer was, with reason, offended; felt it should have been his to publish.

There were authors who could be loved without reservation, such a one being I. A. R. Wylie, always Ida to her friends, who lived in a big house in Princeton with Dr. Josephine Baker, known as the first female pediatrician in the United States, and Dr. Louise Pearse, who had something to do with discovering that the tsetse fly was the cause of sleeping sickness. I remember the New Year's holiday my wife and I spent with them, and the terror with which we kept our eyes on the bull terriers who were the women's pets and protectors. The agent Carl Brandt had

* Produced later as a play called *The Bat*.

told me about a novel Miss Wylie was completing. Called *Keeper of the Flame*,† it was about a national hero, who could have been taken for Charles Lindbergh or General MacArthur, who was planning to overthrow the Roosevelt government and set up a dictatorship. There was the possibility the story would be misunderstood, considered offensive to citizens of right-wing sympathies. I had doubts about the wisdom of using it, but its power and suspense prevailed and I bought it. I believe any editor with any sense would have bought it. Miss Wylie, however, regarded publication an act of courage and we became closer friends than ever because of it. She and the two women who shared the household were a peculiar trio, it was hard to imagine what brought them and kept them together, but they were always exuberant, full of fun. Dr. Baker and I had something special in common. As a boy I had lived in Poughkeepsie for a few years. She had been born there.

Writer and gentleman, Edward Streeter was only twenty-six when he achieved fame for his *Dere Mable*, and his fame swelled thirty-seven years later when he created Stanley Banks in *Father of the Bride*. By that time Mr. Streeter was an officer of the Fifth Avenue Bank, and banking then was a respectable business, not as now more like a junky discount store with windows filled with cheap radios and carpet sweepers given away "free" to people gullible enough to withdraw their savings from one bank and deposit them temporarily in another. After *Father* came *Mr. Hobbs' Vacation*, we published it, it got a fine reception, I offered to take Mr. Streeter to lunch at any fine place of his choosing. "Haven't been to the Automat in years," he said, "let's try it." Which we did, inserting coins in the slots for our sandwiches and coffee. I thought Mr. Hobbs might make another book, could be a sequel, in which by popular demand of his townsmen he would be a candidate for

† Later an enormously successful movie starring Katharine Hepburn and Spencer Tracy.

mayor of Cleveland. "Would he win or lose the election?"
Mr. Streeter asked, and I said he couldn't help but win.
"Then it's no book," Streeter sighed, "my Hobbsie would
have to lose. He always loses." I don't know which man I
liked more, the real Mr. Streeter or the fictional Mr. Hobbs.

As for difficult authors, there were some very special
specimens, one of them being Ayn Rand. She made no
bones about declaring my conservative liberalism too radi-
cal for her taste. In her novel *Atlas Shrugged* the character
John Galt makes a radio speech that goes on for some
fifteen thousand words. When asked if she didn't think it
could be shortened a bit, her response was: "Would you
cut the Bible?"

In whatever exalted terms a magazine editor thinks of
himself, he knows he does not have the stature of a book
editor. Magazine editors write autobiographies. Biographies generally are written about book editors. But whatever the magazine editor/author relationship, the book editor is in a more vulnerable position; experience tells him a
manuscript should be condensed or need drastic revision
but he must be careful not to offend the author lest the author decide to take his wares elsewhere. The magazine editor has greater options; a too unyielding author may be
dispensed with altogether, unless he is one of the few absolutely indispensables. For magazine publication the author
is less obstinate about cutting or making requested
changes; what matters most to the author is the book, the
hard-cover format likely to attract the attention of established reviewers. Whether occupied with magazines or
books, the editor must be mother, father, nurse, cajoler; and
in the end is obliged to concede that the story is the author's, that assistance can be construed as interference, that
there is a point beyond which suggestions will be neither
welcome nor tolerated.

I know I could not have been successful as a book editor; would not have had the patience to wait for a year,
sometimes two or three years, between acceptance of a

manuscript and its appearance in print. I'd have had no composure in the face of authors' complaints about the absence of displays of their books in the shops. The loyalty of authors can be notoriously thin, and that would have distressed me. Their recollections of happy association can be conveniently set aside. All of us who have labored in the book or magazine vineyard have had our vexations; more annoying than serious, most of all disillusioning. When Adela Rogers St. Johns was planning a sequel to her very successful *Final Verdict,* she wrote, "You are still the greatest editor in the world and for me to start a book without your help is impossible. Please help me because I don't know where to start. You may remember you solved this problem for me for *Final Verdict* in one luncheon at the Oak Room. Dear Herbert, do be my editor again for just a little—give me some direction on how this book should be written."

I did try to be of help to that woman who had been a fabulous newspaper reporter and became one of the most facile fiction writers in the country. But Adela, for all the big money she made, was somehow always short of it; improvident, generous, she frittered it away. On occasion, to get a few thousand dollars in a hurry, she would dash off a story that was far from her best, and once I had to return one. Accompanied by a gentle, almost apologetic letter, it hurt her and she never forgave me. In the sequel she had in mind, called *The Honeycomb,* there is a single reference to me, and that an unpleasant one. It has to do with the rejection of the one story.

"You are the best editor I ever worked with," Jerome Weidman wrote, "the most wonderful and natural editor I have ever known." He was as wonderful and natural an author as I ever worked with. I miss his personal warmth and amiable chatter, such a statement as that until he was married he didn't know bicarbonate of soda wasn't automatically brought to the table at the end of every meal. "All I need is you sometimes, to straighten me out," Charles Jackson wrote after we worked together on several stories during difficult days that followed his confessional *The Lost Weekend*. He was one of the many who didn't forget such days and the close relationship that developed between us. "You've loaned me money," he wrote, "you've been patient with me when I was desperate for understanding, and I'd like to be remembered as your friend."

Every editor of magazines or books receives adulatory letters, sooner or later is told he is the best, the greatest, the most helpful. It is to be assumed neither that the letters when written are insincere nor that the editors to whom they are addressed do not accept them as genuine expressions of gratitude at a given moment.

On the whole, my difficulties with authors were few. With, for example, Edna Ferber, who seldom used the normal salutation in writing letters. Not "Dear So-and-So," but "There is something I want to discuss with you, dear Arthur," or "I want to thank you, dear John, for the enjoyable evening." Her letters to friends were often signed Ferb. She could be kind, thoughtful, generous. Knowing that my younger daughter was in love with her books, she had a complete set bound in leather and wrote an endearing inscription in each one. She could be spiteful, referring to those she thought her enemies as "members of the well-known Legion family." She had a love-hate relationship with her sister Fannie, begrudged her whatever successes she achieved, though they never approached Edna's. I recall no lunch or tea or dinner with her when I was not ill at ease. One never knew—I think no one ever knew—when that feisty little woman for no reason would launch an offensive. At dinner one night in my home a reserved, quiet young man suddenly became her target. "What do you do?" Ferb asked imperiously. And was answered with "I work for British Iranian." "British Iranian!" snapped Ferber. "One of those thieving cartels, I suppose. Why aren't you in uniform, over where you belong, fighting for your country?" The poor victim stayed silent, could not explain he was an American, an intelligence officer operating under cover of a British company. When I was talking with her about *A Kind of Magic,* her follow-up autobiography,‡ she assailed me with "You paid that Zsa Zsa Gabor a hundred thousand dollars for *her* book and you're daring to offer me *less?*" (We did not pay Zsa Zsa Gabor a hundred thousand dollars, we paid her half of that for talking it and the other half to Gerold Frank for writing it.)

Sooner or later Edna Ferber fought with every friend she had, though usually the quarrels were patched up—until the next time. She made no attempt to disguise her fury when she saw an unfavorable notice of one of her books or plays, and she wrote a goodly quantity of both, including *American Beauty, Giant,* and *Show Boat,* and plays that included *Stage Door, The Royal Family* (with George S. Kaufman), and *Dinner at Eight.* Her work, I think, has not stood up well over the years, but I think also that someday there will be a revival of interest, her regional novels particularly possessing a very special merit. At her funeral service, where along with playwright Marc Connelly, publisher Bennett Cerf, and editor Kenneth McCormick, I spoke a few words, I chose the words carefully lest Ferb return to haunt me. After her death, I was asked by Doubleday if I would be willing to edit a book of her letters, and the letters were sent to me to examine. One of them to her mother said—I don't have it and can't quote verbatim—"If you only knew how I hate people who are namedroppers!" The letter ended with reference to a dinner she had attended the night before. "Noel was there," she wrote, or approximately that, "and Bea and good old Johnny Gielgud, and our darling Alec, and Grace who is just as beautiful as a princess as she used to be in the movies."

I am glad to have been, however uncomfortably, a small part of her life. I am glad not to have been subject to the

‡ The first was *A Peculiar Treasure.*

venom she reserved for anybody who confused her with
Fanny Hurst, whom she loathed. Of Miss Hurst I was not
myself enamored. The calla lily that was her trademark and
that she always had pinned to her dress or coat was no
symbol of peace. She wrote a few popular novels, of which
Back Street and *Lummox* became best known. She wrote
good short stories, of which "Humoresque" became most
famous. Early in our relationship we disagreed about the
title of a story she had written. From then on, though she
continued to submit stories, she never addressed me except
as Mr. Mapes, and I had to pretend not to notice.

Fairly soon after we published John Steinbeck's *Winter
of Our Discontent* he was awarded the Nobel Prize.
("Congratulations. There is only one man I would rather
see get it," read the telegram sent by John O'Hara. For
O'Hara, that was fairly gracious.) The novel was far from
Steinbeck's best and I thought it detracted from his reputation. But when we had lunch together I spoke more enthusiastically of it than was warranted. "I'm glad *you* liked it,"
Steinbeck said, "but I'd say it's a rotten job—the worst I've
ever done." What I haven't learned to this day is to be totally honest with authors. I'd prefer not to be, when their
work isn't their best. What wounds writers have to suffer I
am disinclined to inflict.

In his devotion to himself Sinclair Lewis was single-
minded; about his greatness he had no misgivings. A sometime friend of Upton Sinclair, he could foam at the mouth
if confused with him. Lanky, his thin face pocked with acne,
his awareness of his ugliness affected most of his relationships. Now and then he could be amusing—more than
now and then—and he was a grand mimic. I got along
with him, found him generally kind, but suffered when he
gave vent to rage, which also was more than now and then.
His conduct could be irascible and irrational. During an
evening I had taken him and Edith Haggard, his literary
agent, to a late supper, he became furious over some fancied slight on the part of a waiter, picked up a knife, and

shattered a champagne glass to splinters. On another evening, in my home, he disrupted the dinner party by lashing out at Lester Markel, then the Sunday editor of the New York *Times*. By his friends, Lewis always was called Red because of the color of his hair. He misunderstood and thought Markel had called him *a* red.

Of the writers whose peccadilloes I have read about, I think Arnold Bennett's were the most eccentric. He was particularly neurotic about punctuality. A maid, preparing tea, would have to tell him the precise moment at which she poured the boiling water into the pot. Pulling out his watch, Bennett would time an exact four minutes from that moment, then give the signal that the tea should be served. Of the writers I *knew*, Sinclair Lewis was the most neurotic about punctuality. "What the hell makes you think you're more important than we are?" he snarled at Arthur McKeogh, an associate of mine, who had been delayed for a few minutes in getting to a meeting with Lewis, Alexander Woollcott, and me at the Plaza, then rose abruptly and stalked out of the hotel. Woollcott, himself no benevolent soul, then said, "Who does Red think *he* is, leaving me here?" He didn't add "with the likes of you two," but that's what he meant, and he left also. "A couple of rats," I said. McKeogh had known them longer. "A couple of bastards," he said, "and I'd slit their throats gladly." McKeogh was the man who could do it, too. He had been with Major Whittlesey's "Lost Battalion" in France, and creeping back to rejoin the American lines had at point-blank range shot the heads off three German soldiers.

Though he was declared winner of the Pulitzer Prize for literature, which he rejected, and winner of the Nobel Prize for literature, which he accepted, not all of Lewis' novels, though always best sellers, were of first magnitude. I have thought of most of them as magnificent social histories in the form of fiction, with *Arrowsmith* the best. He saw himself genuinely a genius, for half his writing life he *was* a genius. A short Lewis novel—*Harri*—never saw the light of day as a hard-cover book, and for good reason: it was twaddle. The author was usually willing to make reasonable changes, but this thing was hopeless, so bad that I had it rewritten in the office, rewrote part of it myself, without consulting him, which didn't make it much better. I knew Lewis wouldn't have taken the necessary time on that one. However, he didn't utter a complaining word; I had just done him a favor important to him—found a place on *Good Housekeeping* for a favorite young friend he had been trying to mold into an actress.

A pleasanter man than Lewis who had a passion for promptness was the "Conning Tower" columnist, Franklin P. Adams. "Promptness is a worthy cause," he would say, "but costly. You call the doctor and he says he'll be at your home between three and four to have a look at your wife. You wait. He arrives at seven. You have an appointment with the dentist for 3 P.M. sharp. At 3 P.M. sharp you are in his reception room. So are six other patients waiting their turn. You buy tickets for the theater. The curtain will rise on the dot of eight, or so the announcements say. Fifteen minutes earlier you are in your seat and already have memorized the pages of program notes. You also have read all the ads and decided on which sandwich you'll order later at Sardi's. At 8:17 the curtain rises. Slowly. I have wasted a year and a half of my life waiting for curtains to rise, and seven years waiting for people who were late."

On a Christmas Eve I was interrupted by a phone call from John O'Hara, who had been writing short short stories for us during an interval he was on the outs with *The New Yorker*. He said he would be glad to show me the manuscript of his new novel, *Ten North Frederick*, if I sent him a check for twenty-five thousand dollars. I said I supposed he wanted immediate payment of that amount if I decided to take the novel, with the balance, whatever might be agreed on, to be paid later. No, O'Hara replied, I would have to pay him the money just for the privilege of being the first magazine editor to see it. I thought he was daffy and said so. In much less of a Yuletide spirit O'Hara bellowed forth a stream of profanity. "You're not daffy, John," I said, "you've been drinking again." Whether he was or not is of no consequence. A few months later, when I was sitting in the office of Bennett Cerf, his publisher, Cerf suddenly looked at his watch. "You'd better be leaving now," he warned. "O'Hara is due in a few minutes. He told me he's going to break every bone in your body." I am no coward, but I don't go in for brinkmanship, either. I left.

After *Catcher in the Rye*, J. D. Salinger's alienation novel that brought a new dimension to modern writing and became the most sought after of books by the high school generation that wallowed in Holden Caulfield's explicit language and youthful musings about sex and the purpose of life, I published a Salinger story he called "Wien, Wien," about a young American who fell in love with a girl in Vienna, a Jewess, who was engaged to marry a man in Poland. After the war the boy learns the girl had been killed by the Nazis. Not very much of a story line but distinguished for the kind of observation and dialogue intentionally and tauntingly trite at the writing of which Salinger is a master second to none. Because a sentence in the story said, "Probably for every man there is one city that sooner or later turns into a girl," I thought "A Girl I Knew" would be a more appropriate title. The blurb we used was a line taken direct from the story. The illustration was a fair representation of the girl described by Salinger—as fair as any magazine representations usually are; and the caption under it also was a line taken direct from the story. I don't know what upset Salinger but he protested vehemently and ordered his agent, Dorothy Olding, never again to show me any of his manuscripts. Miss Olding, whom I consulted on the matter recently, could not herself remember exactly why and at what the author took offense. After all, the incident occurred about thirty years ago. I would have suffered to see Salinger's stories published elsewhere, but there was little occasion; the author is almost as

famous for hiding away and not writing, or if writing anything not letting it be seen for anybody to read, as for creating at least a minor masterpiece in *Franny and Zooey.*

It isn't strange, when one thinks about it, that so
many of the civilized engagements with writers are tucked
away in the back of the mind while more poignant memory
remains of less rewarding ones. A quarter of an hour in the
bar of the Vanderbilt Hotel with Somerset Maugham
leaves no faint trace of subject discussed, most likely a
word or two about the weather and the state of his health
and how long he would be staying in town, but what is as
clear as though it were made yesterday is an agreement we
had entered into: he was to produce four short stories
within twelve months and to receive ten thousand dollars
for each one, a new high in short story compensation and it
was what persuaded him. The first of the quartet—"The
Colonel's Lady"—was one of his particular triumphs. The
second—"A Woman of Fifty"—contained a passage that
seemed spurious and he was asked to delete it. When he
objected, I wrote a long explanation and then another, always deferentially, on why it seemed out of place; urged
him for the story's sake to make the concession. He wrote
to say that what was described in the passage objected to
had really taken place, it had happened, he had seen it, and
therefore it belonged. For a moment he may have forgotten
a line he once used in connection with writing: stick to the
point and, when you can, cut. Further, he knew as well as
any editor that what may be true to life isn't necessarily
true to fiction. Finally, not graciously, he gave way.

Some months after we had sent his literary agent,
Jacques Chambrun, one of the checks due, Maugham wrote
to Kenneth McCormick, his editor at Doubleday, to ask if
Good Housekeeping was in financial difficulties. McCormick assured him the magazine was quite solvent but
called me to inquire when the check had been mailed. As
was anything but unusual with Chambrun, he had with-

held payment to his client. Later, talking with Maugham, I asked why he retained as his representative a man known in the trade to be tricky and dishonest. "Well," Maugham replied, "I've caught him once and now he knows I'm on to him. He won't ever dare do that to me again, so I'm going to keep him." And he did.

When he was sixty years old, Maugham wrote *The Summing Up*, a philosophical exposition of his attitudes toward religion, life and death, his experiences as a student in medical school, of his frequent travels to distant lands, the pleasures and discouragements of the writer's trade. In that book, in reflecting on his own status in the world of letters, the author of *Cakes and Ale, The Moon and Sixpence*, and *Of Human Bondage*, whose plays included *Our Betters, The Circle*, and *The Constant Wife*, and whose short stories still seem so well constructed, was almost embarrassingly modest. He was candid in explaining his approach to writing, saying he was more concerned with the obscure than with the famous. However, once an author has made a great name for himself he may be inclined to make up as many stories about himself as about others. Maugham's statement that he would rather spend a month on a desert island with a veterinary surgeon than with a prime minister appeared long after he had met prime ministers and been feted by those who stood high in society, and one could be forgiven for not taking it at face value. My meetings with him were few and far between, and I never noticed the stammer he was reputed to have, probably because he had as little to say to me as I to him. He had acceded to my request to make a change in "A Woman of Fifty" but I guessed he resented my intrusion into the story and I felt later I should have accepted it as written. Maugham, it seemed to me, was not a man who took kindly to ordinary people; even in the game of bridge, which he loved, he desired the company of professionals and was flattered when asked to write an introduction to a book on bridge by Charles Goren; made him feel, he said, as proud as an ensign bidden by his admiral to lead the flagship into battle. His private life, though fairly well publicized, was none of my business, and the friendship I had formed with Beverley Nichols terminated when he wrote *A Case of Human Bondage,* a disagreeable book about Maugham's marriage relationship with Syrie Wellcome.

About ten years after *The Summing Up,* Maugham's *A Writer's Notebook* was completed. Unlike the former, it is an accumulation of observations of persons met during his excursions to far-flung places—details of how people dressed and talked and acted, so many of which, like his notes about the characters who became the basis for *Rain,* became the basis for much of his literary work. Included are odds and ends of ideas and situations he had never gotten around to using and which, it seemed, he might be bequeathing to writers of the future. There were disquieting reports about Maugham's health at the time and he suspected this could well be his final literary contribution. We acquired magazine rights and then Maugham learned he was in as good health as ever; with writing years still ahead he was not in a mood to leave to anybody what might be salable property—it was possible he could use it all himself. For which reason, or so I suspected, he asked us to postpone publication for a while, which we were obliged to do. He lived to be ninety-one.

I have not gone back to reread any of Maugham's stories or novels but I remember them as always absorbing. If he wasn't a literary master, at least he was a master craftsman.

"In lapidary inscriptions," Samuel Johnson once wrote, "a man is not upon oath." It can be added that neither is a man who keeps a diary. From Evelyn Waugh, deservedly eulogized as one of the superior satirists and stylists of our time, we had received and published a story about an Englishman who was planning to murder his wife but whose wife managed to get her licks in first. Some while thereafter, in February of 1947, Waugh was in New York and

through his agent's office arranged for a visit to mine to talk
about another story. First, however, he groused about the
service at the Waldorf-Astoria Hotel, where he was staying,
which he said was abominable; the abominable food and
wine served, the abominable filth in the city, and the taxi
drivers, who were *most* abominable. When we got around
at last to discussing his projected story he said that instead
of his four-thousand-dollar fee he would prefer to have us
get him, in part payment, a Ford station wagon and have it
delivered in Dublin, where he would pick it up. It was obvious that by receiving a car in lieu of a check he hoped to
avoid paying his government's income tax. To his growing
irritation I had to explain that on no basis would it be possible for the magazine to withhold a declaration to his
country's Inland Revenue. We sent him the car, notified the
British authorities, and Waugh probably paid the tax. I
wouldn't bet on it.

The title of the murder story was "Tactical Exercise,"
which, after receiving his consent in writing, we changed to
"The Wish." In the *Diaries of Evelyn Waugh*, edited by
Michael Davie and published by Little, Brown in 1976,
Waugh introduces in this manner his entry about his session with me: "I then went to see Mr. Mays, the editor of
Good Housekeeping which is the most prosperous paper on
the continent. He was an emaciated Jew lately promoted
within the Hearst organization from editing a weekly paper
devoted to commercial chemistry." I must pause to say,
first, that the man spelled my name wrong. Secondly, that
though prosperous indeed *Good Housekeeping* may have
ranked about fifth in the order of periodical prosperity.
Thirdly, that "commercial chemistry" referred to *American
Druggist*, a monthly not a weekly pharmaceutical magazine, from which I had departed a full thirteen years earlier. Fourth, I have always been fairly slim, never emaciated.

Waugh's entry then proceeds astonishingly to say not
that he asked for part payment in the form of a station

wagon but that the suggestion was mine. He quotes a conversation about the illustration used for the story in which he makes me sound like an advanced case of dementia praecox. I have been told by acquaintances of his in England that at least half of what is in his diaries is false. Writing of his brother, Alec Waugh said, "He was often snubbing, he could be cruel, but basically he was gentle, warm, and tender." Cruel yes, but warm and tender sounds like hyperbole. Michael Davie wrote that Waugh destroyed portions of his diary during "periods of near lunacy," that he was "quite incredibly depraved morally," and then goes further: "Publication of the verbatim text will not be possible for some years, because of the English laws of libel. In this edition, twenty-three libellous references have been altogether excised. Another twenty phrases have been omitted, not because they are libellous but because I have concluded that their publication would be intolerably offensive or distressing to living persons or to surviving relations of persons recently dead." Mr. Davie also refers to Waugh's "taste for exaggeration and fantasy."

I have read five novels from the interesting *Vile Bodies* to the magnificent *Brideshead Revisited* given us by that quirky genius. As a human being, from what I came to know of him, I think he was a creep.

9

Man hasn't changed a great deal since Adam discovered he was one, and human nature is about the same as at the beginning of time, an observation to which even Euripides beat me by a mile or two. Judging from the papers, not excluding the funnies, we have just as much mayhem today, the same elements of love and hate, envy and greed, generosity and self-sacrifice. From way back, writers have always taken all of them into account. Regardless of different styles in which current novels are written, basic subject matter is along the old lines, except that now we may have reached the ultimate in a cycle of obscenity. There is thumping emphasis on crapulous copulation, glorification of pornography and deviant conduct, a tell-it-like-it-is, let-it-all-hang-out approach. Hester Prynne had a child by the Reverend Arthur Dimmesdale, then wore the scarlet "A" proclaiming her adultery. No details of the transgression. None necessary. Hawthorne's modern counterpart has the parties in bed in the first chapter, snorting and exulting in every turn and tumble. Only a few decades ago magazines wouldn't dare show an illustration in which a woman was holding a cigarette in her hands, much less a man in her arms.

Not people but customs were different then. For better or worse is not my business to say. At the start of this century, *Scribner's* carried an article about French art embellished by a picture of a nude. An angry subscriber wrote in protest, I quote verbatim: "A young female in my house-hold saw the article, uttered a low cry, and fled to her room." The old magazine *Chic* was alarmed about women's sleeveless dresses. "In the name of all that men hold sa-cred," it said, "let us ask where this is to end." In 1932 a Mickey Mouse cartoon was barred in Ohio because it showed a cow reclining in a field while reading a copy of Elinor Glyn's *Three Weeks,* the banal novel that es-tablished "It" as a synonym for sex appeal, was excoriated as "fit only for the garbage pail," and banned in Boston by the Watch and Ward Society. It's a bit hard to believe now, but in the 1940's *Reader's Digest* got a great hand for pub-lication of Margaret Culkin Banning's "The Case for Chas-tity." As late as 1954, for *Good Housekeeping,* Phyllis McGinley wrote—no fooling—"Let Us Dare to Say It Out Loud—Unchastity Is a Sin." In 1959, in *McCall's,* Abby Van Buren was saying to teen-agers, "Stay cool, kissing power is stronger than will power—girls need to 'prove their love' like a moose needs a hatrack." We were already well into the morals revolution. While taking it more and more into account, the old established women's magazines still had to endorse the traditional mores. Not in fact a morals revolu-tion, we were in a freer-talk-about-morals revolution. Morals hadn't changed, girls as well as boys had a good grip on the facts of life and indulged in them, but on the quiet. Sex, in effect, simply went public.

Making no claim to virtue—heaven forbid or forfend—I state merely as fact that only once do I remember using the word "sex" on the cover of a magazine, the blurb "My Husband Won't Talk to Me About Sex, Money, or the Chil-dren," not likely to arouse anyone's libido. We weren't prudish, not trying to set any ground rules for behavior, but we weren't going to let anybody else set them for us. Nevertheless, an editor must be of his time, he is expected to change course, though not necessarily all the way. I con-fess to a personal preference for privacy and an aversion to public use of gutter language. Instead of being told how and when a single woman hopped into bed with a man, I sort of liked to read that "she anticipated the marriage ceremony." Anyway, it sounds more genteel, and I do miss the old-fashioned asterisks. I can thumb through *Penthouse* without going into a tailspin; it hasn't taught me one thing I didn't know or shown me one thing I hadn't seen. It's quite all right with me and I don't mind at all if people like to see in print delirious explicitness of what goes on between the sheets. My only objection is that so much repetition gets to sound adolescent. Kid stuff, for needy cases. Not at all like the real thing.

10

Even though the British weren't all that familiar with S. J. Perelman's work, there were enough Americans in residence there when he was who would have given their eyeteeth for a chance to entertain him. Some of them did give their eyeteeth. I gave mine. All of us had heard what fun it was to be with Sid Perelman, what great company he could be. He may have committed some sin and been under a vow of silence during his months in London. We wined and dined him, walked him, flattered him, fluttered around him. Nothing seemed to bring him out of his muteness except mention of a foodmonger where Campbell's soup or some other American product was on sale. "Where's it at?" he would ask, and whip out pencil and notebook.

If there was a lugubrious man in London, it was Perelman. He lived in a flat there, alone, had nobody to look after his needs, did his own shopping for household supplies. He could have afforded such comfort as he wanted. He seemed to have gone spartan. I know of nobody to whom he extended reciprocal invitations to lunch or dinner.

One night I found him a fellow guest in the home of Max Wilk, the American writer, who seemed to know everybody in town worth knowing, and I figured now I'd have a chance to see Perelman brought to life. In my home he had simply sat, eaten, had his drinks, looked benign, said nothing. In Wilk's home he said nothing, looked be-

nign, had his drinks, eaten, and sat. He was, during his sojourn, our enigma. He went around our London world in
eighty words.

Of course, there were other writers from whom one
learned to expect disconcerting silences. Except for Richard
Sherman, so much of whose work I published, from his
"Love in Minneapolis" to "The Life of Riley," and from
The Bright Promise to *A Kindred Spirit*, there was no
fictionist who became my long-lasting intimate friend. A
complex, introverted man, he had a constitutional shyness
and would spend a long evening lounging quietly, taking a
sip of scotch, staring. I don't think he knew for sure what
he wanted, or wanted to be. Writing seemed to be his way
of escaping from his doubts and feelings of guilt about his
lapsed Catholicism. Most writers of fiction have fears of
running into writing blocks—periods when they can't write
at all—and they suffer. Sherman was among them. Their
moods can come close to destroying their faith in themselves; can destroy the peace of mind of their families. Recognition and hoped for rewards don't always materialize.
They bemoan the fate that got them embarked on so peril-
ous an occupation.

I liked Perelman. I loved Sherman. And wasn't successful in making conversation with either one. Whatever their
capriciousness, one had to learn to live with the short story
writers and novelists. I could get along without trouble
with such authors as Elizabeth Janeway, Allen Drury, William Fay, Noel Langley, Paddy Chayefsky, and go home to
swallow some aspirin after an hour with Anne Morrow
Lindbergh, Dorothy Parker, or Carl Van Vechten. Writers,
like everybody else, like editors, have their private problems, they are individuals of varying dimensions of opti-
mism and despair, each day brings some mental or physical
turmoil. It is a good day when the writer has produced his
quota of words, found the solution to a thorny story line,
come away from conference with agent or editor feeling

that life for all its perplexities is tolerable. The creative writer knows much more loneliness than an editor.

Louis Bromfield, whom I had gone to see at his experimental Malabar Farm in Lucas, Ohio, turned sullen because I could not promise to make the story he was writing for us the lead story in the issue for which it was scheduled. If that could not be assured, then he said he'd insist on being paid more money, as though the positioning of a story bore particular relevance to its quality. The first story in an issue may be what the editor considers the best. It may be a lesser story, a lighter one. The most important story sometimes may be in the middle of the well—the main editorial section—because the editor wants the reader to come across it unexpectedly and be shaken up a bit. Bromfield compromised: decided to submit the story elsewhere. He sent us another, later, and it was of his usual competence, so that we were denied the dubious satisfaction of returning it.

If not about positioning, a few authors complain magazines fail to give sufficient prominence to their names (until the middle of the nineteenth century much editorial fare was published anonymously, the *North American Review* being one of the first magazines to print authors' names). To book publishers, authors complain about a conspiracy of silence—too little advertising or none at all. The writer of a detective story sometimes resents the editor's questions: how did the missing key get to be in the trunk in the first place, why didn't the police sergeant lock the door, where did the dead man's wallet suddenly come from? "The detective story is a kind of intellectual game," wrote S. S. Van Dine, creator of the omniscient dilettante of the arts, Philo Vance. "It is more—it is a sporting event. The reader must have equal opportunity with the detective for solving the mystery. All clues must be plainly stated and described." Howard Haycraft, author of *Murder for Pleasure*, put it somewhat similarly: "Stripped of its decorations and embellishments, the detective story is at bottom one thing only: a conflict of wits between criminal and sleuth, in which the detective is traditionally victorious by out-thinking his adversary. Each important plot incident, every structural step of the story, must be the perfect and logical consequence and result of this central conflict of crime and pursuit, just as each move in a chess game determines and is determined by a counter-move. In basic structure it must never vary by a hairsbreadth from absolute logicality."

The new author of a mystery sometimes fails to realize that an editor in charge of mystery fiction is trained to spot inconsistencies, missing links, false leads. Dedicated readers of mysteries are expert in detecting when an author is cheating and the editor's job is to save the author from himself.

In O'Neill's *Where the Cross Is Made*, the right arm of Nat Bartlett has been amputated at the shoulder; a little later he goes to a table, "turning the lantern low, and sits down, resting his elbows, his chin on his hands." The playwright's editor should have caught the error. In Defoe's *Robinson Crusoe*, the hero, who has removed all his clothes in order to swim back to the shipwreck, says, "I went to the bread room and filled my pockets with bisquit." Today's alert copy editor would latch on to that sort of anomaly instantly. In several of Horatio Alger's juveniles a character starts out with one name and has a different one a few chapters later. It wouldn't have bothered my mother; but Alger wrote so much and so fast that no editor had time enough to stay caught up.

For sheer persistence, Samson Raphaelson would have won any award. Author of *The Jazz Singer* and *Accent on Youth*, one of the better Hollywood writers, he was a favorite of Ernst Lubitsch. He deserved more compassion than I was able to offer, his distressing habit, born of egotism, of marching to my home on a Sunday morning to read his stories aloud, driving me to the point of rudeness. There was no way to stop him. One could fidget, frown, yawn, utter a low moan—Raphaelson read on. "Pretty good, eh?" he would say on coming to the end of something like "Lost on Forty-fourth Street," and then without waiting for comment would go right on: "The idea came to me while I was shaving, just one of those things, like way back when I thought of *Skylark*, I was shaving then, too, and now I'd like to do a serial for you, I have the outline here—" He was such a kind man, and so dedicated to his craft, and so supremely good at it, and I wish I had been kinder to him and been able to say to myself, "Patience, my soul—thou hath suffered worse than this."

Patience is a priceless gift, an editor needs much of it, but I didn't have enough. Edna Ferber once phoned to announce an imminent call on me by Marc Connelly, and to say he had a magnificent story for me. A story by the man who was one of my favorite playwrights? Who had written *Dulcy, Beggar on Horseback*, to say nothing of *The Green Pastures?* This was to be my lucky day. When Miss Ferber had used the words "magnificent story" I could not know Connelly had been sitting right alongside of her. When the famous man arrived two hours later, what I heard was a meandering rigmarole he seemed to be making up as he went along. "May I ask what you want from me?" I interrupted after some fifteen minutes. "Well, right now I could use a couple of thousand dollars—if you don't like the story I'll give the money back." I wanted to go home. Promised to send a check the next day. When his story came in it was not remotely related to what Connelly had been describing in the office; but it was, nevertheless, fine. The next time I saw Miss Ferber, she thanked me for being courteous to her friend. "He needed the money in a hurry," she said, "and you've always been a soft touch. By the way, what was that story of his all about?"

When Betty MacDonald followed *The Egg and I* with *The Plague and I*—the book based on her bout with tuberculosis—she materialized out of Puget Sound without notice and intimated I might take her to dinner. To spend an evening with that gallant woman seemed a pleasant prospect, so I invited her to stop at my home first for a drink. She came, and brought along her mother, an aunt, and two other members of her family. They'd decided it would be ducky to dine at the Plaza and then go on to "21" for a nightcap. Without an expense account an editor cannot always manage to pay his bills. *With* an expense account it isn't always easy.

In their own way readers, too, can grate on one's sensibilities, as when several wrote angrily because *Cosmopolitan,* just before I came to it, had published *The Foxes of Harrow.* Frank Yerby was living in Spain or France and we'd never met. Didn't we *know* Yerby was a Negro? We hadn't known and couldn't have cared less.

During the nine years following *For Whom the Bell Tolls,* Hemingway had not written another. It was then he said he had a new one, still untitled, in work; we agreed on a price and in *Cosmopolitan* announced the forthcoming serialization. On the staff of the magazine was A. E. Hotchner, who had become chummy with Hemingway, so to Hotchner I assigned the task of staying in touch with him to make certain the famous but often aberrant author remained actively at work. I had met Hemingway only casually, we had gotten along with a minimum of politesse, but I shared the universal respect for his wizardry as a writer.

Hotchner's ensuing verbal reports on the progress of the novel were disconcertingly vague. When Hemingway whimsically decided to go abroad, presumably to complete the book, he was eager to have Hotchner with him for companionship; between them, like a couple of delinquent schoolboys, they concocted a story that would persuade me to let Hotchner go along. Hotchner seemed as good a babysitter as any around, so I agreed.

From being vague, Hotchner's reports from Europe became suspiciously inconsistent and it was suggested his desk might give us a clue. In consequence came a disagreeable but necessary decision: to make a search of the desk. The decision was endorsed by the company's legal department, the desk was opened by a locksmith in the presence of four witnesses, including an attorney and the superintendent of the building. In the desk were correspondence from Hemingway to Hotchner and carbons of letters from Hotchner to Hemingway, making clear that the two men had been conniving to keep us misinformed. I reached Hotchner by phone, ordering him to return to New York immediately. He came, and the completed manuscript bearing the title *Across the River and into the Trees* finally was in our hands.

As a serial in *Cosmopolitan* the novel was a flop. The Hemingway name had lost some of its spell—the public wasn't even interested in sampling the first installment. About the book when issued by Scribner's, John O'Hara, with his typical lack of restraint, declared it, in a first-page review in the book section of the Sunday New York *Times*, to be the best writing since Shakespeare. Most of the notices, however, were unfavorable, the critics thinking, as we did, that the novel was inferior Hemingway and saying so. I have not reread the novel but I have thought back on it often and long ago concluded it may have been better than any of us thought at the time.

In 1966, Hotchner himself produced a book, *Papa Hemingway*, an account of his fourteen years as a Hemingway crony, following which, in a *Saturday Review* column, I said the following: "Speaking of *Cosmopolitan*, A. E. Hotchner was a member of the staff at a time I was in charge, and I assigned to him the Hemingway book project which turned out to be *Across the River and into the Trees*. In his interesting and successful *Papa Hemingway*, Hotchner tells the story of that venture. It makes good reading, but it happens not to be true. Indeed, Hotchner's handling of the project for *Cosmopolitan* was so unfortunate that, in February 1950, the very month we published the first installment, it became necessary to ask for Hotchner's resignation."

Agitated, Hotchner wrote a denunciatory letter to *Saturday Review*. Norman Cousins, then editor of the magazine, forwarded a copy of the letter, thinking it fair I should be given an opportunity to respond in the same issue. I did, vigorously and in detail. Cousins then thought it reasonable that Hotchner should see my response before the correspondence got into print. "On seeing your reply," Cousins then wrote in a note to me, "Hotchner opted to withdraw his letter. Under the circumstances I think this was a wise decision, as I am sure you will agree." Cousins wrote further: "This is strictly a case of no contest. Hotchner gets so much the worst of it that the Humane Society would be after us if we ran it." In a lengthy article in *The Atlantic Monthly*, analyzing Hotchner's effort, Philip Young, research professor of English at Penn State and an acknowledged Hemingway scholar, wrote: "Several reviewers have expressed deep misgivings about the taste and propriety of this book ('disgraceful,' 'shameless,' 'contemptible'). But no one seems to have called any substantial part of it into question, though little more than common sense is required to question Hotchner rather early in the game, and to doubt as well that Papa was much concerned to tell him the truth. Almost at the start Hemingway appears to have discovered that his fawn would relish almost anything. And so he fed it tidbits in generous variety as long as he was having fun."

A contentious character as well as a thoroughly competent writer, Hotchner has been party to several lawsuits, with one of which I am familiar. A Spanish author, José Luis Castillo-Puche, had written a book that was translated into English and published by Doubleday under the title *Hemingway in Spain*. "The thing I disliked most about Hotchner," Castillo-Puche wrote, "was his two-faced behavior toward people who were Ernesto's real friends. . . . Though he was very clever at hiding his true feelings, you could tell that Hotchner was really a hypocrite . . . he was such a toady at times that it was sickening." Why Hotchner

bothered to give a second thought to the comment is hard
to explain. Castillo-Puche's book is excruciatingly dull and
the author was nothing more than a hanger-on in Hemingway's years in Spain; so unimportant that Mary Hemingway in her autobiography, *How It Was,* merely mentions
the man once and then only as a member of a group that
one night had dinner with her husband. Being a sensitive
soul, however, Hotchner was so offended that he filed suit
for libel. The case wound up in the United States Court of
Appeals for the Second Circuit, which decided against
Hotchner.

It can be said for Maggie Cousins and me that the
way we earned our living was seldom dull. Whatever the
problems that sometimes made for sabotage of peace of
mind, we counted our blessings and were grateful for the
nature of the challenge. One could set down for pages on
end the unproductive efforts to lay hands on a desired manuscript. There were three or four days spent with Arthur
Kober putting finishing touches on an outline for a story in
which the hero would be an immigrant Israeli bookkeeper
with a "Yiddisher Kopf" who by chance solved a murder
problem and thereafter devoted himself to crime investigation. Because of his *Bella* stories, Kober seemed to me
the ideal choice for creating the necessary language for a
Jewish Sherlock Holmes. His enthusiasm for the idea
seemed boundless. It ended in a week. I felt our idea might
have gone over; several years later one Harry Kemelman
wrote a series of books about a Rabbi Small, "shy, scholarly and slightly absent-minded," who discovered he was
pretty good at solving mysteries.

Sometimes we published a story that resulted in an
awkward postscript, John van Druten's "Gavin" as a case in
point. It had to do with a woman who wanted children but
whose husband didn't. He had a son, he said, by another
woman and that was enough. The son, he said, was "just
twenty, six feet two, weighs a hundred and seventy, a

magnificent specimen, never had a day's sickness in his life; not an intellectual giant but not stupid, either. As a matter of fact, the standard of perfection." In the end the wife gets to see the son, quite by accident. He was misshapen, a hunchback, with one foot dragging behind. Quite a gruesome tale but too compelling not to dare use. Mr. van Druten told me a stranger knocked on the door of his house one night and asked to see him. "I don't know how he got hold of my address," van Druten said, "but there he was, a hunchback, and in other ways deformed." The man had just finished reading van Druten's story. "You know what I look like," he said to the author, "and I just wanted to see what *you* look like." "Scared me half to death," van Druten reported.

It isn't necessary to search hard for sweeter memories. In Moss Hart's book *Act One,* telling how he and George Kaufman met for the first time and began their successful collaboration on the play *Once in a Lifetime,* there was a section I found captivating and told Hart so. I mentioned also that Maggie Cousins had written a rapturous report. Hart pleaded that I go to my office immediately and fetch it for him to see, which I did. Hart could not contain his excitement, insisted on standing up and reading the report to the assembled guests. He declared himself as happy with it as with the success of the play. When our portion of the book was published, Hart took me to a fancy lunch that really should have been for Miss Cousins.

When both of us were young men, and publishing our passion, Eric Hodgins and I became good friends. He was editor of *Youth's Companion* when I was editor of trade magazines. He was editorial head of *Fortune* when I was of *Good Housekeeping.* He had a more beautiful command of English than any other person I knew. He produced *Mr. Blandings Builds His Dream House,* which in 1946 became a best seller, and followed it with *Mr. Blandings' Way,* which we were happy to publish. Hodgins loved words, his speeches were eloquent and his voice the perfect one for making them. One day he woke to find he had voice but no words; had suffered a dreadful disabling stroke but remembered every minute of the tragic occurrence. Ultimately he wrote about it, in a book that is a classic, called *Episode*. I began to read the manuscript at noon, at home, and finished it at midnight, too late to call him. "Call him anyway," my wife urged, so I phoned. His voice was choked with emotion as he tried to thank me; I had said we would publish it. In time he began to regain his ability to walk, if not well at least without assistance; and his speech, if not altogether clear, was understandable. He came to the office, unannounced; took my hands in his, and his big frame shook as he shook my hands; then turned and made his slow way out.

It can be said that from almost all authors we had far more gratitude than grief. Any gripes I have are incidental.

If we had a story from Jerome Weidman that seemed to call for a few changes, he would as soon as not prefer to write a completely new one. Of all writers he seemed to be the fastest. And though his first novel, *I Can Get It for You Wholesale*, may be his best known, since it came out in 1937 he has written more than two dozen other novels of which the saga beginning with *Fourth Street East* in 1971 and going on to *A Family Fortune* in 1978 can be considered among his best and will grow in stature as the years pass on. Weidman is something of a phenomenon. A tenacious, positively brilliant writer of short stories. One of his plays, *Fiorello!*, was honored with the Pulitzer Prize.

What would an editor do without the daily newspaper? Where would some ideas for stories come from? Richard Whitney, member of a distinguished family, had been president of the New York Stock Exchange. After news of his conviction for embezzlement and his sentence to prison, I phoned Adela Rogers St. Johns. What happens now to the man's wife? I asked. Does she go into seclusion? Continue to appear in public, go to afternoon teas, play bridge, try to pretend nothing has happened? What does she say when she goes to visit her husband in prison—does she make small talk about family matters? What I wanted to know, what I said readers would want to know, is what goes on in the mind of such a bereaved woman. "I'll do it," Adela said promptly, "and I'll call it 'Wife, Maid Nor Widow.'" A perfect title for what became a bittersweet story and within a month it was delivered.

Paul Gallico, a huge man, looked like the sportswriter he used to be, like a heavyweight prizefighter who could take on Jack Dempsey, which he once did for the novelty of it, to see how it would feel to be knocked out, which he was. His black hair and dark brown eyes gave one the impression he was a fierce character, but his smile was broad and his laugh hearty. He never looked like a man who could write tender stories, who wrote *The Snow Goose,* which made him famous, who could write so whimsical a tale as that about the romance between a snowflake and a raindrop. After *Mrs. 'Arris Goes to Paris,* I asked if his adorable British char Ada Harris might be brought to America. There was no hesitation, along came "Mrs. 'Arris Goes to New York." Soon after we published Mazo de la Roche's heartrending "Peter—a Rock" and were deluged by mail from readers demanding a sequel in which the dog Peter would be reunited with his master, Miss de la Roche responded quickly. Remembering Daudet's story "The Last Class," I said to Faith Baldwin, "Suppose a woman who has been a schoolteacher all her life is now about to retire. She faces her class one morning—it is to be her last. She thinks back on the children who once were her pupils. One has become a successful merchant, another governor of the state, another went off to war and was wounded. The one she loved best became a priest—" Faith Baldwin called the story "Roll Call" and it worked out beautifully. As a gift for the idea she sent me a cocker spaniel puppy. "But don't cut off his tail," she pleaded, "he was born with it and needs something to wag when he's happy."

Vera Caspary had written *Laura,* a highly successful

suspense novel, and after that the famous *Bedelia,* which we published. Then living in California, the author was impatient to be started on another. I asked her to come to New York, saying I might have an idea. On the evening of her arrival we had supper at the Stork Club. "Must be a great idea," she said, "to make me fly across the country for it. So tell me." "A murder," I said, "right here, this very spot." She stared at me, at Bernard Gimbel, who was sitting across from us, and at Walter Winchell at his accustomed table. "Perfect," she said, "especially if we can get permission to use the real names of the people who come here." The permission was granted. Then for several weeks, day and night, Miss Caspary lived in the place, absorbing background, making notes, putting together her *Murder in the Stork Club.*

It had been getting increasingly difficult to find novels that held up well enough to run serially, even for four or five issues, as against the six, seven, and eight that formerly had been considered normal. Even ten installments had not been considered too many, though hardly matching Harriet Beecher Stowe's *Uncle Tom's Cabin,* which, beginning on June 5, 1851, in the *National Era,* ran in forty successive weekly numbers (John Greenleaf Whittier was an editor of the magazine at the time). For her effort—one could say it provoked more explosive sentiment than any other novel before or since—Mrs. Stowe was paid ten dollars per installment. A total of four hundred dollars! Early in the 1940's we began to give more attention to novels that could be handled in two installments.

Like any other editors, we were elated whenever a story arrived from William Saroyan. One afternoon, from either Las Vegas or Reno, I had a collect call from him. He had lost all his money gambling, he confided, and would I be so kind as to send him ten thousand dollars via Western Union, which he would repay shortly by sending in a couple of new stories. Knowing how erratic that brilliant and ebullient genius could be, and that the promised stories might be a week or a year in coming, I offered to send him a thousand dollars instead. Insulted, Saroyan hung up on me. I sent him nothing. A month later we received "Thank You Very Much for Everything, and Don't Worry," one of his superior stories, whose title may have been intended to convey to me some kind of personal message. One never knows.

In his book *Thirty Years*, John Marquand ranked me third as an editor, declaring George Horace Lorimer and Maxwell Perkins* my betters. In books and articles written about him, Perkins has been held to be the greatest of book editors. The glorification may be well deserved and has mystified me only because of the absence of comparatives. Of which book editors was Perkins greater? Than any at Viking, Knopf, Oxford, Dial, Dutton, or Farrar, Straus? He certainly was responsible for much of the success of Thomas Wolfe, and for what was achieved by Taylor Caldwell and Scott Fitzgerald, among others. But I have not really been able to understand what made Perkins a better editor than Saxe Commins of Random House, as one example. I doubt that Scribner's issued more distinguished books than Alfred and Blanche Knopf during the same period. However, I was pleased that Marquand put me in good company, though I admired him for other reasons. At lunch one day, knowing he was fairly proficient at chess, I suggested he try a story about a man who, like all male members of his family for generations back, had learned to play chess as a matter of family tradition, had gone to West Point, then on to high posts in the Army; who turned out to be the family rebel, resigned his command, ended up in a penny arcade playing chess for twenty-five cents a game with anybody rash enough to take him on. Marquand never had seen the kind of arcade I described, so he went with me to Eighth Avenue and Forty-second Street to see one. He stayed a few minutes, then went on his way, having

* For twenty years until his death in 1947, Perkins had been chief editor of Charles Scribner's Sons.

made no comment. Recruited into a secret service area of military life dealing with biological warfare, he spent part of the war period in Europe. When we met again, about two years later, it was quite by accident. "I've got your chess story," he remarked, as though we had just been talking about it. "Am checking a few details. It'll be over to you in a week or two."

The story—a novelette—deftly worked out, not a soft spot in it, was called "The End Game." Referring to it in his book *The Late John Marquand*, Stephen Birmingham said, "Though it was admired, several critics pointed out the artificiality of the surprise O. Henry-esque ending and John became quite sensitive about this. He began, in fact, to talk about the story, saying that he himself liked it 'in spite of the tricked-up ending tacked on by Herbert Mayes.'" I hadn't tacked anything on. Quite the contrary, my suggestion for the ending was exactly the opposite of his. I had wanted the "hero" to remain a maverick, his old age spent in a penny arcade, not finally reaching a higher military rank than his brothers, as Marquand had him do. But in my opinion Marquand's ending was better than mine, no matter what he said about it; and the notion that I would have dared change so radically what he wrote is an absurd one. Normally an editor may reserve to himself the right to cut a manuscript but never the right to add to or change an author's point of view. When it comes to changes, the author generally is the best person to make them. Marquand's defensive attitude in the matter was an indication in part of his vanity, and in part of his inferiority complex, and of the latter, for all his success and patrician bearing, he gave evidence often enough.

He had constant curiosity about other writers, in particular Lewis, Maugham, and Richard Sherman; wanted to know how I worked and got along with them. He liked to believe he was at least as highly paid as any other author, with rising inflection would say, "I suppose Maugham is very well off?" and "Do magazines pay Lewis as much as I hear sometimes?" Maugham was near the top of the scale, but not all the way, which it wouldn't have been wise to tell him.

During an office conversation Marquand asked if I had ever seen military service. I hadn't. My draft notice was received a few days before the end of World War I, but it had no significance—a heart murmur, with me from birth, would have kept me out of any active war service. When we got into World War II, when I was forty and thus disqualified by age for active service, I wrote to Frank Knox, who had been for a short time a Hearst executive and now was Secretary of the Navy, requesting some kind of appointment. Knox replied by saying I should stick to my job as editor where I might do more good than by trying to be a hero in Washington. "Knox must have been right," Marquand commented, "but in your place I think I'd have wanted to be more directly involved, just so it would be on the record." I saw no sense in trying to contradict him.

In the beginning it wasn't easy for me to get close to Marquand. He seemed reticent, not ill at ease, just wanting to keep me at arm's length; but as time went on he opened up, spoke frankly and sometimes disparagingly about his reputation, saying he was on the whole regarded as more "popular" than literary. He was pleased that I did not cut his stories, let them run at the length he wrote them. The *Ladies' Home Journal* published several of his novels. "Over there," he complained, "the editors hack me to pieces," a statement that could be doubted.

Marquand took pleasure in popping in at the office, I suspected because his oldest son, Johnny, was an editor on the *Cosmopolitan* staff. His affection for Johnny was undisguised, as was his opinion that the young man did not work hard enough. He said Johnny had considerable talent as a writer, that he could be one, but questioned whether he would make the necessary effort. Now and then, perhaps to his own surprise, he talked of minor family problems. The eight-year-old Ferry, a daughter by his second wife, had shocked him with her use of scatological language. "I ordered her to get a sheet of paper and a pencil," he told me. "Then I said, 'Now I'm going to call out all the dirty words there are. I want you to write them all down, so you'll know them. After that, you will tear up the paper. And if I ever hear you use one of those words I will do something very unfatherly—I will spifflicate you.'" He guessed *that* would hold her. It certainly held me because I hadn't run into the word before.

When I suggested to Marquand that he might write a story about the president of a railroad—a man who wished to retire and spend the remainder of his life on ships but didn't dare quit because so much and so many were dependent on him, a man whose failure in life was his success in business—Marquand said irately, "You seem to have it so firmly in mind, why don't you write it yourself?" I was too good an editor and had read too much of what had writing style to know I had none myself, so I told Marquand I was no writer. "Well," he replied, "I am no railroad man," and the idea died then and there. I could visualize characters in detail, have them progress orderly in plot from one situation to another, but it is true I had no skill in putting any of it on paper, and had no desire to. Often, night after night, instead of reading to my children when they went to bed I would sit alongside and make up stories for them to listen to. But I couldn't write them. My dear, dear children! When they were very young I took them on a journey through New England, wanting them to see the birthplace of our history. I began to point to roads Paul Revere had traveled to spread the alarm of redcoats on the march. "We're coming close to where the Old North Church was built, the one with the belfry arch," I explained. And in response they shouted "Idaho!" and "West Virginia!" and "Louisiana!"—being more concerned with identifying states from license plates of passing automobiles. In Concord would they care to hear again of the hurrying hoofbeats of

Paul Revere's steed? "We want *Little Women*, we want to see the house where Louisa May Alcott lived!"

The commitment of Daphne du Maurier to the *Ladies' Home Journal* was of long standing. Our blandishments in seeking to steal her away were unavailing. Then Miss du Maurier wrote a horror story the editors of the *Journal* rejected as being too frightening for their readers and it landed on the desk of Margaret Cousins. We read it —"The Birds"—with mounting suspense. The thousands of birds, millions of them, tens of millions, attacking. The radio report: "This is London—a national emergency has been proclaimed." Then no more bulletins. The gulls, the hawks, their stabbing beaks, set on destruction. Mankind to be destroyed. What a setting, what a scene! It is the story of Daphne du Maurier's most often anthologized. We were pleased to have published it, lucky to have had the chance.

Acquaintance with Ben Hecht began through Helen Hayes, whose husband, Charles MacArthur, was Hecht's companion in fun, games, and mischief. Of all men I knew, Hecht was the most violent on the subject of the persecution of Jews in Europe and what he held was lack of fervor on the part of their coreligionists to resort to any physical means to defend themselves. His collective hero was the Irgun, his support passionate of their terrorist tactics in Jerusalem. His personal villain was President Franklin Roosevelt, who in his opinion was interested only in saving the British from the Nazis and fundamentally cared little about the fate of the Jews. Among Jews I thought he was the most activist. He gave no small part of his life to their cause. He berated me for giving so small a part of mine.

When in a writing mood his output could be enormous. He could spin off short stories, novels, plays, and scripts for films that proved to be spectacular successes. I think that "The son-of-a-bitch stole my watch," the last line in *The*

Front Page, which he wrote with MacArthur, is still the best last line I ever heard in a play. I had been trying to persuade him to speak to my weekly class at Columbia University. "What could I say that your gang would want to hear?" he asked, and I said a description of his writing habits. "If I told the truth your kids would swear never to try writing. It's a terrible business." It was not the writing itself that was so awful, he went on, but what happened when he got through. "I'm alive and well when the typewriter is going full blast," he explained, "but when the final paragraph or scene is done I hate myself—I'm sure I've got a disaster."

Other writers have spoken similarly, and it is no exaggeration to say that a writer's exhilaration when he is in the throes of composition can be totally dissipated when he is through. There can be a descent from high tension to despairing depth. He wonders if it is as good as he wanted it to be, if it will be recognized as the best that could be done. Then the time waiting for reaction to its reception can frazzle the nerves. Knowing which, no experienced editor holds on to a manuscript for any undue length of time without sending word to explain the delay. No matter where, or what else there was to do, I did not let manuscripts accumulate; set aside everything else to write a report to the author or agent or to Maggie Cousins, so that it could be known, as it always was, that we had no greater concern than for the authors. I never left my office without a briefcase packed with manuscripts—an editor is fortunate in that he can always carry his work with him. What editor has not gotten home from the theater close to midnight and sat up until sunrise to finish with stories calling for attention? An office is seldom congenial for reading—too many visitors, too many interruptions.

If not satisfactory, manuscripts should be returned immediately. For a short story that can be read in an hour or less, there is small excuse, even remembering the number of manuscripts a magazine receives, for delaying return more than ten days. On the other hand, it is not unreasonable to hold a novel or long book of nonfiction for two or even three months.

Whether to the author of a first story, to a Daphne du Maurier or a Ben Hecht, there can be no kinder gesture from editor than that prompt word, favorable or otherwise. If favorable, payment should be made quickly, to be followed where appropriate by note or phone call to literary agent or direct to author. No matter how experienced, hard-boiled, and well established, writers thrive on compliments. When Samuel Johnson declared any man a blockhead who wrote except for money, he was only partly right. Writers write out of egotism, for fame, to be gossiped about, for the satisfaction of being able to write, for seeing their work in print. For the sheer joy of exercising their gift.

11

It's a gamble. Writing is a gamble. Editing is a gamble. The editor guesses a little, hopes a lot, prays that the issue being put together will succeed. He can't be dogmatic about what readers will like most or least. Statistics reveal in advance only readers' sex, age, locale, approximate income. Nothing definitive about what they'll like. Here I could be as gobbledygooky as when I was preaching to youngsters on the must-haves and must-dos of an editor; but he must surely possess perception, insight into human beings and human affairs. He relies on subconscious impulses. Hunch. Intuition. Instinct. He needs wisdom more than learning.

I'd explain it better if I could. If I could explain it better, I'd be a writer. Writers become writers by writing. Editors become editors by editing.

We assumed our readers to be fairly intelligent and have modest intellectual curiosity. Middle Americans. Middlebrow. In every way middle. It would be foolish to patronize them. A mass audience is not visible, not seen in the flesh. What is called an average reader is a nebulous being, a myth. Few readers know one another. Commonality of interest may be assumed if the editorial appeal, as in the once popular *American Weekly* under Morrill Goddard, is on a low enough intellectual level. Goddard's formula was based on what he described as the sixteen basic human interests: love, hate, fear, vanity, selfishness, ambition, immortality, evildoing, cruelty, superstition, curiosity, veneration, culture, heroism, science, and amusement. Somehow in that comprehensive catalogue he managed to ignore sex, which made all the rest of his pontificating suspect. However, his audience became so huge that he kept trying to explain it by virtually apologizing for what achieved it: *"American Weekly*—yes, it is sensational, but the great events of history have been sensational. Because a thing is sensational it is not necessarily objectionable." Commonality of interest, but limited, also may be assumed if the appeal is on a high enough literary plane as in *The Bookman* when under John Farrar, or when there is a well-defined religious or political bias, as in *The Catholic Sentinel* or in William Buckley's *National Review.*

Magazines like *The Atlantic* and *Harper's* make an incalculable contribution to our cultural life, but neither in its history has gotten a circulation of more than a few hundred thousand. Most authors would prefer to be published in them than in a "commercial" magazine like *Redbook* or *Good Housekeeping,* but the scale of payment is too low to warrant such indulgence often. Other "quality" magazines such as *The Century* and *Scribner's* also served a laudable purpose, but for none of them did circulation grow to proportions of appeal to advertisers, and all of them disappeared.

A magazine isn't always measured by size, nor should it be. The biggest is seldom the best, the smallest hardly ever the worst. Influence can count for more than size. But where the influence is and how far it carries is a matter not readily determined. Yet for all the failures it is comforting to realize that counterparts of the departed quality magazines will again be fostered by bright young men and women who will derive their nourishment from hope if not from income; they will attend stoically to tales of magazine misfortunes past but keep in mind the likes of the deceased *Story,* which found a place for the masterpiece "Address—Unknown," and the likes of the abandoned *Dial,* which found room for the unforgettable "The Gentleman from San Francisco." "Little" magazines and small book-publishing houses are sometimes first in recognizing literary value and with them many famous writers got their start.

Literary merit in novels is no barrier to popular success, though one has to distinguish on the one hand between the psychological analyses of a Proust and the obscurant prose of a Joyce, and on the other hand the sentimentality of a Dickens and the romanticism of the Brontës. All of them are part of literature and need to be known enough by an editor if only to find out he doesn't care for them. More of what is good literature might be more popular if, as complained by young people, it wasn't forced down their throats, as *Silas Marner* is—or was—in school. Assigned reading, as they call it, with every chapter having to be examined microscopically and every motive dissected and interpreted. Great writers of the last century, from Hugo and Balzac to Dumas and Thackeray, were published in popular magazines in the United States and abroad. Trollope's *The Eustace Diamonds* was serialized in *The Galaxy*, Shaw's *Pygmalion* in *Everybody's*, as was A. S. M. Hutchinson's *If Winter Comes*. Wilkie Collins' *The Moonstone* appeared in the United States in *Harper's Weekly*. Booth Tarkington's *Alice Adams* and Edith Wharton's *Age of Innocence* were serialized in *Pictorial Review*. American novelists ranked as the best in their part of the present century —Willa Cather, William Faulkner, Ellen Glasgow, John O'Hara, Scott Fitzgerald, and Ernest Hemingway among them—all wrote for the big-circulation magazines; and if others such as Frances Parkinson Keyes and Pearl Buck were not always in the same league, they were compelling storytellers and it was a delight to work with most of them.

In an earlier time, because publishers didn't make much money either, literary values and compensation bore little relationship. O. Henry's first story, "Money Maze," was bought by *Ainslee's* for $50; the maximum payment he ever got was $200. Mark Twain accepted two cents a word for his stories. *Tarzan of the Apes* was serialized in *All-Story Magazine* and for it Edgar Rice Burroughs was paid $700. For *Graustark,* George Barr McCutcheon received $500. For *Pride and Prejudice,* one of the finest novels ever written, Jane Austen, who was all of twenty years old at the time, got $500. It is regrettable that now, when magazine publishers are making the greatest profits in history, their payment to writers is below my own time when I regarded $1,800 as a modest price for a short story and $100,000 for a serial. Once upon a time authors were paid a flat fee for a manuscript and thereafter had no financial interest in it at all, all profit going to the printer or publisher. I recall reading that Milton's total compensation for *Paradise Lost* was the equivalent of $75.

On the whole I found novels less pleasurable to be concerned with than the short stories on which magazines depended for so much of their fiction fare. What a short story is has been defined numberless times by authors, editors, teachers, and critics. It may have a well-defined narrative line—a beginning and an ending, if beginning and ending then obviously a middle, a *plot*. It may be a perceptive satire, or "sketch" or vignette. It may be a character study, as of aging Gustav von Aschenbach in Mann's long story *Death in Venice,* or merely a mood, like Galsworthy's "Buttercup Night," and still leave editor and reader emotionally drained. The novel demands characters and character development; the short story, situation, action. The novel builds, the short story happens. The short story calls for more to be told in less space.

What Margaret Cousins and I sought to publish was the better fiction, which didn't always mean by "big" names; we did not mistake reputation for quality. Ours was a declared goal, attainable in no small part because we paid high prices. I think of Doris Peel's "The Beginning," a few hundred words that tell little more than how a hapless, hungry, tiny child living on charity hands a flower to a lady: "I gived somebody something!" And "The Shining Thing," in which Sidney Carroll paints a portrait of Mister Beau Brummel, the English gentleman, bankrupt, destitute, who presents his one possession, a priceless ormolu clock, to a wealthy visitor who covets it. "I do not sell to friends. It is yours. I pray you accept it. My pleasure, sir, my very great pleasure."

We gave our readers many memorable stories, wish we had given more. I have stayed awake at night, like every editor, brooding about authors whose talents we should have sought out, about stories we should not have rejected. I chastised myself about "The Light in the Piazza," the story by Elizabeth Spencer of the mildly retarded American girl whose parents acquired an Italian for her husband, which I thought too special for our readers and recommended to *The New Yorker,* which gratefully accepted it. I remember with regret a story called "The Lottery"—the assembling of the people of a small town, the collecting of stones, the drawing of the tickets, the first stone thrown that struck Tessie Hutchinson, the first scream of fear and pain. I had met the author in the home of Leah Salisbury, an agent. Shirley Jackson, wife of Stanley Hyman, one of the country's foremost literary critics, said she had finished a story I might like and I suggested she send it to me. She didn't, she brought it, in person, a carbon copy, and left it with a secretary. Two days later I phoned Miss Jackson and asked her to come to the office. "Mrs. Hyman," I said— and she said, "Please call me Shirley"—"Shirley, this 'Lottery' of yours is so absolutely perfect that I can't get it out of my head. It's a gem, we'll be thrilled to have it." "I'm so glad you liked it," she said, "and I'm sorry you haven't heard, but *The New Yorker* has taken it." Her husband, on *The New Yorker* staff, had handed a copy to one of the editors there. "The Lottery" remains one of the most startling stories I have ever read.

I think of Elizabeth Thomas' "Traveling Salesman," about the man who took to peddling gadgets from door to

door in hope of some day coming across his wife, who left
his home one evening, not a word being said, and never returned; of Brendan Gill's "The Test," of the boy snitching
on his roommate Edward Carter, who had written a kind of
love letter to the dean's wife; of William March's "October
Island," in which Irma Barnfield returns to the savages she
helped to civilize, is received with joy and decorated and
revered and worshipped and then, like any other deity of
the tribe, is deposited in a volcano. We published George
Sumner Albee's "Little Hiram," Colored Person Number
One, who said, "Lawd, let mah people go," which caused
all the coloreds of the world to vanish in the twinkling of
an eye, with His Soo Preme Excellency the President of
the United States calling on Hiram and pleading with him
to pray them back again; it could be held dated now, but if
one's mind unrolls to when old Satchmo was tooting his
trumpet and Jackie Robinson was whanging the ball for the
Dodgers (the *Brooklyn* Dodgers!), it is still one of the most
seductive of fables. We published Mary King O'Donnell's
"A Pair of Shoes," about poor old Timothy Berry, who
wanted to keep his shoes on even when lying near death on
a hospital cot, and Paul Gallico's "Never Take No for an Answer," about the love of the orphan Pepino for his donkey
Violetta (who had a Mona Lisa smile), and William San-
som's "Vertical Ladder," with Flegg taking the pretty girl's
dare, and climbing, climbing, the terror in him growing,
and the wind echoing, "Don't look down, for God's sake,
don't look down." And there was Grace Amundson's Greco,
who played for age-old stakes in an ancient bunco game in
"A Man of Parts" and Phil Stong's Waino and Ivar hoping
to find something to aim at with their rifle in "Honk the
Moose" and—well, they're still around and I think their glit-
ter has not been tarnished by time, and I hope one of my
vintage may be forgiven for thinking back to an age when
stories, magazines' short stories, many of them, were literature. I hope it will be remembered that mass circulation
magazines, unlike television, did not choose the lowest

common denominator of taste as the final determining factor.

However wispy the plot of a story by a Katherine Mansfield, who died at thirty-four, or the dramatic power of one by a Joyce Carol Oates or the tantalizing back-in-time motive of one by a Jack Finney, we envy the thrill of the author at the moment of conceiving it. There is a wealth of invention in the world's short story heritage. "It is the product of effort," Wilbur Daniel Steele said of the short story, "to be dreamed up, contemplated, gone over, groped with, twisted, turned around, sighed over, chiseled, polished, and sometimes begun over again from scratch." I think the short story is itself an art form, though it must have fewer characters than a novel and cover less ground; it demands quicker resolution, has no room for discursive rumination. A short story can be the epitome of imaginative skill but does not have to have a contrived ending. "It is not always desirable," as Sinclair Lewis noted, "to add to the pot some 80,000 words of tediousness in order to call the resultant stew a novel."

A good many books have been written that seek to explain how stories can and should be written. I never thought they really served their purpose. The critic Edward O'Brien went so far as to prepare a "case book" in which he analyzed every paragraph in a dozen or more stories. All the pulling apart and reassembling is stuff and nonsense, a waste of time. I thought the book a futile effort then and doubt I would think better of it now, because it seems to me the only way to learn to write stories is to keep on reading stories, perhaps two or three a day, and then going ahead and trying to write. What I would urge the would-be's against is reading collections of stories, anthologies, one story after another, in quick succession, without stopping. Stories shouldn't be lapped up that way, the reader needs time for a little reflection, a savoring of the emotion aroused. I feel stories are not to be gone at like a textbook, but absorbed, inhaled. A dozen or more stories engorged at a sitting are for gluttons, not gourmets. Old stories, good old stories, may not be good *now* stories, but hundreds of them are still worth reading, bearing in mind that the world's fashions change, in thought, style, humor; one needs to remember the time and circumstances in which they were written. For me, in fiction, there is only the first time around. I don't want to chance being disillusioned by reading again what once I may have cherished.

There aren't and can't be effective textbook rules, unless, for the fun of it, one cares to make an exception for Ring Lardner's *How to Write Short Stories,* which begins: "A little group of our deeper drinkers has suggested that maybe boys and girls who wants to take up writing as their life work would be benefitted if some person like I was to give them a few hints."

When asked how an idea for a story came to her, Carson McCullers said she didn't know for sure, that she just sat and gazed out a window, or dozed in a chair, and a situation and a set of characters suddenly were alive in her mind. Sometimes, she said, the denouement came to her first and she would begin to work backwards from it. The idea for a story may come to a writer who sees a face in a crowd, a cloud in the sky, a clock on a shelf, or hears the cry of a child, the bark of a dog, the patter of rain. It was one of the crime authors, I believe Raymond Chandler, who said, "I suppose there's a kind of magic to writing but don't hand me any kudos for it—it just happens, like red hair." But for others, the process of literary creation is purgatory and is nowhere as dramatically portrayed as in Tess Slesinger's stream-of-consciousness "A Life in the Day of a Writer" (which is the correct title, not "A Day in the Life of"). It appeared in *Story* about forty years ago and nothing I have read since has come up to it in visualizing the pain and psychosis endured by a man or woman struggling to set the first word on paper.

I believe the best description of how a writer knows what a story is, is what I read in an interview by Jean F.

Mercer with the writer Mignon Eberhart. It appeared in *Publishers' Weekly* and I can't do better than quote from it exactly. "A young man who wanted to be an expert on jade," Miss Eberhart told Miss Mercer, "went to learn from a talented teacher, a very old man. The gentle man put a piece of stone into the boy's hands and told him to hold it tight. Then he began to talk about philosophy, men, women, the sun and almost everything under it. After an hour, he took the stone back and sent the boy home. The next day the student returned, the procedure was repeated and so it went, for several weeks. The boy was quite frustrated—when would he be told about jade?—but was too polite to interrupt his venerable teacher. Then one day the old man put a stone into the boy's hands and the student said instantly, 'That's not jade!'" Likewise, anybody who reads enough knows soon enough when a story is not a story. Anyone who reads Katherine Anne Porter's "Noon Wine" knows *that's* a story. With beginning, middle, and end. With characterizations of people so real the reader can see, hear, and touch them, can smell the dairy farm and hear the sounds of Mr. Helton's harmonica.

For reasons unclear to me, some stories continue to rate a reputation they don't deserve. As an example I cite Mark Twain's "The Man That Corrupted Hadleyburg." It still finds its way into anthologies. To me it is, or was, a long, rambling, pretty dull job. There's no law says anybody has to agree with me.

All too often I have held guests captive (and myself enraptured) while repeating almost word for word from memory Manuel Komroff's "The Packed Suitcase" and Richard Sherman's "Barrow Street," which we published. There are people like me who hate to be read to, but that does not stop me from reading aloud to others. I keep my eyes riveted on my wife, willing her to stay awake, though she has been through this exercise and heard the same stories so many times before.

At one point in his life Manuel Komroff was a faithful

follower of one of the professional consumer organizations
that advised members how to save money by making their
own products. Told it was senseless to pay twenty-five
cents in a store for a bottle of ink, Komroff went out and
purchased all the recommended ingredients. Then, in line
with instructions, he mixed them in a bathtub half full of
water. "I got enough ink," the author reported, "to satisfy
the needs of a thousand writers for a thousand years. My
tub is still smeared with black stains." It seemed too amusing a tale to die there, so I suggested Komroff create a
character who would set out to make himself famous by
writing the longest story ever written. "I'm afraid it's been
done already," he said in an effort to put me down gently.
"Don't you remember Scheherazade and her thousand-and-
one nights?"

The once so popular short stories are less often seen
these days in big-circulation magazines; two or three,
maybe only one in an issue, as against the six to eight that
in another day gave readers infinite variety.

Highbrows called the multi-million circulation
magazines "slicks." Derisively. Said they presented only
predictable formula fiction, which was only sixty percent
true. Sometimes what they called formula stories were really so-called because of their deftness. They said formula
fiction always had a happy ending, which was fifty percent
true. A hundred percent true would have been the claim
that the stories had *satisfactory*, not necessarily happy, end-
ings. Many stories were less superficial than their critics.

World War II marked the short story's fall from
favor. Fact became more impelling than fiction. The most
facile storyteller found it difficult to compete with events as
dramatic as the London blitz, the evacuation of Dunkirk,
the Japanese assault on Pearl Harbor, the landing of our
troops in Normandy on "D Day," the escape of MacArthur
from Bataan to Australia. It was impossible to create heroes

and villains of the proportions of Churchill and Roosevelt, Hitler and Mussolini and Stalin. Magazine editors were hard-pressed to find stories that had the impact of events to be read about in the newspapers, the intensity and immediacy of nightly radio reports from abroad from Edward Murrow, William Shirer, Eric Sevareid, Cecil Brown, Martin Agronsky. Before long a soldier portrayed in a story as standing before a firing squad could be watched on television as he was shot and fell. The viewer could see his fear and his death. Stories in magazines were black ink on white paper, without sound or movement, no current dateline. Born abroad, brought to its zenith in our country as an art form, the short story is quiescent now; not dead, only hibernating. The great short story will have a renaissance. Somebody will start a new short story magazine and get it under way.

Where the magazine editor shows up big is in the nonfiction category. There he is likely to be more creative, subject matter as often as not originating with him and with staff. He knows what he wants and to which writers given subjects should be assigned; thinks up ideas for articles and books, brings ideas and writers together. No matter how prolific the editorial minds, however, as many ideas as theirs fly in over the transom. A witty unordered essay can invest a dreary morning with a kind of splendor and the editor pats himself on the back for being so worthy as to receive so worthier a contribution.

It could be a really mean day, everything going wrong for a change, everybody out of sorts, and on the desk one might pick up something—well, a manuscript—from H. Allen Smith, one of the naturally funny writers of our time. It could be madly titled "Write Me a Poem, Baby" and be composed of letters collected by Smith of inspired writing by young children; a note from a little girl to her grandmother: "Thank you for your nice present. I always wanted a pin cushion, but not very much." Or a letter written to his parents by a little boy from New York who had gone to visit an upstate farm: "There were all these little pigs. They saw a great big pig and chased him all around the pen and caught him and then threw him on the ground and started chewing the buttons off his vest." Or an excursion into the realm of fiction by a nine-year-old girl: "Once upon a time there was a little girl named Clarise Nancy Imogene LaRose. She had no hair and rather large feet. But she was extremely rich and the rest was easy."

Gratifying to remember are the happy hours spent in talking with another Smith—Robert Paul; recalling the pieces he wrote about the way things used to be, the ghoulish artifacts and ornaments, including stuffed owls, with which homes used to be adorned, the games like stoop ball and one o' cat we played in childhood. What he remembered, and what I, or what we thought we remembered, makes little difference; when dining rooms had potbellied stoves with tiny isinglass windows through which one could see the red-hot coals glowing; when Friday was always fish day, not just for Catholics but for everybody because it was the day fish markets received fresh fish; when a crape on a door signified a death in the family—black for a grown-up, white for a child; six-day bike races in the old Madison Square Garden; when men sat at upright pianos on horse-drawn wagons and played the newest popular tunes and then sold the sheet music to gathering crowds; Welsbach mantles that had to be so gingerly handled; when all butchers wore straw hats in their shops; drip pans placed under iceboxes; signs hung in windows calling for delivery of cakes of ice; other signs, on house doors, that warned passers-by of measles inside, diphtheria, or scarlet fever; pneumonia, when patient was covered with ice and everybody waited tensely for the "crisis"; short corduroy pants and the whining sound they made when we walked; men's socks that were held up by "Boston" or "Paris" garters.

Thanks to Louis Untermeyer I could be reminded of what he called penny candies from heaven—the licorice shoelaces, chocolate cigars, marshmallow bananas, jawbreakers we got two for a cent, caramel-chocolate miniature dolls affectionately named "nigger babies," tiny sugar hearts that said "I love you truly," all-day suckers, and . . . And there was Frank Sullivan, who wrote for us so many of the pieces that ended up as chapters in his books, his fascination with proverbs and the glee with which he reupholstered them—"A penny saved is a pound foolish," "Sleeping dogs make strange bedfellows," "An apple a day is the evil thereof," "Two heads are better than one but not on the same person." And there was Joseph Caro, advertising friend in Chicago, who collected malapropisms for us, about the girl who woke up starch-naked after having been raped over the coals, who lost her job, she said, because she couldn't pass mustard, and the one who could read behind the lines and did everything in a half-hazard way, and who after a torrid night woke up feeling bed-raggled.

———— The prime objective of a magazine is to survive. Most magazines don't, for three principal reasons: first, overoptimism concerning potential market—the kind and number of readers who will be interested and the companies that buy advertising space; second, undercapitalization—the amount of money needed to achieve a viable circulation, plus the cost of staff and paper and printing and distribution; thirdly, the failure to recognize new competition soon enough and that readers and advertisers can change quickly and drastically.

All magazines with colossal circulation embraced in the editorial mix writing that appealed to readers of varying interests, intelligence, age, and income and geographical demographics. They didn't by any means always play it safe by avoiding material beyond the average in intellectual content, but for their readership bracket it was as crucial not to talk up as not to talk down. The appetite for "think" pieces and polished prose was relatively small; for the personality feature, insatiable; but some of all of it had to be included. We covered the Joan Crawfords, Bing Crosbys, and Marlene Dietrichs up to our eyebrows. I hesitate to estimate the number of "real life" stories that have been published about the same person, in the same magazine, not one story more than another containing more than a grain of truth. On checking back I have found that on three different occasions, deliberately, with no help from anybody, I published the "true" story of Judy Garland, one—"There'll Always Be an Encore"—written by the performer herself.

Naturally we found more readers more attentive to Joseph Wechsberg's report on "Maxim's, the Most Famous Night Spot in Paris" and Prince Rainier's "Seven Years of Marriage to the Former Grace Kelly" than to Mrs. Willy Brandt's monograph on the building of the Berlin Wall during her husband's service as mayor of West Berlin or educator Arthur Bestor's brilliant series on the deterioration of teaching techniques. John Kobler's roguish article about Madame Tussaud's waxworks in London, with the enchantingly grisly drawings by Charles Addams, was more popular than our "Inside the Kremlin" report written by John Gunther. Publishing the Duke of Windsor's personal story of his life following abdication was more enthusiastically received than what we published after sending John Barlow Martin to Norway to determine whether true or false the rumor that operatic soprano Kirsten Flagstad had been a Nazi collaborator. (He found she had not been.)

It is nice to be able to say that professional critics consistently downbeat about the popular book or magazine were the exception. The book editor who saw a devastating notice of a book he issued with confidence took it as part of the game. A saving grace was that here and there a perspicacious critic found an element of excellence overlooked by the editor and gave the book a happy send-off. Only once in a while did a critic have so strong a personal bias that it was impossible for him to be objective. The otherwise dispassionate Oliver Herford ("A gentleman is one who never hurts one's feelings unintentionally") always spoke of Arnold Bennett with disdain, even hatred. When a friend asked him why, he said, "Well, I'll be very frank with you. When Bennett published his first book—*Buried Alive*—I reviewed it for the New York *Times,* and that review so prejudiced me against the man that I never read another word he wrote!" Few critics were so pigheaded; they understood what power they had and used it with discretion. They knew they had to view with equanimity the inferior material that along with the good streamed from the inner sanctums of book and magazine shops, even from the most prestigious ones. Not without a sense of proportion, they realized no publisher could earn an honest living by feeding the public a diet of highbrow fare exclusively.

It used to annoy us to hear the sophisticates pour scorn on our reports of a Washington soiree presided over by Perle Mesta, the antics of a Harpo Marx, Debbie Reynolds, Marilyn Monroe, and forget, in that awful time when with the advent of summer the first sign of a sniff or fever in a child made infantile paralysis the terrifying thought, that we published the first comprehensive analysis of the disease together with a meticulously compiled list of every hospital in the United States equipped to cope. We had to swallow our rage when carpers picked on us for running Maurice Chevalier's autobiography and gave us no credit for our compendium of small colleges, specifying type, size of enrollment, curriculum, cost, and scholarships available, which took us months to investigate and put together. The know-it-alls turned up their noses at the autobiography of Kate Smith when we published it, and bothered not at all to notice that, with the approbation of the American Medical Association, we published the first cancer chart, identifying all cancer sites along with symptoms, treatment, etc. Except by our readers, barest acknowledgment would be given to Mrs. Khrushchev's article about the life of women in the Soviet Union, though months of effort and reams of correspondence were necessary to procure it. Nor would there be, except from our own readers, recognition of the story by Golda Meir of her responsibilities as Israel's Foreign Minister.

Of course, the cover lines of magazines placed emphasis on popular personalities and personal problems. Only an imbecile wouldn't know them more likely to attract readers than an analysis of East-West détente or the plight of the underprivileged. As editors we knew we had to present Art Buchwald and Corey Ford but that there was nothing to keep us from presenting at the same time a report on the hazards of nuclear power plants. Admiral Rickover was no more reluctant to write for us than we were to ask him to do so. Thomas Mann was as pleased to tell our readers of the long links of human generations that impregnated the Bible with piety as Cordell Hull was to urge our younger readers to take up the study of Spanish.

I'd like to go at it from the other end. It never occurred to us that advice on how to look and dress and cook better, how to make a home lovelier to live in, was less important than a polemic on the Christian ethic. The multimillion-circulation magazine was under no obligation, and isn't, to try to sway the populace with proposals for reforming society. It does not print for eternity, but for today. It performs its duty and performs it well if it offers an amalgam of fact and fiction, some of it entertaining, some enlightening, some defiant, and some practical. It fails in its obligation if it doesn't carry promise of hope and escape from the too generally depressing state of the world. It is unrealistic to pretend to despise the popular presentation, which serves to anesthetize, at least a little bit, the recurring pains and bleakness of the ordinary life. The works of a Harold Robbins or an Arthur Hailey are not to be looked down on because they are popular enough to be bought by the millions. They have done nobody any harm. They have given much pleasure. We had no more hesitation about using the starry-eyed illustrations of Jon Whitcomb and the human-interest pictures of Norman Rockwell than about having Grandma Moses and Salvador Dali paint pictures for us or about publishing reproductions of paintings by Picasso and Raphael. The multimillion-circulation magazine is a reading supermarket, with much to choose from and at a price almost everybody can afford. To cheer a little, inform a little, challenge a little—such tasks represent no mean achievement.

13

When Hollywood was capital of the movie world dominated by Louis B. Mayer, Samuel Goldwyn, Darryl Zanuck, and the Warner brothers, two women who ruled as queens of gossip could scare the pants off all of them, neither being more inaccurate than necessary to hold her massive audience. Of the two women Hedda Hopper was the more literate, meaning only that her syntax was better. Neither cared whose reputation and/or career might be damaged.

I had an idea, which was to have each woman write her autobiography. The first lunch was with Louella Parsons, who introduced me to Mike Romanoff, proprietor of the restaurant, as her old and dear friend. We had met exactly once before. It didn't take long to come to unreasonable terms. Louella decided to call her story *The First to Know,* something of a misnomer, because she wasn't always. On the following day, same place, same time, I had lunch with Hedda Hopper. In a crowd of women Mrs. Hopper could be identified by whatever grotesque hat she wore. The one she wore on this day was modeled after an eagle's nest and I wouldn't have been surprised to find an eagle in it. A live eagle. When Mrs. Hopper said no, she was definitely not ready to write her life story, I said, "Well, readers will be awfully disappointed when they find Louella has done hers and hear you're not going to do yours." That did it, and *The Whole Truth and Nothing But* came through (with the help of a writer named James Brough). It was not quite the truth, which could have turned out to be dull.

"Her virtue was that she said what she thought," Peter Ustinov wrote of Hedda Hopper, "her vice that what she thought didn't amount to much." A valid observation. In her book Mrs. Hopper more than suggested that Michael Wilding, who had been Elizabeth Taylor's second husband, was a homosexual. Really? A man who had been married to Elizabeth Taylor? Absolutely. "How do you know?" I asked. "*Every*body knows," the columnist said. I didn't know and wouldn't let the statement stand. When the autobiography was issued in hard covers, the statement remained intact, Wilding promptly sued for libel, Mrs. Hopper was obliged to apologize and share with her publisher the sum of a hundred thousand dollars that had to be paid to Mr. Wilding.

The popularity of William "Billy" Lyon Phelps as a professor at Yale was as protracted as Charles "Copey" Copeland's had been at Harvard. I did not meet Phelps until after his college retirement and then found him as lively and gregarious a companion, a complete extrovert, as one could hope to meet. His *Autobiography with Letters* still is, I'm sure, as engrossing a book as I found it. I remember his remarks in that book about the traits of dogs and cats, which could not have been better described by a professional canine-feline naturalist. When I mentioned that to him he said he once had a dog to which he would read from the Bible, which caused the pet to fall asleep, but which would smile and nod its head in approbation when he read from *Tom Sawyer*, would shake from head to tail with laughter when he read from the *Pickwick Papers*, and would cry real tears when he read about Little Eva going to heaven. I said I would gladly have spent half of my life as a student in his classroom, the other half in a classroom under Dr. Copeland. "Well, I think you would have liked us," Phelps said, "because both of us were hams at heart—

our job wasn't to teach literature so much as to get the boys themselves interested in reading."

His conversations with Galsworthy, George Moore, William Howard Taft, Thomas Hardy, Thomas Edison, James Barrie—with men and women famous in every walk of life—are recorded in the autobiography in enchanting detail. When heavyweight champion Gene Tunney accepted an invitation to address Phelps's class in Shakespeare, the event made news everywhere.

I had written to Phelps to ask if he would be willing to do some pieces for *Good Housekeeping*, which he did, and we became fairly constant dinner partners. One evening he told me he was planning an address to students at the University of Michigan at Ann Arbor, and I wanted to know the subject. "I'm not sure yet," he said, "but I think I have a beginning. I'd like to tell the kids that in England, a country smaller than the state of Michigan, there were living and writing at about the same time such a band of literary lights as the world has seldom seen." He spun off the names of Kipling, Anthony Hope, Max Beerbohm, Kenneth Grahame, Arthur Wing Pinero, Hall Caine, Ford Madox Ford, Arthur Conan Doyle, George Bernard Shaw, A. A. Milne, Galsworthy, Maugham, Israel Zangwill, W. H. Hudson, Walter de la Mare, Conrad, Chesterton, Arnold Bennett, Hilaire Belloc, and H. G. Wells.

I may have forgotten a few, but it seemed an imposing galaxy.

On another evening Phelps was rambling idly about a series of pieces he'd like to write about boys who had been his most promising students. I said I'd commit for them sight unseen. A few weeks later I was in New Haven to attend his funeral. He was seventy-eight years old. I had thought him fifteen years younger.

Though I once promised to give a talk on how an issue of a magazine is put together, the students at the Annenberg School of Journalism in Philadelphia had to settle for another subject. I didn't undertake the original assignment because it would have been too unsatisfying to the students, the business of assembling an issue too formless in my mind to define. I can as little explain the procedure as why suddenly I began to hum a few bars of a tune, then switch to another, neither having any relationship to the other or to anything I am thinking at the moment, or doing. In starting on an issue, naturally one begins with the cover. What subject? Painting or photograph? Then, what should be the opening feature, how much fiction, which departments? Three short stories or two? One serial or none? There is no system or rule of thumb, the programming is based on the year's month, the month's weather, the day's news, perhaps whether one had Wheaties or oatmeal for breakfast.

It is impossible for me to say why I thought we should publish an article about wigs, but we did, photographing a model wearing wigs of varying hair styles. "How Would *You* Look in a Wig?" initiated a nationwide trend. What brought the subject to mind is out of the question to say (even a good answer wouldn't make front-page news). It is part of the by-God-and-by-guess routine, with a little experience (not much) thrown in. When *Good Housekeeping* at the first home-furnishings show at the Coliseum in New York set up an exhibit of children's rooms, one of the model rooms was for a seventeen-year-old girl. On the night before the exhibit opened, I made a final inspection, without forethought walked over to the exhibit of the New York Telephone Company and borrowed ten of its model instruments and placed them in the girl's room—one on a dressing table, one on the bed, another under the bed, one on a chair, and so on. That small unpremeditated action brought the repeatedly heard expression "My, how our Janet would love to have all those phones!" and became the talk of the whole show. What prompted the approach to the telephones could be anybody's guess.

"But don't you have a philosophy about editing?" I was asked. No more than about how I take a shower in the morning. Does anybody think about soaping himself? The soap is there, you use it. I had no concrete procedure for the way I worked. Didn't think about it. Most of all my purpose was to put issues together that would keep readers from tossing them aside. A reader anticipates an evenness of quality. The editor is doing well who can maintain it. Elsewhere I used the word "surprise," and I return to it because according to my lights it's what helps encourage a reader to renew a subscription. An issue is not a failure that doesn't carry something that jolts, startles, disconcerts; for all the searching and scrambling it is not possible for editor and staff to come up with something in every issue that will hold the reader in thrall. Readers found an issue satisfactory if it carried something as madcap as "The Mud-Pie Cookbook" for children, as amusingly informative as "How the Nicest Women Cheat at Canasta," as touching as Gary Cooper's confession of his failure as an actor, as provocative as "The Kennedy Children Can Be Accepted in This School But Your Children Haven't a Chance."

On no regular basis, only when the spirit moved, I asked associates to submit half a dozen or more ideas they were positive I'd reject. They could be as far out and off-base as they chose. If they wished, they could be almost insane. Now and then a seemingly insane idea had in it a germ of sanity, maybe for use a year later. We were ahead if we could isolate the germ.

The oddest, most useless scraps of information are embedded in my mind. I couldn't eradicate them if my life depended on it. A man named Hunt invented the safety pin and sold his patent for a hundred dollars. Crazy? Samuel Goldfish and Edgar Selwyn were partners in a film studio and when Selwyn died Samuel Goldfish changed his name to Samuel Goldwyn. Significant? Barns were painted red because red paint was cheaper than any other. Imperishable knowledge? But if I could remember such trivialities, what could the magazine print that would make some impression? That was the ever-niggling question, I believe

it remains the most important. So, such as it is, my only
philosophy might be said to be: Never consider a magazine
schedule ready to go unless it is at least as good as the last
one, and when possible introduce an unexpected feature.
That won't make editorial history but it's the best I can do.

14

Ideas that come in the night can be lost forever if not promptly written down. You must put salt on their tails, as Samuel Butler admonished, or they fly away and you never see their bright plumage again. In bed at night you think of the best idea you ever had and by morning you never had it. On a bedside table I kept pencil and over-sized pad on which in the dark I could jot a word or phrase that hours later would recall the thought. In jacket side pockets there were always scraps of paper for notions that came to mind during a walk, at the theater, while attending a concert. Some of the scraps ended up being useful.

In the inside pocket of my jacket I kept three sheets of paper, often returned well creased from the tailor to whom my suits were sent for pressing. A monthly magazine editor must always be a full season ahead in his planning, except for Christmas, about which we began our planning in early July. Each of the three sheets carried the tentative schedule for one of the three forthcoming issues. At whatever time or place, it was convenient to excise, insert, make any desir-able changes. With a deadline coming up, I took a last look; and in no particular order asked questions. Does the sched-ule have balance? Is there sufficient variety, adequate pac-ing? Is there something that will compel the reader's attention—some feature the reader is bound to remem-ber, that would make a good topic for conversation? Is there a report, chart, point of view to make the reader feel the magazine was worth buying? Could a title be improved, a story blurb, a picture caption? Should this illustration be discarded and another substituted?

With what might be called a visual mind it became easy to think in terms of layouts. Not at the outset, but with practice, I was able to keep whole issues in my head, the pages in proper sequence. Anybody can do it who wants to make the effort.

In the art department it was the custom to pin on a story board miniature photostats of every layout as it was completed. Thus one could see not merely in the mind's eye but in fact exactly how an issue would come out. I spent as much time in art departments, to the discomfiture of art directors, as in my own office, shuffling and re-shuffling pages. Art directors need to be pampered, praised, loved, especially in public. Now and then an art director could begin to feel he should be left to his own devices, his work not subject to the editor's veto. Permitted to get away with it, he becomes a burden. If I have said it before, it's worth saying again: There can be only one boss. It can't be the art director.

Once in a while some of the troops felt I demanded too much, maybe expected more than was warranted. But I did not get terribly upset, not often, though naturally it's a biased view. I wasn't even upset when Joseph Heller, a young fellow in our *McCall's* promotion department, seemed to be banging away at his typewriter but handing in no staggering amount of promotion copy. Somebody told me he was author of some stories that had been published in *The Atlantic* or *Harper's,* but I didn't think so. He looked too dour to have that much imagination, and when I tried to talk with him he seemed preoccupied, too monosyllabic to have words enough in him to write a story. A secretary confided that Heller was afraid of me, because when I would say, "Hello, Joe, what's doing?" he would lean back in his chair, stare at the ceiling, never at me, mull things over for a moment, and then reply, "Nothing." People in

the office said Heller clammed up at my approach, though
I couldn't understand why, even if everybody else could.
Anybody who can say "Nothing" isn't clammed up. A clam
wouldn't say a single word, but Heller always had that
word ready, for me. Maybe I can make everything clear by
saying he was the introspective type. Anyway, he could put
together a promotion plan that was a beaut and I figured
maybe he's a little smarter than I think, but not much. A
little, not likely, but possible. He was so close to his typewriter and so unconcerned with my presence whenever he
sensed it that I tended to keep my interruptions to a minimum. What somebody guessed he was writing in the office
was a book. No matter where he wrote it, when it came out
it was called *Catch-22*, and it was a success. Success? It
was a smash hit and squashed all the other titles on the
best-seller lists. Betty Weston, one of the darlingest and
brightest assistants, who was sure Joe was using office time
for a book, who could inevitably think of the right thing to
say, said, "It would have been very quid pro quo of Joe to
have dedicated the book to the company." The truth of the
matter is that Miss Weston only assumed Heller had been
working on a book in the office, and certainly not a soul on
the staff would have begrudged him a moment of anything
that gave him pleasure. The book Heller wrote after
Catch-22 was called *Something Happened* and was
packed from beginning to end with voluptuous office dialogue. The office might have been a takeoff on our own. All
those girls who could be fussed with and mussed up!
Where was I all that time?

15

One can be engulfed in the day-and-night cycle of editorial routine; the stacks of manuscripts to go through that first readers have passed along for attention; letters to answer; conferences to go to. An editor finds surcease in different ways; part of mine I found in classrooms, most of all, at the invitation of Carl Ackerman, the dean, spending Monday afternoons with students in Columbia University's Graduate School of Journalism. It was refreshing to be with ambitious young men and women anticipating careers in communications. The girls were pretty and that didn't hurt.

Professional periodical people usually had no patience with neophytes descending on newspapers and magazines straight from schools the pros complained were staffed by instructors not qualified for jobs in the journalism workaday world. If I had any such opinion it was quickly dispelled. To me the instructors seemed experienced and capable, the students in a hurry to finish with the classroom and move on. There was a Richard Baker at Columbia who was an exemplary teacher.

Of the three hours on Monday afternoons half were set aside for the appearance of guests—friends who had long since made their mark as writers and editors. Carl Van Doren was such a one, to talk about his disciplines as a biographer; Roy Alexander, to talk about his responsibilities as an editor of *Time;* Leonard Lyons and Earl Wilson, to describe their chores as daily newspaper columnists. Now and then, to vary the routine, there'd be two guests: Sinclair Lewis, to talk of his problems as a novelist, along with Bennett Cerf, his publisher, to complain about his problems with Lewis; or Phyllis McGinley, to offer cheerful tidbits about her life as a poet, along with Louis Untermeyer to discuss the perquisites—lecture fees—available to poets. Advised in advance of who the guests were to be, the students came prepared with pert and sometimes impertinent questions.

Once a month a committee chosen by the students would come to the office to suggest ideas they thought would be suitable for *Good Housekeeping*. The student selected to write an article would be paid $50, the magazine contributing an additional $400 to the school's scholarship fund. "What Do You Call Your Mother-in-Law—Ma'm, Jane, Mrs. Bellamy, or Just 'Hey, You'?" was the first of such articles accepted. The visits of the youngsters kept us perked up. Some were sassy. All were ambitious.

The students—all students—wanted to know if choice of editorial content was dictated or influenced by advertisers. Everybody thinks so, but everybody is wrong; as out of order as Ann Watkins, once an important literary agent, who said, "Circulation and advertising departments govern and control the editorial policy of big-circulation magazines." Miss Watkins didn't specify which circulation and advertising departments of which magazines. She didn't know of any. Challenged to prove otherwise, she admitted she had been talking nonsense.

To set out deliberately to antagonize advertisers would be senseless. But when there was reason to investigate and expose, there was no hesitation. Disclosures of unfair airline practices ("Going to Fly? Another Look at the Airlines"), or of the diamond monopoly ("Diamonds Are a Girl's Most Overpriced Friend"), or life insurance sales methods ("Let's See What the Insurance Companies Offer"), meant we might never get the advertising of the companies named; such possibility never deterred us.

Common questions from students were "How does a magazine find new writers and what chance has a new writer of making a sale?" To begin with, new writers themselves do the finding—they find the magazines, either by submitting manuscripts cold or by engaging (not always easy for a beginner) the services of a literary agent to represent them. Nothing pleases a magazine more than to discover a new talent; even first readers on a magazine are trained to recognize a manuscript's chances. It has been said often and is worth repeating that every prejudice is in the new writer's favor. In our experience about 15 percent of what we published came in the slush pile—what Charles Hansen Towne called "the unrush mail"—submitted by men and women who had not before been in print.

It would be pointless to stand before a group of students in a journalism school, and a graduate school at that, and have to say that manuscripts must be typewritten, double-spaced on one side of the paper, each page numbered in sequence, with name and address on the first sheet, and that a stamped self-addressed envelope should be enclosed. If any of them had to be given any such information they had no right to be in the school and I had no right to be there.

How does a writer learn what his rights are in regard to a manuscript? An agent knows all the answers concerning advances, royalties, second-book option clauses, serial and other rights, participation in paperback or film or other sales, responsibility in the event of libel. Normal royalty paid for adult trade books is 10 percent of the book's retail list price on the first five thousand copies sold, 12½ percent on the next five thousand copies, ten or fifteen percent on copies sold in excess of fifteen thousand. They are considered minimum percentages. Established authors sometimes get more favorable terms. By making application and paying $35 in annual dues, almost any person may become a member of the Authors' Guild* and receive a copy of the

* 234 West 44th Street, New York, N.Y. 10036.

"Recommended Trade Book Contract" and "Guide to the Authors' Guild Trade Book Contract." The Guild is any author's best possible insurance, especially in the event of dispute. The Guild's overriding interest is in safeguarding the rights of its members.

Marchette Chute is unusual in that, among other things, she does not use the services of a literary agent. Everything that concerns her work she handles herself. Three years prior to her *Ben Jonson of Westminster* she was known for her *Shakespeare of London,* written before she ever had been abroad, all of her background information deriving from what was available in and through libraries. One book she called *The Search for God* was submitted to forty publishers before it was accepted by E. P. Dutton, the forty-first.

A dozen times in the course of a seminar students would ask guests how and in what circumstances they went about their writing. There's nothing wrong with the question except that there isn't a satisfying answer, because every author has his own method, or several methods. When a story or book is done it doesn't matter whether it was written with pen or pencil or on a typewriter, or done standing up, sitting, or lying down (as was the practice of Artemus Ward), or dictated to a stenographer or machine. Some writers need music while they work, others solitude and silence. Some are night writers, others can get going only in the morning. Some have visual minds and "see" a story complete in their minds, others start with nothing more than a character and let him take over. Faulkner said he ran along behind his characters, pencil in hand, trying to keep up with what they were saying and doing. Concerning novels, Trollope declared an author must remember that each month his characters are a month older and that as characters advance a month in age their thoughts and actions have to be a month older. Mary Roberts Rinehart rented an office for herself in which she could compose in peace, Rebecca West chose the impersonality of a hotel room. Edna Ferber claimed the ideal view for daily writing, hour on hour, is the blank brick wall of a cold-storage warehouse. "A room with a view," she said, "is not a room in which a working writer can write." Nelson Algren has been quoted as saying he was never sure where he was going when he started a novel, simply kept writing "until something happened." Algren made little money out of his *Man with the Golden Arm*, but he got and deserved the first National Book Award.

Margaret Lee Runbeck would bring to the office the outline of a story and talk details into it as I listened. As she heard herself talk, she would say, "No, that isn't going to sound right, let me try it this way and see what you think." Prentiss Ingraham, who wrote Buffalo Bill stories, said he just opened with some element of action. "I begin," he declared, "with 'Crack! Crack! Crack! Three more redskins bit the dust.' From there on, it's easy." George Moore's dictum was that a man must write two novels to teach himself to write a novel. Thackeray's that he couldn't get going until he knew his characters inside out, that he had to hear the sound of their voices. While writing about the suicide of Emma Bovary, Flaubert, most meticulous of writers, said he was able to detect the taste of arsenic on his own tongue. H. G. Wells was never without two fountain pens in a pocket of his waistcoat—"The big one for the long words, the little one for the short ones." It sounds too much like a joke, but he was quoted as saying it. Charles Reade, author of *The Cloister and the Hearth*, had a formula for writing serials: "Make 'em laugh, make 'em weep, make 'em wait." Allan Seager said he wrote the opening pages of his caustic story "Sham" while having breakfast, that three days later on a five-hour bus tour he finished all but the last page. The story was set in a small town in the Southwest to which a crowd of Hollywood technicians had come to make a movie of the life of Jesse James. During the action several horses were deliberately pushed off a cliff because the script called for it. Hank Childreth, the local old-timer who had been watching the filming from the start, couldn't take any more. He got hold of a shotgun.

"I'll bet I rewrote the last couple of lines ten or twelve times," Seager told me. "I got them right, though, when I stopped for a drink in a bar. Want me to repeat them? Well, Old Hank said, 'Damn 'em, the movies, the automobiles, the tourists, all of 'em. Damn the whole twentieth century. Damn it—damn it—damn it all to hell.'"

I knew the ending myself; and the beginning, and the middle, because I had published the story.

My recollection is that, because of its massive circulation, second only to *TV Guide,* students expressed more curiosity about *Reader's Digest* than any other magazine. Lila and DeWitt Wallace, who founded it in 1921, originally did all the condensing of articles—"pick-ups"—that already had appeared in other periodicals. Later, because they suspected some magazines might refuse to grant reprint rights, they began to publish "originals"—articles they commissioned and then "planted" in other periodicals, later picked up for their own use. The *Digest* paid handsome fees to all magazines whose articles it used, as it still does, and as it still pays handsome fees to the authors.

Early in the game, Harold Ross and I agreed we would no longer permit the Wallaces to use anything from our magazines. We became the two holdouts. Who did they think they were? The nerve of the Wallaces—picking our brains! But after a while I had to concede and gave in to pleas from our authors who welcomed the bonuses that used to come from the Wallaces' pick-ups. It did *Good Housekeeping* no harm. Ross, however, stuck to his guns, and to this day, I believe, *The New Yorker* adheres to the old Ross policy.

The paternal *Digest* has served as a harbor for many men who once had been editors of and then retired from other magazines—they included *The Saturday Evening Post's* Ben Hibbs, *Woman's Home Companion's* William

Birnie, *Liberty*'s Fulton Oursler, *American Mercury*'s Eugene Lyons. Along with *Time* and *Newsweek*, the *Digest* employs the largest number of editors. There may be as many as two or three dozen people involved with the condensations. Each month the staff scans hundreds of articles and books likely to have something suitable to its purpose. J. C. Furnas' *Digest* original "—And Sudden Death," about fatal accidents on the highways, is said to have been reprinted more often than anything else in magazine history.

At this writing, at age ninety, DeWitt Wallace (and his wife Lila) is still in total control. It would be hard to deny that no editor has been more successful or grown richer; as equally hard to deny that no editor has been so modest and unassuming as Wallace. He's the only one who hasn't written his autobiography.

Students wanted to know if I could name one magazine more than any other that had an influence on my life. I mentioned those I'd edited, but said otherwise it would be impossible to be specific. I think no magazine, however, gave me more satisfaction than *St. Nicholas,* the most entrancing magazine ever conceived for boys and girls. For three decades it had been in the hands of Mary Mapes Dodge.† It was where Kipling's brave mongoose Rikki-Tikki-Tavi had appeared, Frances Hodgson Burnett's Little Lord Fauntleroy (with the enchanting drawings by Reginald Birch), Gelett Burgess' "Goops," the Uncle Remus stories, Palmer Cox's "Brownies" (little-girl readers complained because there were no *girl* Brownies). Among the magazine's contributors were Richard Harding Davis, Robert Louis Stevenson, Louisa May Alcott, Mark Twain, Tennyson, Bret Harte. It was where one was introduced to John Kendrick Bangs's Little Elf-man, the Ralph Henry Barbour baseball stories, and the great illustrators from Arthur Rackham and Frederick Remington to Howard Pyle. Katharine Lee Bates wrote "America the Beautiful"

† Also famous as author of *Hans Brinker, or, The Silver Skates.*

for *St. Nicholas;* and Mark Twain *Tom Sawyer Abroad.*
The magazine had a St. Nicholas League, with chapters in
cities and towns the country over. Young readers contrib-
uted verse, prose, and drawings to that department's pages
in the magazine—boys and girls who were awarded gold
and silver badges and who later became famous, among
them Edna St. Vincent Millay, Eudora Welty, Carolyn
Wells, Cornelia Otis Skinner, Robert Benchley, Ring
Lardner, William Faulkner. I believe I would rather have
been editor of *St. Nicholas* than of any other magazine I
ever knew. Oddly enough, I could have been. The magazine ultimately was acquired by the wife of David Stern, a
prominent Philadelphia newspaper publisher. For various
reasons, Jill Stern was unable to continue publication.
Knowing of my great affection for it, and my wife's, she
turned it over to us, lock, stock, and barrel. It was too late.
We had then too many other responsibilities.

"What would you say is the difference between women
writers today and those of earlier years?" was a question
raised by one young student. Many more women then, I
said, had triple by-lines—a first name, a second, and a third.
The student thought I was trying to be humorous, but
among the authors popular earlier in the century were
Fanny Heaslip Lea, Marjorie Stoneham Douglas, Mary
Hastings Bradley, Dorothy Canfield Fisher, and at least
thirty others. There was even a writer who could boast of
five names. Deserted by her husband, left to fend for herself and their two small children, Mrs. Emma Dorothy
Eliza Nevitte Southworth wrote novels—more than sixty of
them. All got published, a few were best-sellers, in particular *The Hidden Hand,*‡ later produced as a play starring
John Wilkes Booth. The titles of Mrs. Southworth's novels
offer some clue to their nature: *The Unloved Wife, The
Discarded Daughter, The Deserted Wife, The Fatal Marriage, Retribution, or The Vale of Shadow.* I could not

‡ Published in 1859, the one copy in the possession of the New
York Public Library, which I was determined to read, had been stolen.

resist reading one, *Cruel as the Grave,* to its bitter end. Nor can I resist passing on a typical passage in it in which the suspicious wife, Sybil Berners, speaks her mind: "To you, viper, who has stung to death the bosom that warmed you to life—to you, traitress, who has come between the true husband and his wife—to you, thief, who has stolen from your benefactress the sole treasure of her life—to *you* I have this to say: I will not drive you forth in dishonor from my door this night, nor will I publish your infamy to the world tomorrow; but in the morning you must leave the house you have desecrated! For if you do not, or if ever I find your false face here again, I will tread down and crush out your life with less remorse than ever I set heel upon a spider!"

A number of the triple by-line women were still alive and active. My reply, of course, was not to be taken seriously. There were just as many male authors with names parted in the middle—Ford Madox Ford, James Oliver Curwood, Harry Leon Wilson among them. But when one of the women's names was featured on a magazine cover, excellent newsstand sales were almost assured. Which is why when I received a first story from Fannie Fox I decided to implement her name in the middle with her better known maiden name. Fannie Ferber Fox promptly berated me, saying she did not wish to trade on her sister Edna's reputation. Nevertheless, from that time on, whatever she wrote was under the by-line that had been foisted on her.

"Some people, if they can learn to write badly enough," Flannery O'Connor said, "can make a great deal of money." Then she added something that wouldn't have been appreciated by, let us say, Jacqueline Susann or Kathleen Winsor, and I quote it only because I love it: "Many a best seller could have been prevented by a good teacher." However, the sale of just a few stories or articles can go quickly to a new writer's head. Contemplation then of being a full-time professional is intoxicating. Little does one know how rapidly a few rejection slips received in quick succession can depress the spirit and to what extent and how fast worries accumulate with the incoming bills for rent, groceries, and unfortunate sudden illness. Panic takes the place of peace of mind. The salary that once came in from a steady job is thought of with nostalgia.

It is trite enough to say that anybody with the will to write will write. But every week has a weekend and seven nights. In that available time anybody with something to say can come close to saying it, because writing for the natural writer is almost a physical need. There are so many successful authors—such as Edna Ferber, Paul Gallico, and Erle Stanley Gardner—who stayed at their less glamorous tasks while they wrote and did not give them up until enough time had gone by to assure continued success as authors.

A writer with several successes in the short story field says he would like to take a year off to tackle a novel. It is a risk if he has an idea for a novel clearly in mind; it is a bigger risk if the idea has not yet been formed. And why a year? Where is it prescribed that a year is required for writing a novel? (It might take five years.) Anthony Trollope's mother was fifty when she wrote her first book, begun and finished in four months. In the remaining thirty years of her life she produced another hundred and fourteen volumes. They weren't always very good, but they got published. Trollope himself was over thirty before he wrote his first novel. For most of his adult life he remained in one position or another with the British postal service (he originated the idea of having letter boxes on public thoroughfares). During his post office period he wrote most of his forty books. "It was my practice to be at my table every morning at 5:30 A.M.," he said in his autobiography. "By beginning at that hour I could complete my literary work before I dressed for breakfast." He declared that "three hours a day will produce as much as a man ought to write." He added that one must not merely want to tell a story but should have a story to tell. What a wise man was Trollope! "If it be necessary for you to live by your work, do not begin by trusting to literature," he said. "The career, when success has been achieved, is certainly very pleasant; but the agonies endured in the search for that success are often terrible. And the author's poverty is, I think, harder to bear than any other."

There were would-be writers who couldn't write, which didn't minimize their persistence. They kept on, relentlessly. I found nothing more disagreeable than the need to say to one here and there, "Give it up, you can't make it, you haven't a chance." I preferred to say it in person, found difficulty saying it in a letter. It was easier, face to face, to try to be kind. Arthur Hoffman, long the distinguished editor of *Adventure*, said that to an elderly woman who had been referred to him by a mutual friend and become a pest, he wrote, "You are wasting your time, you are wasting mine, and that isn't good for either of us. Writing demands talent, and you have none. Why don't you try to learn Turkish?" The vicious question was prompted, he said, by a package of Turkish cigarettes a visitor had left on his desk. Then he said he spent a restless night, ashamed of having been cruel. "I never learned how to say it graciously," he said. I never learned, either.

Most writers I knew who came to grief quit their jobs too soon in favor of the literary life exclusively. The matter is of such consequence I ought to add the opinion of Struthers Burt, a fine and very successful author of fiction and verse. "I firmly believe," he said, "that the best way to begin writing is to slowly creep up on it, by, at the start, earning your living in some other way. Since life itself is the material of writing, the best place to find it is in somewhere else than in writing or editorial circles; it is a very thwarting thing to young writers to be so poor they have to depend on writing for their living or, equally bad, so rich they write only when the classic and mysterious effluvium overpowers them."

I'd like to try to envelop it in a single line: For the beginner, writing should be an avocation.

The conclusion of Trollope's *Last Chronicle of Barset* still moves me when I re-read it, and it is one of the very few novels I do re-read. Though not nearly so passionate a Trollopian as my wife, who can quote verbatim from much of Trollope's work—I have not had her patience with the author's repetitious recitation of his characters' traits—I can recommend to any beginner the autobiography that Trollope left to be published after his death. It is as forthright and enduring a record of a person's writing career as can be found in all literary history.

The manuscript of a novel is returned with a rejection slip; may already have been returned by two or three other book publishers. The author of little faith falls for an advertisement: "Discouraged by rejections? Do not think your time has been wasted. We will publish your book immediately. It will be printed by us and bound and distributed. You can be a published author!" The advertisement is sponsored by what is known as a "vanity press." It is true the book will be published. A few copies may appear in bookshops, most likely in the city in which the author lives. What the author isn't told in the advertising is that he must pay for it in advance; that included in the cost of printing is a substantial profit for the vanity publisher; that only a few copies are sent out for review; that no reviewer ever gives a second glance to a vanity book; that the vanity press has no standing; that it is the refuge only of writers who do not know the ropes.

"Do editors of big magazines get much graft?" "Is there some payoff for editorial favors?" One could laugh or one could try to answer seriously. No graft, I said, no payoff. "But I get loads of free books," I told the journalism students. "They're sent to me by publishers, and those I have no use for I give to schools, libraries, the Salvation Army. I can tell you what Christopher Morley did with some of the copies that were sent to *him* for review," I added. "He scrawled long, passionate inscriptions on the flyleaves, full of loving sentiments and veiled hints, from one fictitious person to another fictitious person. Then Mr. Morley would 'lose' the books, in subway stations, in telephone booths, on park benches, on counters in stores. And would delight in imagining the imaginings of the finders of those books."

As a class project the Columbia students elected to investigate and report on the reference books that might be most useful to them. Out of approximately three hundred titles they voted for twenty. It is as good a list as any of the kind. At Simmons College in Boston the students asked for a list of books that could give them an overview of early-century "popular" literature. It resulted in a string of the fifty best-selling titles published from 1900 to 1930.*

A digression for a moment to talk of Andrew Lang, who was known during his lifetime as "editor-in-chief" to the British nation. He was master of three literatures—Greek, French, and English; translated the *Odyssey* and the *Iliad*, was a poet ranked with Stevenson, whose close friend he was, and highly esteemed as a critic. Above all else, Lang's name was associated with fairy tales, but he died protesting his reputation for authorship. "I do not write stories out of my own head," he explained. Most of them he did not even translate himself. Lang *edited*. For the *Blue* fairy book—the first of the "color" group—he did the research, traced sources, made his choices from the works of Hans Christian Andersen, Charles Perrault, the Grimm brothers, and dozens of other foreign narrators of folklore, and assigned them for adaptation and translation to his wife and a small coterie of friends. Yet Little Red Riding Hood and Cinderella and their knighted and sometimes benighted fellow creatures we know chiefly because of Lang. If other men and women recounted identical tales, it was Lang who put the most distinguished and lasting mark on them in English. More than any other person he

* For both lists, see Appendix.

created our fairyland and populated it with giants and
dwarfs, valiant heroes and distraught princesses and god-
mothers who wafted magic wands. This diversion does
have a relationship to Morley's inscriptions, though I have
been slow getting to it. Lang hoped owners of books would
put their signatures on the flyleaf, saying a written signature was more meaningful than a bookplate. It would be
interesting, he said, for the new owner of a book to know
who preceding owners had been and to see their hand-
writing. He thought it would also be interesting if owners
indicated the price they had paid, and where. "Our prede-
cessors in proprietorship," Lang wrote, "probably shared
our tastes, and if they had taken the trouble to write their
names they might receive from us, and we from them, a
slight telepathic impact of a friendly character."

Another diversion reminds me of what I read about
Eugene Field, who may have inscribed more books than
any other author. He always kept handy copies of his more
popular poems, like "Little Boy Blue" and "Wynken,
Blynken, and Nod," which he would sign and give away
even before being asked. When he visited anybody's home
for the first time, he would as soon as possible get to any
shelves containing books and quickly write inscriptions in
them. The owner of *Moby Dick* or *Gulliver's Travels*, for
example, would pick it up and find something like "For
Elizabeth Halstead, whose bosom companion I have been,
with lascivious memories, Eugene Field." Not all individuals whose libraries were titillatingly embellished were appreciative. Others were, because Field's signature did have
some autograph value.

My favorite inscription used to be written by P. G.
Wodehouse. "Tell your friends to buy this book," would appear on the flyleaf of anything of his, "because I need the
money."

Schools of journalism originally were for students
focusing on newspapers and magazines; radio and televi-

sion weren't in evidence. Today the schools have courses in all communication arts. When I conducted seminars—always, incidentally, a labor of love—most questions had to do with periodicals. Then, with the spreading of electronic media, about the future of the printed word. What I said then is what I'd say now. Print came first, print will stay with us. What one has read and forgotten can be gone back to—it's always somewhere around to see and be read again. When I mentioned "The Gentleman from San Francisco" I was remembering the title and the opulence of the prose. For the life of me I couldn't recall the name of the author. I knew the story was about a man from San Francisco who, having amassed a fortune, decided to take his wife and daughter for a long holiday abroad; that suddenly he had suffered a stroke or heart attack and died while on the holiday. I went to the Forty-second Street library and made inquiry; was referred to several anthologies. The story showed up, by no strange coincidence, in *The Gentleman from San Francisco and Other Stories*, was written by Ivan Bunin, a Russian, was translated into English by Bernard Guilbert Guerney, and published by Alfred Knopf.

About a year ago I wanted to get back to O'Hara and Fitzgerald, to see if I'd still get a charge out of *Appointment in Samarra* and *The Great Gatsby*. From my pet Society Library on Seventy-ninth Street I borrowed the books. They had lost some of their magic but nobody could forget how smashing they were, the first time met up with. What I had was the chance to find out.

I can't think of better examples than the above of what I mean about the permanence of print. Technical books with tables, charts, and graphs may be replaced by records and cassettes, their data computerized and instantly retrievable. Books of creative writing won't be going in that direction. *Treasure Island* in print is something to hold in the hand and fondle. On a cassette, it isn't.

16

The day could be counted lost when there wasn't rumor of some blockbuster book under way, somewhere, in some part of the world: the disclosure of a dangerous political conspiracy, the confessions of an exiled dictator, the autobiography of an executioner. I remember being on a London-bound plane in 1946 and seeing Andrew Heiskell of *Life* and an official of the New York *Times* whose name escapes me though he probably was Julius Adler, general manager of that newspaper, when they were on their presumably hush-hush mission to sign up for Churchill's war memoirs. Magazines of the kind I edited had small involvement with historical reminiscences, but William Hillman, a friend and European-based correspondent, mentioned off-handedly that Ernst "Putzi" Hanfstaengl was said to have written a book and arranged for me to meet him in London. Hanfstaengl, German-born, Harvard-educated, knowledgeable about art, accomplished in music, had been close to Hitler when the latter was nothing more than a street-corner rabble-rouser, remained a member of Hitler's inner circle all the way to the latter's rise to unchallenged power. A big, jolly man, Hanfstaengl had acquired the reputation of being something of a court jester, who was able to amuse Hitler with stories and please him with his skill as a pianist. For reasons never made entirely clear, Hanfstaengl was obliged to flee Germany, was briefly a privileged prisoner of war in Washington, then was turned over to British authorities, who kept him under surveillance in England.

Precautions taken by Hanfstaengl to ensure we would not be seen together in the secretly designated Fleet Street office were as childish as unnecessary: a locked door, a sudden yank by the man to open it for a furtive glance along the corridor to make sure nobody was eavesdropping. The war had come to an end a year earlier, Hanfstaengl was then as free as he pleased to move around, it wasn't likely anybody would be seeking him out to do him any harm. Nevertheless, in the event anything "untoward" happened to him, Hanfstaengl told me, he had deposited his manuscript—his full account of his years with the Nazis—with a British bank and for an advance of twenty thousand dollars a copy would be sent to me. I explained I rarely carried that much money with me except when going shopping with Mrs. Mayes, which wasn't very funny, and he didn't think so, either. But surely the great Hearst organization had bank balances in London? True enough, but I was in no position to pay anything without first seeing the manuscript. That, my friend said, was impossible, but didn't explain why; my suspicion was that it had not been written. If there had been a piano in the room I might have asked Hanfstaengl to play a tune or two for me, as compensation for my wasted trip and time. At last, but not until almost a dozen years later, Putzi's story was published. The book—*Unheard Witness*—turned out to be a self-exonerating account of his pro-Hitler-Göring-Goebbels years and I don't recall that anybody paid much attention to it.

Even had Hanfstaengl's manuscript been in existence in 1946, and given to me, even if it had been a great revelation, it would have been out of place in a women's magazine. It would have been right for *The Saturday Evening Post* or *Look* or *Life*. I think most of the books I chose to publish that proved to be popular were popular for different reasons, but that what I published that failed always failed for the same reason: it belonged in some other kind of periodical. The best bet was to follow my instinct, not what I hoped might be favorably received because it had an aura of importance. However positive my estimation of success, and I think any editor's, I always had to wait for the circulation result to find out.

Book editors and publishers are seldom more positive of what on their traditional spring and autumn lists will do well than are magazine editors of issues that will be effective on the newsstands. Most new books are bought in such small quantities they do little better than break even; the handful making the necessary difference to publishers are those that have magazines' advance interest in serialization, are made book-club selections, receive loving reviews, get supported by heavy advertising, are bid for by paperback reprint companies, end up being made into films. Not all such desirable factors are necessary for success, of course, but it is interesting to know that way back, early in the eighteenth century, books sometimes had to be sold by subscription, with publishers announcing their forthcoming titles and then soliciting orders, thereafter printing just enough copies to fill the orders received. No gamble involved. During the same era, and sponsored by publishers, there were what were called "subscription banquets" to which booksellers were invited, to be exposed to panegyrics of masterpieces in work, and then supposed to place orders. That didn't involve much of a gamble, either.

My records don't specify the time but it was around 1945 that three or four magazine editors had an appointment with David Randall, head of the rare-book department of Scribner's, whose reputation was unsurpassed for familiarity with famous manuscripts and first editions. It was nothing more than an hour of tranquil talk with an affable gentleman. However, when one of the group touched on the vast debt that literature owed to magazine editors, Mr. Randall pointed out that as far as fiction was concerned book editors deserved most of the credit. He was, of course, correct. Many magazine serials never are

published as books at all. Novelists from the most to the
least famous almost always wrote with anticipation of book
publication and in almost all instances initial discussions
were held between author and book company editor. When
novels by the likes of Edith Wharton and Joseph Her-
gesheimer or even a Faith Baldwin were to be found in
magazines it was generally because of the substantial payments made for serialization prior to book publication. The
editors who merit a place in literary history, as Mr. Randall
suggested, are the book editors. As far as the origin of important novels is concerned, magazine editors are also-rans,
and they run far behind, which should be mentioned only
to establish fair perspective.

Vital to a magazine are the regular columns intended to
capture readers' issue-to-issue attention. Some for which we
were responsible—Clare Luce's "Without Portfolio," for example, and Mrs. Roosevelt's "If You Ask Me"—I have mentioned earlier; but also to mind come columns by the Duch-
ess of Windsor, writer Samuel Grafton, Variety's Abel
Green, Secretary of Health, Education, and Welfare Abraham Ribicoff, novelist Laura Hobson—too many, over too
many years, to mention. A particular favorite was "Fitz &
Starts," written by Bernice Fitz-Gibbon, the country's ablest
department store advertising manager whose "Nobody But
Nobody Undersells Gimbel's" and whose Macy slogan "It's
smart to be thrifty" alone would have made her famous.

A successful department was called "Date Line—Facts
& Fancies for the Student on Campus." Each semester we
engaged fifty boys and girls who were in their senior year in
high school or freshman year in college, who reported on
current campus slang, fashions, parties, games; on which
radio programs were most popular, which film stars, books,
etc. Not only were students thus kept up to date, but so
were we in the office. Another popular department was
handled by Dorothy Kilgallen, whose syndicated newspaper column billed her as "The Voice of Broadway." Each
month Miss Kilgallen would go to a small town and write

"Big Night in Kalamazoo," or Altoona, or Wilmington, telling why young people patronized jukebox taverns, beer joints, and roadhouses to relieve their boredom. Her pieces were not flattering to the small towns and were always followed by a handful of cancellations from subscribers who lived in them. In one issue we published a reader's letter that wasn't flattering to Miss Kilgallen. She got very uppity and refused to write for us again. As against that, television's Dave Garroway was so pleased with his monthly columns that he asked us to send his checks to our favorite charities. When his contract expired, he came to the office to say thanks for the opportunity we had given him to write. He walked around the office shaking hands with the copy editors who had seen his work through to the printer. So we had our Kilgallens and we had our Garroways. You win some and you lose some, but because of the Garroways you always came out better than even.

There is no large magazine that doesn't rely on continuing columns and departments, discoursing on anything and everything from etiquette, word games, medical views, travel news, gardening hints, and marriage muck-ups. They are the bread and butter on the editorial menu. *Good Housekeeping*'s contents page was originally called "Bill of Fare," very ingenious, I suppose, and revoltingly coy.

The renowned publicity device invented by the *Literary Digest* was its quadrennial straw vote to determine who was ahead in the race for the presidency. Disaster struck in 1936 when the magazine published its unqualified prediction of the election of Alfred Landon over Franklin Roosevelt. Landon carried exactly two states—Maine and Vermont. He vanished from public view shortly thereafter, and so did the magazine, which was absorbed by *Time*. Which is not to imply that such polls are worthless, only that I didn't find them worth anything. Nevertheless, a number of managements, mine included, tried to maintain a cursory check on editors by sponsoring polls, usually called reader-interest surveys, that were supposed to prove which features in given issues of their magazines, and their competitors', had highest and lowest readership. All publishing companies distributed copies of such surveys when they showed that their magazines came out ahead. None called attention to surveys in which they came out last, or even second.

It is depressing to have to say so but reader surveys always pop up with information after the fact. By the time a research outfit walks in, perhaps in April, with the unfortunate results of the preceding January issue, it is a bit too late to remedy the situation. In any case, an editor can guess a good portion of the time which stories and articles are going to get most attention, and which least; a juicy Hollywood scandal is surely going to be widely read, and a column whose subject is whooping cough in infants will be at the bottom of the list because it isn't going to be read by people who have no children, or by most parents of infants who at the time the column appears don't *have* whooping cough, or by parents of children who have had whooping cough already.

It is true that an editor may get a little lazy and take too much for granted and find out from a reader-interest survey that a long-established feature has lost some of its following. A "How This Marriage Was Saved" department, for example, may have lost half its readers because continued for too many years, or because the pediatrician in charge of a "Bringing Up Baby" department may have gotten as out-of-date as Dr. Benjamin Spock before he discovered that a good whack on the backside could do a child a world of good. Gertrude Lane, when she was editor of *Woman's Home Companion,* put the matter quite simply. "To get a hundred percent readership," she said, "all you have to do is run a big cartoon on every page and give it a one-line caption." Miss Lane was right. Miss Lane was a smart editor.

I found reader surveys not worth their cost. Not worth half their cost. To be honest, they bored me. To be honest,

I am sick and tired of them, of everybody being polled, of all those questions about why you did it, when you did it, how you did it, how much you did it. I didn't give a damn about reader surveys and one could bet I wasn't going to let an Elmo Roper with a bunch of tabulated answers from a computer show me how to run a magazine. Circulation, and *only* circulation—newsstand sales and subscription renewals—is what gives an editor the key to how he's doing.

The aforementioned Mr. Roper once was convinced that by analyzing old magazine covers he could discover why they had been newsstand successes or failures and that with such information in hand an editor could have reliable guidance for the future. Roper was so positive that in a somnolent moment I took a chance and agreed to underwrite the cost of a study that embraced half a dozen previously published issues of *Collier's, Ladies' Home Journal, Good Housekeeping, The Saturday Evening Post,* and *Cosmopolitan.* Roper was furnished with newsstand sales figures for the specific issues. I hadn't any confidence in the procedures Roper proposed to follow but respected the man's integrity when later he admitted the experiment had been a flop. The successful issues, he found, had covers with one large illustration, with red the dominant color, and three blurbs. The unsuccessful issues had covers with one large illustration, red the dominant color, and three blurbs. For that kind of information, who needs a computer?

Researchers live by numbers. An editor lives by instinct. It isn't infallible, but nothing is. One must remember that to some extent an editor is paid to make mistakes; if he doesn't make a few once in a while he's playing everything too safe, which is no prescription for success. Once there was an issue of *Good Housekeeping* that I felt couldn't miss. Unfortunately, it appeared during a month when there were fantastic news events. That month the Russians launched their first Sputnik, and then another with a little dog named Laika aboard; President Eisenhower, to the consternation of Arkansas's governor, Orval Faubus, dispatched troops to Little Rock to escort a little black girl to school; there was a fiercely competitive World Series in progress; the country was frolicking in the loveliest Indian summer in a decade. What magazine could compete when all the cards were stacked against it?

When news is spectacular, people naturally buy more newspapers and fewer magazines. When the weather is propitious, people naturally stay home less and buy fewer magazines. My issue did not do well. Readership figures available after a magazine has been off sale for three months are useless. For all my experience, I am pretty bad at forecasting news and weather three months in advance.

In 1936, the editors of *Ladies' Home Journal* assigned a corps of researchers and writers to assemble a report on the forthcoming coronation of Edward VIII. Every conceivable detail of the ceremony was covered: prayers to be said, music to be played, costumes to be worn, who would sit where and stand when; as comprehensive and magnificently prepared a feature as anybody could imagine. The feature appeared in the *Journal* just before Edward abdicated. Like the rest of us, the editors of the *Journal* could run into a snag.

In 1970, Oscar Lubow, who was head of the Starch organization, asked Leo Burnett and George Gribbin, two of the country's outstanding advertising executives, to review and comment on some thousands of magazine ads that had come up with highest scores on the Starch computer. It may have been a sense of humor or mere recklessness that prompted Lubow to bring me into the act as a third commentator, because he was aware of my cavalier attitude toward readership ratings. I went through those high-rated ads diligently and poked fun at a lot of them, including those for Chevrolet and Pontiac cars, Palmolive dishwashing liquid, Avon cologne, American Dairy Association, Pequot sheets, Bulova watches, Kodak film, the American Tobacco Company, Olivetti typewriters, and TWA. I was pretty sure Mr. Lubow would throw my stuff out, especially when I suggested he give up his computer and try using an abacus. But he kept his promise and printed every word as I wrote it, in his two wildly expensive volumes called *Best Read General Magazine Ads of 1969* and *Best Read Special Interest Ads of 1969*. At least Mr. Lubow is a gentleman.

— All I could conclude was that high readership scores are no guarantee of big sales. There was a shoe ad in the Starch study that got an A for reading. Did it make people buy shoes? The sales manager of the shoe company would know, the computer would not. Of what value was the high rating if the shoes didn't sell well? I will venture a guess: the account executive says to the client, "For Pete's sake, look at the terrific score. Our ad was great—your marketing strategy must have been wrong and, who knows, maybe your shoes are lousy." Of course it is a comfortable reason for the agency to use research.

If a shoe ad gets a low score but the shoes sell like mad, the client wants to know how come the ad didn't score higher, because then the shoes might have sold even madder. The account executive then can say, "For Pete's sake, you sold the shoes, didn't you? Who knows what goes on with those crazy computers?"

Advertisers naturally like to know how many individuals read a single copy of a magazine. You buy a copy, one or two or three members of your family may read it, and then it's loaned to a friend who reads it. That's called pass-along readership. What happens? One research group finds that a total of fifteen million people have gone through it. Another group finds only ten million. Quite a difference? But the same kind of research will go on. There is no getting away from it. If it doesn't come up with anything reliable, at least it's always a good topic for conversation.

It may be irreverent to suggest the whole advertising business is afflicted with an inferiority complex—there's so much checking up all the time. Starch, Roper, Nielsen, Robinson, Simmons, Magazine Research, Inc., Gallup—forever checking up on something, and sometimes on one another, to find out if what was done was done right. A few of us may remember when General Motors used to send out questionnaires to learn what motorists wanted in cars: size, shape, horsepower, colors, price, gadgets. Replies were tabulated, scrutinized, patted and petted, and some of the cars General Motors produced thereafter were duds. I haven't a glimmer about the advance research if any that Ford initiated in connection with the Edsel fiasco; all I believe is that people guess right sometimes and wrong sometimes, that advertising is no science, it's an empirical art, precisely as editing is, and the best a computer can do is confirm you guessed good or bad, which you know already because the sales figures come in before the ratings do. I like what Sir Alexander Fleming said: "A good slug of whiskey at bedtime is recommended for a cold—it may not be very scientific, but it works."

Market studies by manufacturers are not to be confused with the Roper magazine type. Whether it's a bar of soap, a package of cereal, a detergent, a cosmetic, or anything else of standard manufacture, a potential market may be investigated for a new product that for some reasonable period will not change in size, shape, color, fragrance, or anything else. A manufacturer can learn which existing competitive products have how much share of a market, sales tests in limited areas can provide invaluable data. A magazine, however, is not a standard product—*Reader's Digest* the most notable exception because the cover always lists the table of contents and has little other variation; for most magazines the covers differ from issue to issue.

With the same procedures as a manufacturer, a magazine can test a new cover price on newsstands in limited areas, but that's about the only research I found that mattered. On the whole, research is big with advertisers and agency media departments. Editors are big on insight and subconscious impulses. Advertising men's minds react more favorably to figures. They have a greater affinity than editors for charts, slide rules, and computers. It's said they don't think so much as count. Sometimes they surface with quixotic information. I remember when the esteemed advertising executive Jack Tinker declared his study of pupil dilation had a distinct relationship to creativity in advertising. What could one say? Pupil dilation—my eye!

As a guide, letters from readers are about as useful to an editor as reader surveys, no more, no less. "I think your magazine is swell" is what most of them say in effect, or "I don't like it." Too many of the former are as interesting to subscribers as a cold in the head, so once in a while the editor, making up a name or two for himself, feels it necessary to address a few scathing remarks to his magazine, to even things up, an idea by no means as silly as it sounds. Henry Luce admitted to writing such letters to *Time* during his early years of ownership.

Once in a while we'd get a letter from a long-time subscriber whose sensibilities were deeply offended by some article or piece of fiction. We'd try to mollify her with a gentle response, usually trying to agree partially with her point of view, but that didn't always serve its purpose. We'd get another letter from her, virtually demanding an apology, preferably to be made in person, which suggested we'd have to get on a plane and fly to Albuquerque to make it. When it got that serious we had a solution. We'd say we had fired Genevieve Gooch, the editor responsible for accepting the article or story in the first place and that Miss Gooch's name would no longer appear on the magazine's masthead. Obviously the reader would wait for the next issue or two to be sure we kept our word, and would find that indeed we had, Miss Gooch's name was no longer to be found. Of course, there never was a Miss Gooch, we simply made up a name like that and tacked it on at the end of the list of associate or assistant editors. Then we could eliminate it without doing anybody any harm. The device could not be regarded as, well, ethical, but it had its value.

If there is heavy derogatory mail after a particular issue it may serve as a warning, not necessarily an edict. Reader letters can't be a blueprint for running a magazine. There are too few of them—several thousand letters from among ten or more million readers indicate something but don't prove anything except that an editor can make a whale of a wrong guess. Margaret Farrar was considered the country's most qualified composer of crossword puzzles at the time we asked her to prepare for *Good Housekeeping* what could be billed as the world's hardest crossword puzzle. She accepted the assignment and we published the result, anticipating angry cries from experts who would say it was unsolvable, impossible, a cheat. We were as surprised as Mrs. Farrar to have several hundred addicts write to say it was a snap.

Because of its extensive service departments, *Good Housekeeping* was always swamped with mail from women asking advice on personal grooming, cooking, sewing, a myriad other personal and household concerns. About 95 percent of such letters could be handled by forwarding a pamphlet or booklet or form letter. As far as I know, *Reader's Digest* is the only mass-circulation magazine that doesn't carry a letters-to-the-editor column.

Newspapers receive less mail than magazines. Of all newspapers I used to read regularly, *The Times* of London elicited the most literate and fascinating correspondence and to such an extent that once I spent a week in *The Times* morgue sampling issues going back more than a century. I made a record of some of the topics covered in the "Letters" columns, which had to do with the origin of "Sing a Song of Sixpence"; the distance a gorilla can jump; the disgrace of seeing a soldier in uniform carrying an umbrella; the absurdity of calling a telephone box a kiosk; why apes commit suicide; the advantage of sand over blotting paper; the skill of Egyptian magicians; the awful noise in the night produced by neighbors' chiming clocks; how to identify poison mushrooms; why counting sheep can keep one awake; the question of whether the eyes of Mary Queen of Scots were hazel (as described by James Barrie) or blue (as asserted by Algernon Swinburne); the educational value of crossword puzzles (from Eden Phillpotts); why men should be permitted to go bathing with their manly chests exposed (from A. P. Herbert); "if manly chests (from Rose Macauley), then why not the womanly chest, too?"; the observation (by A. A. Milne) of a cormorant flying over St. Paul's.

By no means the British paper with the largest circulation—far from it—*The Times* nevertheless is the most influential. "To have a letter in your columns," one Englishman wrote, "is felt to be the duty of the distinguished; it is ever the ambition of the obscure." There was an era when Britons paid for the privilege, preferring to have their letters labeled "Advertisement" to not having them appear at all. With *The Times* a notable name carried no weight; only the subject matter mattered. Disraeli's fulminations were as often ignored as published.

The romance of Edward VIII and Mrs. Wallis Simpson brought more letters to the paper than anything else in its history. Not one was printed, the editor construing the affair as strictly private and none of the public's business. John Arbuthnot Fisher, First Sea Lord during World War I, set a record by having twenty-four of his letters printed in *The Times* in a single year, all of them pleading with his successors in office to concentrate on submarines and aircraft. In 1894 the paper published a letter about the Dreyfus case. It covered a full page and ran for twelve thousand words, another record for any letter to any editor anywhere. Queen Victoria, for the only time in her long life, wrote a letter to a newspaper—*The Times*—to explain why she was so often absent from London after the death of the Prince Consort.

Letters, *The Times* once said, represent a literature of protest, not so much a remedy for individual grievances as an outlet for the purging of personal emotion. In its judgment individual letters are so important that it has a department headed by an "Editor of Letters to the Editor." On a printed form, notation is made of every letter received, and the date; each letter is given a number, the name of each writer is entered, the subject of each letter described. At the day's end the editor of the department sorts out the letters he feels deserve the attention of the editor-in-chief, who alone determines which will be sent to press that night.

What the post office delivers to a magazine in greatest bulk other than home-service mail is poetry. It is not true that more people write poetry than read it, though to an editor it often seems so. On magazines for which I worked, everything except poetry got at least one reading. Not merely is it impractical to read all poems submitted, the possibility of plagiarism is forever present. Surprisingly often, poems reached us that could be recognized instantly as swipes of old familiar ones. Out of curiosity, Maggie Cousins occasionally would tackle the poetry slush pile— the unsolicited poetry—and one day came across a poem she herself had written and that had been published years before in *College Humor*. For our protection we generally paid attention only to verse from poets with whom we were acquainted, in most other instances took refuge in rejection slips because there was no suitable alternative.

For some years the *Good Housekeeping* poetry department was called "Between the Bookends" and was edited by a man whose name I think was Russell but who chose to call himself Ted Malone. Every day on a radio network, conducting a program also called "Between the Bookends," Malone read poems to his audience, made up mostly of

women who were followers of his magazine department.
They would swoon over the sound of his mellifluous voice
and in the course of a month ten or twelve of them would
show up at the office to have an adoring look at the man.
That's no great shakes when one remembers the thousands
of teen-agers who prostrated themselves before an Elvis
Presley, but in our less rarefied operation it was quite impressive.

Somebody asks what I would say is the most important
ingredient in writing for a mass-circulation magazine.
Every editor must have the same answer: clarity. With
books the situation may be different, though I don't like to
have to beat my brains out trying to make sense of a con-
voluted sentence structure. I like similes to be simple and
am put off by metaphors that I have to sweat to understand. Almost sixty years have passed since James Joyce
wrote *Ulysses*, which since its appearance in print has been
acclaimed by most, though not all, discriminating critics as
the greatest literary innovation of the century. The same
point of view is likely to prevail sixty years hence, but for
the average reader the book won't provide much satisfaction. Some parts of it, for me, were impenetrable mum-
mery—I recall making note of a word containing ninety-
nine letters of the alphabet. Edith Wharton referred to the
book as a schoolboy kind of pornography.

Joyce's *Dubliners*, the penetrating little portraits uncon-
nected except by locale, is unencumbered by the author's
later language complications. After the first thirty or forty
pages, when the rhythm took hold of me, I found pleasure
in *A Portrait of the Artist as a Young Man*. Some of Joyce's
poems came across as lyrical. When I caught up with *Finnegans Wake* I knew nothing but stupefaction. Roy
McMullen, an educator and author, quoted the last lines of
the book: "End here. Us again. Finn, again. Given! A way
a lone a last a loved a long the". And then McMullen said,
"Here we are in the substance of what is probably the
closest thing to a pure art novel that will ever be written."

It's my misfortune not to know what is meant by a pure art novel. In *Finnegans Wake,* what Joyce created for me was not a new literary dimension but literary anarchy. Literature demands new boundaries, but it should be possible to cross them. It can rise to new heights, but they should be scalable.

When I told Henry Morton Robinson of my despair, he, who had co-authored *A Key to Finnegans Wake,* spent an hour with me, explaining how I should make a new approach. The more he talked, the deeper my confusion. What acknowledged scholars have written about *Finnegans Wake*—their infinite interpretations as incomprehensible to me as what was being interpreted—has left me stumped but not intimidated. I am merely admitting, not boasting.

Not so much an apology for my ignorance as comfort for myself, I mention a conversation with Carl Van Doren, a good friend, biographer of Franklin, Swift, and Cabell, a consultant sometimes in my editorial programming. "I've read Joyce, of course," Van Doren said, "and regard his works as masterpieces. But I can tell you that several of my former Columbia [University] colleagues put Joyce down in short order, saying he demanded more time than they had to spare for getting the drift of him. I don't think I knew more than two or three who had a glimmer of what *Finnegans Wake* was about. It's refreshing," he added, "to meet people who don't claim to have all the answers. Joyce is over the heads of ninety out of every hundred people who say—who *say*—they have read him."

Inability to grasp an author's transcendental symbolisms and private allegories and his propensity for invoking mythological images is no reason for decrying his greatness, which I am not foolish enough to do. But when I sit for a half hour with a poem by E. E. Cummings and see a single word separated by parentheses, commas, colons, semicolons, question marks, and exclamation points, or at least two of them, I keep asking myself, What goes on here? When I see Cummings spell "bright" as "bRight,"

and "who" spelled "wHo," or a line like "n:start
birDs(lEAp)Openi ng," which is in a poem listed as 221 in
Collected Poems of e. e. cummings (published by Har-
court, Brace & World), I am not so much upset with myself
for lack of perception as angry with the author for a moment for making me feel ridiculous. Parentheses and question marks can't be read aloud. When they break up an
otherwise simple word in print they seem to me to be de-
facing the language. In the same collection of poems, when
the critic Mark Van Doren is quoted as saying Cummings
was "merciless toward pretense and pomposity," I can't
help but ask what *is* pretense and don't feel shy about asking it. I've read that Cummings' "eccentricities of typog-
raphy, language and punctuation are intended to convey a
joyful awareness of sex and life." There may be a plenitude
of sex and life in Cummings' work but I didn't get my
awareness of them, and couldn't, from Cummings. When
he wished, Cummings could speak and write lucidly and
beautifully. He did so, often. At Harvard he gave lectures
that were in the kind of English that makes one swell with
pride for having been born to the language. I wondered if
he really had to go so far afield in his poetry to express
himself.

I don't find my self-respect diminished by having to
confess to a lack of appreciation of distorted syntax and alphabetical acrobatics; nor do I recognize an obligation to
ladle out encomiums for what to me seems abstruse and esoteric. Gertrude Stein's *Autobiography of Alice B. Toklas* is
straightforward enough and can be easily understood by
anybody who, to misquote the author only slightly, has sat
with wives of geniuses, with wives who were not wives of
geniuses, with real wives of geniuses who were not real
geniuses. However, the pseudoliterary toiling to create a
perfect sentence that comes out like a rose is a rose is a rose
strikes me as fraudulent mystification and I resist being
gulled into declaring it genius and saying I'm just not up to
deciphering it. I'm not seeking any defender of my position

but can point out that the critic Van Wyck Brooks hated what he described as the cults of elegant privacy, the T. S. Eliot cult, the E. E. Cummings cult. He called them coterie writers, doubted the integrity of those who overpraised Gertrude Stein, and called her theories gibberish.

Earlier I have referred to Clifton Fadiman as the popular literary conscience of the country, but leaving him at that is like saying nothing more of Casey Stengel than that he was a ballplayer. "Kip" Fadiman still is one of the comprehensible literary critics, writes exquisitely, combines sense with charm, wit with wisdom, and I'm glad to have kept a copy of one of his amusing lines that is applicable right here. "My notion," Fadiman wrote, "is that Miss Stein set herself to solve, and has succeeded in solving, the most difficult problem in prose composition—to write something that will not arrest attention in any way, manner, shape, or form. If you think this easy, try it."

I wouldn't for a moment wish to impugn the literary reputation of Bennett Cerf, whose friendship I cherished despite his horrendous puns, which he was the first to groan over. It was he and his partner Donald Klopfer at Random House who were responsible for having a copy of *Ulysses* seized by U.S. customs officers and engaging the attorney Morris Ernst to process the case in court, resulting in the famous Judge Woolsey decision to lift the ban against the book's importation into the United States, and it was Random House that first published *Ulysses* in this country. On an occasion when I broached the subject of *Finnegans Wake* to Bennett, to learn if he understood any more of it than I, he grinned and said, "My friend, I have a confession to make—"

He could reel off new jokes and peel off old ones and was the first to laugh at them, which made everybody else laugh harder. Generally thought of as a man of no great scholarship, there was nobody who didn't credit him with being a sensationally great publisher. He did not have to understand the whole of a book to recognize its sales potential.

About poetry my opinion in connection with clarity is the same as about prose. I found rough enough spots in Eliot's verse drama *Murder in the Cathedral,* but in *The Waste Land,* that some devotee enthusiastically called a poetic cryptogram, whatever that is, I was altogether lost; had to read single lines over and over to try to fathom recondite allusions. August Irish editor and critic Robert Lynd said of Eliot, "His obscurity seems not due to the difficulties of his material but to his insufficient mastery of his medium, words. In a considerable amount of literature, obscurity is due to the author rather than any defect of the reader." Ezra Pound's* short verses like "A Virginal" and "A Pact" were comforting, but some of his writings, flaunting quotations in half a dozen different languages including Chinese and Greek, were impossible, and I have no hesitation about making the admission. I found his esoteric autobiographical *Cantos* impossible. According to William Hugh Kenner, a noted professor and author, "In the *Cantos,* the place of plot is taken by interlocking large-scale rhythms of recurrence." I hope others understand. I don't. Other critics have written that Pound's motive was to spring verse from its ancient shackles. I wasn't aware of the shackles. The right to write free verse doesn't confer the right to be lawless. One can protest against old-established academic rules and fixed rules of meter without becoming literarily sadistic. Let anybody mock me who will, but I have some feeling of sympathy for the schoolboy who said he hated poems that didn't quite reach to the margins. I am fooling only to the extent that I don't expect the statement to be taken literally, but nobody can talk me out of saying how thoroughly I enjoyed Coleridge's "Kubla Khan," Longfellow's "Song of Hiawatha," Gray's "Elegy," Poe's "The Raven," and Lamb's "Old Familiar Faces." I am not

---

* Most ardent of Joyce's protagonists, even Pound referred to *Finnegans Wake* as "an aimless search for exaggeration."

going to risk being denounced by naming names, but it is God's truth that I have read the published letters of philosopher-authors—letters written to other philosopher-authors on the subject of poetry—that left me convinced they were written to knock the breath out of one another and certainly with the hope they would be preserved and someday would appear in book form.

Without in any way modifying what I have said above, I ought to say I know fashion in literature is ephemeral, often arbitrary, varying with the era. It may be true that experimental English poetry owes its origin to Pound, and extreme stream-of-consciousness novels to Joyce. Some eminent critics have said so. I am not an eminent critic. One cannot disagree that poetry is the highest, most beautiful form of literary expression, what Carlyle called the heroic of speech. I am simply one who does not believe that incomprehensibility makes it so.

The mounds of poetry submitted to a magazine in the course of a single month (I believe that at *Good Housekeeping* we once counted eleven thousand) are proof enough of the hold that poetry has on people. It doesn't have to be as elemental as what Ella Wheeler Wilcox and Edgar Guest and Berton Braley used to produce in order to attract readers and would-be poets. The simplest poem, especially one that's stickily sentimental, can bring about a great to-do. Such a one was published by William Bigelow before I took his place on *Good Housekeeping*. It was written by Violet Alleyn Storey:

PRAYER FOR A VERY NEW ANGEL†

God, God, be lenient her first night there.
The crib she slept in was so near my bed.
Her blue-and-white wool blanket was so soft,
Her pillow hollowed so to fit her head.

† Reprinted by permission of Abingdon Press.

Teach me that she'll not want small rooms or me
When she has You and Heaven's immensity!

I always left a light out in the hall.
    I hoped to make her fearless in the dark;
And yet, she was so small—one little light,
    Not in the room, it scarcely mattered. Hark!

No, no; she seldom cried! God, not too far
For her to see, this first night, light a star!

And in the morning, when she first woke up,
    I always kissed her on the left cheek where
The dimple was. And oh, I wet the brush,
    It made it easier to curl her hair.

Just, just tomorrow morning, God, I pray,
When she wakes up, do things for her my way!

It provoked such a storm of protest via letters and telephone calls that Bigelow vowed never again to publish
anything about the death of a child, and he didn't.

There was a time when pupils were given poems to
memorize to help them in the study of language. As famous
as any is one whose author remains in the anonymous category:

THE LAYING OF LIE AND LAY

While free from care, the other day
Beneath the verdant shade I LAY.
I said, "How charming here to LIE
And view the glories of the sky."
While thus at ease I long HAD LAIN
I saw a trav'ler cross the plain,
And bade him on the sod to LAY

The load that galled him on his way.
Well pleased, his burden down he LAID
And LAY beside me in the shade.

One must admit it's pretty bad. No worse, however, than other oddball verses about language that I have collected and sometimes like to share.‡

‡ See Appendix.

18

An almost lifelong hang-up of mine has been a fatuous resolve not to write prosaic letters, not even to brokers seeking to sell life insurance. Quite possibly I hoped recipients would save them against the day a discerning admirer would undertake my biography. I found perverse pleasure in composing acrimonious letters of complaint. More than once the president of Con Ed must have contemplated resignation from his post rather than be confronted with my diatribes about the deficient eyesight of the inspector who arrived regularly to take a meter reading. To everybody's surprise but mine, subsequent bills were lower.

The day I embarked with one of my daughters on a tour of New England colleges for interviews about her possible enrollment, a snowstorm caused a delay resulting in a missed train connection from Boston to Norton, which circumstance made it necessary to take a taxi to Wheaton College. The snowstorm might have been an act of God but according to my reckoning it was a malicious effort by the railroad to discommode me. On returning to New York I demanded from the New Haven Railroad not merely the cost of the taxi fare but, highly unreasonable, half the cost of the two railroad tickets. Within seventy-two hours the requested check was in my hands. It was so unexpected that I phoned the vice-president in charge of passenger service, first to thank him, then to ask why I had been accorded such extraordinary attention. "Mr. Mayes," the man said wearily, "we keep your name in our *active* file."

And, I supposed, for good reason. When I commuted from Stamford to New York and trains became so crowded there weren't enough seats for all passengers, I issued an ultimatum: additional cars must be put on or I would organize unseated passengers and have them refuse to hand over their commutation tickets for punching. For two successive days some twenty passengers joined in the protest. The morning of the third day the same vice-president called on me. He pledged the extra cars and swore he would give me a private car to ride in all by myself if I would call off the nonsense and stop writing letters. Somebody could write a really interesting book about life with the New Haven Railroad. I'd be glad to contribute a chapter.

As a result of an altercation with Earle & Calhoun, the real estate agency in charge of a building in which I lived, I wrote to Mr. Calhoun to express my low opinion of him, employing a barrage of words not normally used in polite company. I did not hear from him, but Mrs. Mayes did. "I do not think a man who uses your husband's kind of language," he wrote, "should be editor of a ladies' magazine."

For some research about authors' reactions to early criticism of their books, I sent three or four form letters to Thorstein Veblen, wanting to know how he had felt about first notices of his *Theory of the Leisure Class*. There was no reply until I sent a telegram. Then I received a postcard: "Veblen is dead. I just happen to be living in his old house." Veblen dead? He had been dead for thirty-seven years! It seems that sometimes nobody tells me anything. Anyway, the postman, unlike Western Union, had paid attention only to the street number, not to the name of the occupant.

For some people, and I'm one of them, compulsion about answering letters is a kind of affliction. Not necessarily answering promptly, but sooner or later. Christopher

Morley remarked that people who answer letters the day they are received are stunted and queer, like people who go to the movies at nine in the morning. I have held on to letters and then, in response to a question asked a year earlier, sat down to declare under oath that I was not in any way related to the Mayes family in Louisville, Kentucky. I do not relish writing letters and know that most people would be unaware I never answered theirs. Lin Yutang insisted that if one answers letters promptly the result is about as bad or as good as if one never answered at all. "If you keep most letters in your drawer for three months," he said, "and then read them, you realize what a waste of time it would have been to reply." Ben Hecht didn't even bother to *open* his mail unless a check was enclosed, which he could determine by holding envelopes up to the light. The story is told that a friend who had had no reply to several letters did once enclose a check, but it was a blank check. Hecht returned the blank check, but made no reply.

Henry Pringle, Pulitzer Prize biographer of Theodore Roosevelt and also in other respects an honored writer, once undertook an investigation of astrology for us. The Astrologers' Guild agreed to cooperate by choosing four of its members, each of whom was to cast the horoscope of the same two anonymous persons selected by Pringle. Pringle was to provide data regarding the two persons' sex, birthplace, date and hour of birth. According to the plan, each astrologer was to be assigned a separate room in a hotel. The announced purpose was to compare the findings of the four astrologers and it was understood the magazine would take care of all costs of the test, including fees to be paid for the astrologers' time. On the day appointed, without explanation, none of the astrologers appeared. Pringle's report when published in *Good Housekeeping* was, understandably, thoroughly negative. One astrologer who read it and hoped to make me a convert, wrote a letter asking for the exact time and date of my birth, offering without charge to cast my horoscope. That was somewhere in the 1950's. I replied by saying there was no record of the exact moment but that the date of my birth was February 12, 1809. With a better sense of humor than mine, the astrologer forwarded my horoscope, which stated with absolute correctness that I was destined to be the sixteenth President of the United States.

A well-known newspaper columnist, generally very right-wing and vitriolic in his opinions, whose readers grew in number as his blood pressure rose, was Westbrook Pegler. A good portion of the mail he received from readers who hated him was abusive, and any mail of mine to him would have been of a similar nature. Nevertheless, I asked him to write an article for us about his correspondence and the manner in which he replied. He called it "Dear Sir, You Cur!" and did not seek to play down its vituperative character. No matter what his subject, even when it was noncontroversial, Pegler's articles provoked vilifying letters. This prompted him one day to lay out a half-dozen texts by economic savants, from which he composed a batch of impressive incoherence by latching together phrases and snatches of pseudo-scientific jargon taken artfully at random. "I was surprised myself," Pegler said, "by the rolling rhythm of the periodic crash of my prose." As a result, he received condemnatory letters, including one from a man of strong conviction who claimed Pegler had swiped his theories from *him!*

One may listen with skepticism to authors who say they refuse to read reviews of their books, favorable or otherwise, and with equal skepticism to magazine editors who say they leave reader mail to assistants and never glance at it themselves. Every week there'd be at least a few letters that we found interesting and constructive. It's superfluous to suggest editors read *all* mail; most of it is routine in nature and can be disposed of routinely by secretaries. Nevertheless, a batch of letters voicing the same complaint or expressing the same kind of comment can cause an editor to have second thoughts. Reader mail gets sorted, not all of it is summarily ignored. Unsigned letters we tossed into the "Unknown Soldier" file.

One reader wrote to say it would be kind if we asked other *Good Housekeeping* readers to save and then send their newspaper comics and comic books to us for forwarding to England, for the children there who because of the war and the consequent paper shortage were being deprived of their favorite literature. We published the letter and were inundated with so many comics that a representative of the postal service begged that the suggestion be withdrawn. To begin with, he said, the extra work devolving on the post office in New York was interfering with more important activities. And he added that comics could not any longer be sent on to England because our government had established an embargo on them. There were things England needed more desperately.

It was fun sometimes to know where letters came from. "Holy Moses," I'd say to my secretary, "look at this—we have a subscriber named Smith who lives in Jones, South Dakota." "Holy Mary," she'd say, "how unfascinating." Always received with gratification and acknowledged immediately were letters appealing for a certain kind of help, or just thanking us for some service. "Mr. Editor," began a letter from Wakayama Prefecture in Japan, "I am a mother, having a baby two month old. They say American woman feed babies so intellectually that I want to learn it. And then I interest in life of woman who had delivery. If possible I wish to change a letter with mothers who have a baby of two month old." "I saw those rainbows described in your explanation of glaucoma," another letter said, "and didn't waste any time in getting to a doctor. He says I can't be cured, but because of treatment my sight won't get any worse. What sight I have left I owe to your magazine and from now on I will say a prayer every night to bless you."

Somebody once wrote or said that letters are the closest thing to a national literature and I am inclined to confirm the view when I think of the letters that continue to appear in the syndicated newspaper column conducted by Abigail Van Buren. I will limit myself to mention of two. A fifteen-year-old girl had written to say her mother had bought her a strapless evening gown to wear to a party. The girl's father protested, saying his daughter wasn't old enough, and the girl put the question to the columnist, whose reply was: "Try it on. If it stays up, you're old enough." The other also may be called a classic for pointedness. Over a span of days a subject being complained about by her readers was the unpleasant sound of men's snoring. The correspondence ended with a comment from one of the columnist's readers: "Dear Abby, the most beautiful sound in the world is that of a man's snoring. Ask any widow."

One final letter, from John Bainbridge, *The New Yorker*'s man in London and over the years responsible for a number of that magazine's brilliant Profiles. "Have you ever thought of living in London?" Bainbridge asked. That was late in 1968. In my reply I said a man born in New York, as I had been, who loved New York as I did, never could imagine living anywhere else. Later, I changed my mind.

19

Today the intricacies of publishing are as they were in my day, but with agreements for magazine serial and other rights all put in contract form, very legal, very wordy, and formidable. Publishers are surrounded by lawyers, authors and agents by their own. In my time a telephone conversation, a handshake, sufficed to make an understanding binding. I never had a written contract with Mrs. Roosevelt or Mrs. Luce or any other regular contributor, not with such a temperamental writer as Margaret Case Harriman, or with James Street, Maurice Chevalier, Edmund Ware, Ogden Nash, Lucille Ball, Anne Langman, John M. Henry, Hubert Humphrey, Mrs. John F. Kennedy, Art Linkletter, a hundred others. Such individuals said they would write on a subject we agreed on; we said we would pay a specified sum of money. Once in a while a writer would produce something much longer than at first thought necessary and would expect a higher payment, which usually was given. Negotiations were entered into with mutual trust. I recall but one instance of a frustrating experience with a book publisher, which was when Bernard Geis, who knew more about promoting books than inherent literary value, solicited an expression of interest in a memoir being written by former President Truman. I was interested, and a check covering advance payment was forwarded promptly. I did not know and by Geis had not been informed that a duplicate of the manuscript when it came to me had simultaneously been submitted to *Look*.

As soon as word got out that *McCall's* was planning publication, *Look* laid claim to the story, declaring it had been guaranteed first refusal by Geis, which proved to be the case. Geis, assuming he knew better than its editor, had decided *Look* was not likely to pay his asking price. In prospect was a suit, each of the two magazines against the other.

When Geis's lawyer came to see me, he said, "My client has done a stupid thing, there is no excuse for it, but I hope you will be lenient and let him off the hook." The book— *Mr. Citizen*—was not worth a court hearing, didn't seem worth fighting over. Also, something about it seemed to have a familiar ring.

On making inquiries I learned some of the chapters had been published already, years before, in *American Weekly*. Did Geis know? I had no direct evidence to that effect. But my recollection is that in the end *Look* used only the new portions and I believe the original asking price had to be substantially reduced. I have two other recollections: one, that Random House, which had been serving as distributor for Geis's books, terminated the relationship because it called too many of the books sleazy; two, that in 1971 Geis's company entered a petition in bankruptcy. The company is in business now as Bernard Geis Associates, Inc.

Arrangements with literary agents always were as effectively carried out as with most book publishers, with few exceptions. For every Jacques Chambrun, mentioned in connection with Mr. Maugham, there were dozens of agents who were able and honorable. In the latter category was the gentle, scholarly Harold Ober, one of whose clients was F. Scott Fitzgerald. Not many people other than Ober and Maxwell Perkins of Scribner's knew how badly off Fitzgerald was during his periods of depression. It was Ober's kindness and generosity, his affection for the troubled and troublesome author, that put him in the position of a banker, though without a banker's demand for collateral. His patience with Fitzgerald's unending demands for advances, the loans he made, went beyond the call of duty. The time came when that was altogether imprudent and it was then that Ober called at my office. He had with him two short stories Fitzgerald had written and that had been rejected by half a dozen editors. Would I as an old Fitzgerald worshipper care to be a good angel now and buy them? Maybe, he suggested, it would be possible for a Maggie Cousins to straighten them out, Fitzgerald wouldn't object to drastic revisions, he was desperate for money. I did buy them, expecting only to file and forget, which made no business sense; the money had to come out of established editorial budget. But Ober had done us many favors, and I was remembering when Fitzgerald was edifying the world with his prose, a man who, despite a tidy amount of trash he had written, had made a significant contribution to contemporary literature.

When Andrew Turnbull was doing research for his definitive biography of Fitzgerald, he reached an impasse; there were two pieces of fiction about which he had questions: "Make Yourself at Home" and "The Pearl and the Fur." The first I had sold to *Liberty* when it was scrambling for anything with a noted name attached, and the title was changed to "Strange Sanctuary." The unpearly pearl thing must still be interred on some old editorial shelf of mine, in appropriate oblivion.

Ober's paragon of a chief associate, Dorothy Olding, who later became proprietor of the agency, handled the work of Mrs. Max Mallowan, otherwise known as Agatha Mary Clarissa Christie, better and more simply known as Agatha Christie, creator of the dapper, roly-poly Hercule Poirot and spinster Jane Marple detective novels. For a long period I believe only Miss Olding, Mr. Ober, and perhaps two or three others were aware that the short non-detective novels submitted under the authorship of Mary Westmacott were really written by Agatha Christie. One of them, *Absent in the Spring*, about a long-married woman who was able at last to get away from her husband for a few days and review her life and discover her real self, proved to be a work of depth and perception. On October 13, 1970, at Agatha Christie's eightieth birthday party, held in the office of her London publisher, William Collins, I was a guest. The fabulous woman who had written more than sixty novels, more than a dozen plays, including the world champion long-distance runner, "The Mousetrap," and some dozens of volumes of short stories had suffered an accident and sat majestically in a chair accepting the good wishes of her admirers. Approaching her, I bowed and said, "It's so very nice to meet you, Mary Westmacott." "I beg your pardon?" she replied. And then smiled; probably having no recollection that I had bought and published the Westmacott stories.

On that birthday Agatha Christie's newest book, *Passenger to Frankfurt,* was moving up on the best-seller lists. In one episode was the suggestion that Adolf Hitler did not really die in a bunker in Berlin but had escaped to South America. What it brought to mind was a short story by Nathaniel Benchley we had published some years before. In that story Benchley had Hitler, minus mustache but wearing a wig, serving as a shoe clerk in a store in New York.

Another famous agent was, and is, Harold Matson, who among his other accomplishments practically created an industry out of Herman Wouk's *Caine Mutiny*. We had contracted for a new novel Wouk was working on, based to some extent on the life of Thomas Wolfe. When it arrived it carried the title *Youngblood Hawke,* which I didn't like. My beseeching left Wouk cold; he was adamant about retaining the title. As the customer, I think I was right; as the seller, Wouk had the last word. The book was a best seller. Even if written in Sanskrit a Wouk book would become a best seller.

It was Matson who introduced me to Dobie Gillis, or I

should say to Max Shulman, the author who gave birth to Dobie. What an irrepressible young hero—Dobie, of course! And it was F. Hugh Herbert, then without benefit of agent, who introduced us to Corliss Archer and her lovesick suitor Dexter Franklin. Aside from the satisfaction of publishing the Dobie and Corliss stories there was always the anticipation of hysterically appreciative letters from their fans.

Shortly after Frank Sinatra's phenomenal return to popular favor because of his performance as Private Maggio in the *From Here to Eternity* film, we made arrangements through Helen Strauss, another of the really scintillating agents, for a feature to be written around the title "The Rise and Fall and Rise Again of Frank Sinatra." In a temperamental mood at the time, the performer was being difficult about granting necessary interviews. The delaying tactics were exasperating; finally, out of patience, I said to Miss Strauss, "Please get word to that client of yours that he'd better be cooperative and immediately or we'll cut off the end of the title and just run the rise and fall part." In her effective way, as with everything she handled, Miss Strauss got the message across and the required cooperation followed.

Still another leading agent was Carol Brandt, who handled the work of our medical reporter, Maxine Davis. Each month Miss Davis researched and put together a comprehensive report on some major disease. It could be arthritis, mumps, ulcers, cancer—whatever the disease, Miss Davis was instantly afflicted by it. She must have covered fifty diseases for us over the years. She suffered them all. Promptly on finishing a piece about syphilis, she rushed off for a Wassermann test. Her doctor's infinite patience was needed to convince the buxom author she was hale and hearty. Carl Brandt, Carol Brandt's husband, was one of the best agents of all, but even he could make a peach of a mistake; had told John Marquand he didn't think *The Late George Apley* was worth publishing.

One thing is bound to lead to another, especially if

sufficient time elapses. In 1936 I asked two popular illustrators of the day—Bradshaw Crandell and Hans Flato—to paint for *Pictorial Review* the portraits of the enchanting one-year-old Dionne quintuplets as they might look when they grew up to be young ladies. The feature ran under the heading "The Dionne Quintuplets, Twenty Years from Today." How sweet, how beautiful, the girls became in the eyes of Crandell and Flato! In reality they turned out to be anything but appealing. Then, in the early 1960's, I was called on by a pretty and exceptionally aggressive young agent, Rosalind Cole, whose persistence when she had an idea to sell could drive an editor out of his mind before he could drive her out of his office. Mrs. Cole was pressing for a *McCall's* commitment for the joint autobiography of the four still-living Dionne quints, and my reaction was resolutely negative. "They used to be cute as buttons," I said, "but now—well, you've seen photographs of them! And too much time has gone by—nobody will have any interest in them." When I learned the autobiography had not yet been written, I said yes, we would make the commitment, but named so low a price I was sure it would be refused. I was not so lucky—Mrs. Cole accepted and I got rid of her.

Several months later, to my astonishment—perhaps also to the astonishment of the Dionnes, who had no idea of how resourceful Mrs. Cole could be—the manuscript was delivered. Titled *We Were Five*, it made moderately good reading; better reading, anyway, than if the Dionne girls had written it themselves, which of course they hadn't.* All of us in the office doubted it would have any great appeal, but we hadn't reckoned on a miracle. As a matter of fact, two miracles. Immediately the first of the installments appeared, newspapers carried announcement of the almost simultaneous birth of two sets of quintuplets, one set in the United States, the other in South America. If I were less modest, I could claim it was perfect editorial timing. Every

* It was ghost-written by James Brough.

newspaper obviously reported the births. Less obviously, every newspaper called attention to the Dionne story in *McCall's*, which made for extraordinary publicity for the magazine, and extraordinary sales. Well, throw a lucky man into the sea, as some old Arab proverb says, and he will come up with a fish in his mouth.

The function of a literary agent was first conceived by A. P. Watt, in England, toward the end of the nineteenth century, when Watt established his agency. Literary agents can be a godsend to editors. Certainly to authors. For their 10 percent commission they are counselors—editors, in effect, themselves—and they negotiate the advances and final payments to be received by their clients, sometimes they make loans and serve as business managers and marital advisers. Not least, they are more familiar than authors with available markets. The more important agents are associated with counterparts abroad, indispensable allies where sales of foreign rights are concerned. They know all the regulations affecting copyright and charges for authors' alterations. Well-established agents may be reluctant to take on new writers as clients; some, not unreasonably, will demand a fee for reading a manuscript. Until some twenty years ago the largest part of an agent's business was done with magazines, but with dwindling magazine interest in short stories and serials, agents concentrated on hard-cover books and paperbacks, and films. In the earlier time all agents made regular calls at magazine offices; it was part of their daily routine. The Curtis company editor Stuart Rose arrived in New York from Philadelphia one day every week to make the rounds of agents.

A few authors handle their own negotiations and contracts. But an experienced, conscientious agent can be more valuable to an author than the author's own publisher. Because anyone who has the urge may become an agent—no license, no training officially required—writers can run across a hack, incompetent to offer sensible editorial advice, who doesn't take time to read manuscripts submitted but is content to ship them out haphazardly to one publishing shop after another. For an up-to-date record of agents I have asked editors now active to nominate those they consider best, and I compiled a list of the ones unanimously agreed on.†

The first agent who ever called at my office was the senior Paul Reynolds, one of the grandly distinguished old-timers, with whom Harold Ober had begun his career. During our introductory conversation I learned Reynolds had even been literary representative for Tolstoy's estate. He was impressed to hear that as a young man I had the temerity to prepare for a small group a paper on the comparatively close development of Russian and American literature in the nineteenth century, but was depressed to hear I never had been able to finish *War and Peace;* had read long sections, then didn't go back to the book until two or three weeks later; read more, then let a month go by before picking it up again. Reynolds tried to exact a promise I would try again. I had tried, I told him, a dozen times, which was an exaggeration. "Tolstoy had thirteen children," the kindly old gentleman said, "so why don't you give it one more chance?" It wasn't that I thought the novel too long, though it's long enough, but I remembered that when I thought I was getting to know the Rostovs and Bolkonskis I was trying to remember how many strokes Count Bezukhov suffered, couldn't be sure Natasha Rostov was married to Andrei Bolkonski or Pierre Bezukhov, was confusing the battle of Borodino with the one at Austerlitz. I would get to the end of the third part, and when finished with the fifth couldn't keep straight what happened in the second. The panorama of the book, the sweep of armies, the vast cast of characters, all called for sustained reading, not my pick-it-up-and-go-back-to-it-later approach. There were books in between that for one reason or another demanded my attention. Rudolf Flesch, who made a name for

† See Appendix.

himself with *Why Johnny Can't Read,* admitted he never could finish Dante's *Divine Comedy,* and that's one I couldn't, either. As a matter of fact, if I had persevered with more than two of the five or six volumes of Gibbon's *Decline and Fall,* or more than two of the five of Macaulay's *History of England,* I would have lost the time to read such a masterpiece as Monypenny and Buckle's *Life of Benjamin Disraeli,* which I now could read every word of over again with, I think, total fascination.

I have explained my problem with what no doubt is the greatest novel ever written. I wish I could explain my problem with several "little" classics like *The Book of Tea* by Kakuzo Okakura, and Kahlil Gibran's *The Prophet,* and Dag Hammarskjöld's *Markings.* A more recent thingumabob was called *Jonathan Livingston Seagull,* for which I've been told a million dollars was paid for paperback rights. I don't think any one of them took me more than an hour to read. I never understood what had made them so popular and gotten them the acclaim so richly undeserved.

20

The author with a facile pen does not necessarily have a nimble tongue. The statement by Hazlitt that the conversation of authors is better than any other is a generalization needing more support than out of my own experience I could bring to bear. It is hardly different from the phrase that every editor hears, "You must meet so many interesting people," meaning authors, as though meeting them conferred a claim to distinction. An editor does meet a lot of people, and some of them are interesting, including writers. A butcher meets a lot of people, too, and some of them are interesting. The authors who captured my fancy most were those who gave us their best stories. The authors who found me most fascinating were those to whom I paid the highest rates.

Edwin Balmer, who had been a competent editor of *Redbook,* said it is not so important that writers find an editor interesting as that they feel at ease with him. What needs emphasizing is that the author/editor relationship is fiduciary, that what goes on between them must be strictly confidential. The editor may recommend a modification in story line that solves a ticklish problem, or propose introduction of a new character to enliven an undramatic situation. Stories get rewritten in part by magazine or book editors, sometimes by the authors themselves in line with an editor's recommendation. The editor is obliged to keep it to himself. Authors are touchy, not unknown to be haughty, become irate if word gets around that a story has come out of a collaboration, which it often does. Rule one is that a story must be known as the author's, and the author's alone. Rules two and three are the same.

Even minor deviation from the principle of confidentiality can cause problems. Sheila Burnford wrote "The Incredible Journey," a sorcerous novelette about a Labrador retriever, an English bull terrier, and a Siamese cat that wandered around Canada in search of the owner from whom they had been separated. We had no sooner bought it than we recommended it to Walt Disney for possible use as a film, which he made. When I mentioned the fact offhandedly during a writers' conference, I heard Miss Burnford was disturbed. That seemed unreasonable, I thought I was doing her a favor, but I should have been more cautious. Then when during a lecture attended by Allan Seager I said in passing that he sometimes used T. V. Cookeson as a pseudonym, he was visibly resentful; he had not wanted his faculty colleagues at the University of Michigan to be aware, and again I should have known better. Strangely, in *Man of Genius*, Scott Berg's biography of Maxwell Perkins, Berg makes clear that Perkins spared few details in writing to some of his authors about other of his authors; in writing to Hemingway about Fitzgerald, for example, to Fitzgerald about Hemingway, to Marjorie Kinnan Rawlings about Thomas Wolfe. Berg points out that Perkins spoke too freely of advice he was giving to his most famous authors. However, Mr. Perkins had his own style and one would be presumptuous to question it.

If a story contained incorrect references or dates or was minus diacritical marks, we held it our obligation, for the author's sake and our readers', to make obvious corrections. Editorial excellence has been called the art of noninterference, but if we thought a story unreasonably long and the need to make cuts vital, we made those cuts, usually with the permission of the author. Not often, but sometimes without permission, because editors and readers have rights, too.

One thing we never attempted was modification of an author's style, though we knew a copy editor, a dogmatic purist, who did. She wouldn't concede that the awkward style of a writer might be his greatest asset.

There are times when an author will absolutely refuse to tolerate a change of any kind or character, as indicated when Raymond Chandler sent a letter to Ted Weeks of *The Atlantic*. "Would you convey my compliments to the purist who reads your proofs," he wrote, "and tell him or her that I write in a sort of broken-down patois which is something like the way a Swiss waiter talks, and when I split an infinitive, God damn it, I split it and so it will stay split." However, articles do come along with facts badly jumbled, misspellings rampant, sentences overpunctuated, underpunctuated, or unpunctuated. Authors, and top editors, too, owe more than they can repay to the unsung, unappreciated copy editors of magazine and book staffs.

Manuscript problems, if not always easy to resolve, seldom resulted in friction. In a story about the liaison between a nationally famous and then still active magazine editor and his secretary, Booth Tarkington had a passage that could make the editor identifiable. At first staunch in refusal to permit the requested deletion, he capitulated in the end and was glad he did so. Jack Finney, one of the most imaginative of all living writers of short stories, wrote a story called "Of Missing Persons." It would be included in any list of the most compelling stories I ever published. When he undertook his first novel—*Five Against the House* —one of the male students planning to hold up a Brink's truck was named Pearl; when I said I'd never heard that name applied to a man, he maintained he had known at school a boy so named. At last he was convinced he would be confusing his readers and made the change, as I think he was convinced by my plea that he give up his work as an advertising copywriter and apply himself altogether to fiction. He was one writer I knew couldn't miss.

Modern writers generally are sensible about names they give their characters, but I was never reconciled to the nomenclature invented by writers of eras past; Dickens' Zephaniah Scadder, Pumblehood, and Quilp, for example; Scott's Gibbie Goose, Disraeli's Partenopex Puff, Trollope's Dr. Pessimist Anticant, Arnold Bennett's Tertius Ingpen and Louise Loggerheads, Surtees' Pigg and Lionel Lazytongs. Such names, though sometimes supposed to be symbolic or of current political significance, always struck me as witless whimsy. Evelyn Waugh could go overboard, too, as he did in *Vile Bodies*. Nevertheless, a couple of minutes spent with my 1974 London telephone directory listed such names as Sam Smus, Fanny Shill, Mrs. A. Dupe, Bill Sny, Joe Crutch, Jack Yeap, and Carl Crimp. To say nothing of O. Twist, on Rosetta Street. The man who made the draperies for my London flat was named Mr. Snutch.

An editor may be in the publishing business for most of his life and not know the real names of several authors he was dealing with or the real names of other authors he didn't know but whose books he had read. When I met Rebecca West for the first time I assumed I was addressing her by her maiden name, had no idea she was Cecily Isabel Fairfield and had adopted as her writing name that of the emancipated heroine whose part she had played as a young actress in Ibsen's *Rosmersholm*. Once in London I went to meet Sax Rohmer because I had enjoyed his Fu Manchu stories, did not know his real name was Arthur Sarsfield Ward. I did know André Maurois was in reality Émile Salomon Wilhelm Herzog. I suppose most people are familiar with the better-known pen names, including Charles Dodgson's *Lewis Carroll*, Willard Huntington Wright's *S. S. Van Dine*, Louis Farigoule's *Jules Romains*, Samuel Hopkins Adams' *Warner Fabian*, Frank McKinney's *Kin Hubbard*, Samuel Clemens' *Mark Twain*,

Mary Ann Evans' *George Eliot*, Leonard Miller's *Leonard Merrick*, Eric Arthur Blair's *George Orwell*, Cincinnatus Hiner Miller's *Joaquin Miller*, Henry Wheeler Shaw's *Josh Billings*, Sidney Porter's *O. Henry*, Charles F. Browne's *Artemus Ward*, Hector Hugh Munro's *Saki*, Teodor Józef Konrad Korzeniowski's *Joseph Conrad*, Bulwer Lytton's *Owen Meredith;* and while they know that *George Sand* wasn't the author's real name they might not know it was Amandine Aurore Lucie Dupin. It is fairly common knowledge that *Ellery Queen* was the collaborative name adopted by Manfred Lee and Frederic Dannay, but when Ellery Queen first called on me I was surprised to find him two instead of one.

There are swarms of authors whose real names I'll never get to know. I was in middle age before learning *Anatole France* was Jacques Thibault, *Ralph Iron* Olive Schreiner, and *Upton Close* Josef Hall. In my time in the course of work one knew *Ethel Vance's* true name was Grace Zaring Stone, *Jan Struthers'* Joyce Maxtone Graham (whose daughter was one of Maggie Cousins' secretaries), *Max Brand's* Frederick Faust, *David Grayson's* Ray Stannard Baker, *Sholem Aleichem's* Solomon Rabinowitz, and *Leslie Ford's* Zenith Brown. As a boy I was certain Nick Carter was the author of dime novels I read, not just the name of the detective hero, and didn't know the detective himself was invented by somebody not definitely known. It wasn't until we published an article about Mickey Spillane that I discovered his full name to be Frank Morrison Spillane. Dylan Thomas said that Spillane was his favorite author!

Many other well-known writers did not always use their full names. Several on my list are *Samuel* Dashiell Hammett, *James* Vincent Sheean, *Hannibal* Hamlin Garland, *William* Bliss Carmen, *Joseph* Deems Taylor, *Matthew* Heywood Broun, Ring*old Wilmer* Lardner, *Alfred* Joyce Kilmer, *Henry* Havelock Ellis, *James Henry* Leigh Hunt, Anthony Hope *Hawkins, Harry* Sinclair Lewis, *William* Wilkie Collins, Nevil Shute *Norway, Henry* Hector Bolitho,

Nicholas Vachel Lindsay, *Enoch* Arnold Bennett, *Frank* Gelett Burgess.

What happens when the day comes that finds an editor no longer an editor? He ceases to be of interest, at least to authors, who are now busily in conference with his successor. Some editors take that amiss. But an editor dispossessed for any reason is like a politician who has lost the power to make lucrative appointments. If not altogether forgotten, at best he is in limbo. What he had, he no longer has. What he was, he now isn't. Yesterday's sycophants become today's hurrying passers-by. If he has become accustomed to heavy attention, and sought it, he must become reconciled to lack of it. His status quo fades, and not imperceptibly. He becomes non status quo. It happens in every business, not merely publishing. It's natural. It's human nature.

A pathetic spectacle is a once powerful editor who clings to old haunts and longs for once freely given deference. He'd like to reminisce. He has the time. Active authors don't have it. If the editor's psyche suffers, he may move to Florida, or some cousinly place, the golf course and fishing his refuge. Here and there, not often, one has sufficient initiative and determination, and the necessary competence, and acquires the dignity of an elder statesman by delivering a significant address to a significant audience, writes a challenging paper that gets published in *Foreign Affairs* and is quoted in *Pravda*, dares anybody to count him out, which doesn't necessarily keep him from being counted out. Just barely, he may keep something of his old reputation alive. A well-known author he once published may stop him on the street and say, "I'm so glad to see you, I miss you, your magazine isn't the same without you." Translated, that means the well-known author's work isn't being bought so readily by the once well-known editor's successor.

Tom Costain was an editor for some twenty-five years,

half of them with *The Saturday Evening Post,* before he made up his mind to become an author and wrote a dozen novels, among which were successes like *The Silver Chalice* and *The Black Rose,* after which we had an afternoon together. "Authors used to be my intimates," he said disconsolately. "Now I'm an author, too, so I'm a competitor. A kind of threat. Maybe a book of mine will get more attention than one of theirs. I'm no longer looked on as a friend. I expected it might happen, but not quite so fast."

21

When he was editor of *U.S. News & World Report,* David Lawrence said success for him meant having unequivocal control, the freedom to write and print what he wanted, with nobody anywhere to say him nay. It is obviously the reason why he founded and owned that magazine. Few editors ever own their magazines. For most of them success must lie in uncovering and developing literary talent, achieving greater circulation, a more bounteous income, the growing respect of their peers. All editors want, I think, what they so rarely get, which is the kind of uncontested authority that was Lawrence's. The tragedy, it has seemed to me, is less that so few editors achieve the goal than that so many give up striving for it, and more talent is wasted for want of use than is used for need of it.

The editor can grow weary of hassles, sick and tired of business department harassment. What he often does is settle for what can get him by. "The publisher wants this? I don't want it but the hell with it, I'll let him have it." He cheats himself into a so-what's-the-use state of mind. The first problems that bring it about may be minor ones, but the seed of concession is sown, because if he succumbs the first time the next may be easier for him to lose than for the publisher or management to win. He broods about dependent wife and children, security gets ranked above everything else, he takes the line of least resistance. Thereafter life isn't too bad, not for him any more than for the branch manager of a chain grocery store who takes orders from the main office. It isn't too bad for anybody, which is everybody who has to work for a living. But something is missing. The editor knows what it is, and hates himself for not having it.

It's been bandied about by management and all too often that I placed too much stress on the editor's right to be let alone, but other than to be his creative self I think an editor has insignificant reward. Paid well enough during tenure, it is almost never enough to make him financially independent. It is management that receives the big money, salary being but part of it. Management gets the profit-sharing deals, the really fat bonuses, the company-owned apartment to live in free, the munificent pensions, stock options, company-leased car, the enormous "consultant" fees after retirement. Management signs the contracts for the tens of millions of dollars' worth of paper needed to produce the magazines, and management gets its cut in the way of free accommodations in paper-supplier yachts and planes, in their hunting and fishing lodges. Members of management take seats on their directorates and vote the perks for themselves. Editors rarely get to be board members, are almost always rigidly excluded. They do not end up poor, but one only has to look around to see that management ends up bloody rich. I think I have rarely heard a publisher make a speech without declaring the editor is the end-all and be-all of publishing. It is all so fulsomely earnest, and all so totally insincere.

Freedom to be on his own, to be creative, is little enough for the editor to demand and expect. When I was a member of the American Society of Magazine Editors, I was disheartened by rejection of a proposal that editors should form a union, disheartened most of all by Dan Mich, the marvelous editor of *Look*, who favored the proposal but voted against it because he said Mike Cowles, the head of his company, would regard it as disloyal. I felt the time had come for editors to take a stand, to have their

scope and authority clearly defined. An employment contract is not sufficiently protective, it guarantees little more
than income during tenure. Who ever heard of a contract
that defined, much less guaranteed, an editor's right to editorial discretion, relieved of the tyranny of management
second-guessing? In Hollywood I had seen four of the most
successful, highest-paid film directors form a union in order
that limits be set on the authority of the producers they
were working for. My question was: if them, why not us?

Management can thank its lucky stars that editors love
what they do and would rather do it than what management does and get what management gets. Editors know
and have the satisfaction of knowing they have what management has not, which is the creative skill to produce a
magazine. Publishing would be nothing but another business if it weren't for the editors who give it some sem-
blance of a profession.

However alluring its nature, the job of editing calls
for some respite. The editor needs a breather, an outlet for
excess of energy, or relaxation that has nothing to do with
writers, manuscripts, and staff. The concert here and the
theater there are not always enough. Commitment to a
hobby, some outside pursuit, may also be needed. Sumner
Blossom, who had been editor of *The American*, chose
fishing; Harry Burton when editor of *Cosmopolitan* chose
billiards; James Quirk of *Photoplay* took to hunting; Arnold
Gingrich, first editor of *Esquire*, was up at sunrise every
day and played the violin; Byron Dobell when editor of *Esquire* and *New York* took several days off each week for his
painting. Strictly a spectator, I had no active interest in
sports or hobbies. I stayed with what was allied to my
major work—words, but not those that had anything to do
with office obligations. My own agreeable extracurricular
activity was in excerpting or condensing portions of novels,
plays, speeches, and literary curiosa, in assembling them in
some order, and in turning back to savor them, as I still do.

Suddenly all the bits and pieces piled up began to look like a publishable anthology. No Bartlett or Stevenson *Familiar Quotations,* of which there are enough imitations, but one, more like Ralph Woods's *A Treasury of the Familiar,* that would have ampler passages, not just one- or two-sentence famous expressions. I sensed it as an ongoing project, new volumes to be added at regular intervals. It became not only a pastime but a dedication. In later years, hours snatched from editing made it possible to put together the first two volumes, totaling more than twenty-one hundred pages containing some three thousand items, with material left over to fill another dozen volumes.

What's formidable? The job of indexing such a vast quantity of odds and ends. More formidable, acquiring permissions to use what was still protected by copyright. Alfred "Pat" Knopf, Jr., of Atheneum undertook to bring out the first two volumes; for permission fees, though 70 percent of what I intended to use was in public domain, he allotted $25,000, all of which was needed. It was sometimes a tiring experience but always enlightening. I learned I could use the name Samuel Clemens free but would have to pay two cents a word if I used "Mark Twain," which was still in copyright. (It no longer is.) That for a Robert Frost poem I would have to pay $100; for a bit of verse like Milne's "Sneezles" the charge would be $3.00 a line even if a line contained only a single word. For the sixteen lines comprising A. E. Housman's "When I Was One-and-Twenty" the charge was, peculiarly, twenty-one dollars.

For a needed permission for a selection it might be necessary to go from agent to publisher to author to lawyer to banker to estate trustee. In connection with something written in a foreign language it was always necessary to discover which of two or three translators was the one to credit. Everybody concerned with *Mary Poppins* said the author, P. L. Travers, would positively refuse permission for any part of it to be excerpted. Everybody seemed to be right. In the end it was necessary to locate Miss Travers in

England and remind her of the Hershey bar I had given to her little boy immediately after the war, when sweets in England were hard to come by. Miss Travers gave in, and for $500 allowed me to use a few hundred words about the arrival of Mary Poppins at Cherry-Tree Lane. Publishers of sheet music were usually firm in refusing to permit the use of a mere two lines from a popular song; almost always it was necessary to resort to personal friends who had composed them. If it had not been for the kindness of such as Irving Berlin, Richard Rodgers, Ira Gershwin, and Arthur Schwartz, the anthology would have appeared without any reference to their work. Many literary agents went out of their way to be accommodating. Cooperation from librarians was fabulous. To use some paragraphs from Anne Frank's *The Diary of a Young Girl* I had to find Otto Frank, the girl's father and only surviving member of the tortured family. Some payments that had to be made were pathetically small; for a section from Virginia Woolf's *A Room of One's Own,* her husband Leonard wrote to ask, "Would $2.00 be a reasonable sum?"

Unfortunately the Atheneum undertaking proved to be too costly to make publishing sense. The typesetting expense was horrendous. The changes I made in galleys were so far in excess of the allowance for author's alterations that I reimbursed Atheneum with a check for $4,000. The twenty thousand sets purchased by the Literary Guild to be used as premiums were not enough to balance the deficit. The project had to be discontinued; there were to be no more volumes after the first edition of the first two was exhausted. There are no more left. But I haven't for a moment regretted the labor and time that went into *An Editor's Treasury.*

Anybody can compile an anthology, not necessarily for publication but for purely personal enjoyment, something to look back on and spin through again and love again. It can be a group or class project, for a twosome, or exclusively for self. One can begin at any time, any age, and soon enough have a scrapbook of clippings or copies of historical sentiments or literary tidbits. It can be recommended as a part-time or lifetime pastime, especially for the young. Years and years after first reading—a phrase from *The Little Engine That Could* ("I think I can, I think I can"), or from *The Wonderful Tar Baby Story* ("'Do please, Brer Fox,' sez Brer Rabbit, 'do please don't fling me in dat brier-patch'"), or from *The Wind in the Willows* with Mr. Toad singing to a nonexistent audience ("The trumpeters are tooting and the soldiers are saluting, and the cannon they are shooting"), or a favorite comic strip or a page from Dr. Seuss—can swing back a world of memories. Doing an anthology is a seductive hobby, worth trying to get a small boy or girl interested in, to begin to keep a notebook that will record a joke heard at school, a rhyme learned at play. Other and more serious items will follow soon enough.

Try it! Later, the child may thank you.

22

The editor who has center stage, whose magazine is on top, has the world on his side. Everybody is his friend. Take his magazine away, let the magazine put him away, or let him put himself away, and he is a nonentity. For editors whose active years are behind them there is no lingering glory. Of the editors who were writers as well as editors, more are remembered for what they wrote than for what they edited, one exception being Henry Mencken, who was as well known for editing *Smart Set* and *The American Mercury* as for writing *The American Language* and *Prejudices*. It isn't likely anybody today would think of Thackeray as editor of the British *Punch*. The name of Theodore Dreiser (who wrote the lyrics for his brother's "On the Banks of the Wabash") evokes *Sister Carrie* and *An American Tragedy;* who associates Dreiser with *The Delineator,* the women's magazine of which he was editor, or Walter Hines Page with *The Atlantic Monthly, The Forum,* or *World's Work,* of all of which he was editor at one time or another? Page might be remembered, though not much, as author of *The Rebuilding of Old Commonwealths* but most especially as United States ambassador to Great Britain during World War I. Disraeli's name connects first with his reign as England's prime minister, but he was author of once popular novels such as *Vivian Grey, Coningsby,* and *Endymion;* it isn't likely one person in a thousand knows he was the moving spirit behind the birth of *The Representative*, a periodical that was a dream become nightmare. One may say some editors who have written books were inferior writers; I have effrontery enough to make the statement about Edward Bok.

Of the better-known women's magazines during Bok's administration, *Ladies' Home Journal* was by almost unanimous consent foremost. Its competitors were *Pictorial Review, Woman's Home Companion, Good Housekeeping, The Delineator,* and *McCall's;* but the *Journal* was best known and could boast of most readers. Of the editors of those magazines, Bok's name was predominantly the leader. In 1919, after three decades as editor of the *Journal,* Bok retired and in the following year wrote his autobiography, *The Americanization of Edward Bok,* which Ben Hecht called the worst ever written by anybody. Done in the third person, it reads much better than a book about the Bobbsey Twins, which is anyway a compliment. The quoted conversations—with Longfellow, Oliver Wendell Holmes, Emerson, Phillips Brooks, Henry Ward Beecher—seem little better than puerile, some of his statements aren't true and a number of his observations are vacuous. A single example won't suffice but is in fairly honest context. "During my years of editorship," Bok wrote, "save in one or two conspicuous instances, I never was able to assign to an American writer, work which called for painstaking research. In every instance, the work came back to me either incorrect in statement or otherwise lacking in careful preparation." Which is neither a gracious nor cogent remark from a man who for three decades handed out assignments to the most competent writers in the country.

Bok described American women as unpatriotic because they followed French fashions, called them fools because they did not heed his advice to ignore them. He was long an unrelenting foe—this man was editor of *Ladies' Home Journal!*—of woman's suffrage. It was his strongly held view that music was effeminate, not suitable for the masculine character. He wrote that to Mrs. Curtis, who preceded him as editor of the *Journal*, "the unprecedented success of the magazine is primarily due." And then in total contradiction he wrote, "We may well ponder whether the full editorial authority and direction of a magazine, either essentially feminine in its appeal or not, can safely be entrusted to women." Toward the end of his career he predicted that "because of the total merging of men's and women's interests, magazines like the *Journal*, essentially feminine in appeal," were likely to disappear. They have multiplied and grown bigger. The weekly *Saturday Evening Post*, which Bok believed would thrive forever, disappeared.

Greatness is a quality that must be left to the future to determine, and at best it is a relative matter. Bok was more than an extremely fine editor; could be credited with having done much to embellish Pullman cars, encourage improvement in small-home architecture, and to some extent his campaign to do away with unsightly billboards was effective. The best authors of the day appeared in his pages. Strangely, Bok cited as among his worthy accomplishments such bland and shallow editorial fare as "Side Talks with Girls," "Clever Daughters of Famous Men," "When Jenny Lind Sang in Castle Garden," "Mr. Moody's Bible Class," "When General Grant Went Round the World," "When John Wesley Preached in Georgia."

In reassessing a career, in writing or editing, it is all too easy to be wise and wiseacre-ish, and it would be unchivalrous not to take into account the era in which Bok was active, when women's lib was not yet a public issue and when most women were not greatly concerned with having the right to vote, and it would be churlish to emphasize Bok's bland and shallow editorial fare without saying that it was no blander and shallower for its day than much of what I and every other editor has published. Of course Bok made asinine statements, but anybody who wanted to do the necessary checking would find I made as many and more myself. I go back a few pages and note my remark that books by O'Hara and Fitzgerald had lost some of their first impact. However true for me, it is the sort of comment that might be more tenable if made by an Edmund Wilson or a Malcolm Cowley.

Bruce and Beatrice Gould, from 1935 to 1963 jointly in charge of the *Journal,* were editors as brilliant as any anywhere, with no exceptions. Not until they took over did the *Journal* reach and then rise above the plane to which Edward Bok had lifted it. One of their extraordinary innovations was a series of monthly reports called "How America Lives." They themselves roamed the world, interviewed and wrote stories about the world's dignitaries. Their adoption of "Never Underestimate the Power of a Woman" was as perfect a choice as could have been made; no slogan, with the inspired cartoons that accompanied it, ever exceeded it in effectiveness. If the Goulds faltered during the last few years of their quarter-of-a-century dominance it was because they lost perspective and could not bring themselves to acknowledge that *McCall's* had taken the play away from them, had passed their magazine in circulation, advertising, and prestige. Yet it must be said that from the start they were no less illustrious and inventive than Mr. Bok, their more celebrated predecessor. It must be said also that the *Journal,* everything considered, was for the longest time the very, very best of all the women's magazines. It ranked higher in public esteem. As for *McCall's,* for the few years it was in my care it was a publishing prodigy but the circumstances were special and credit for it belonged at least as much, probably more, to Norton Simon as to me and the editors around me.

I have cast some aspersions on Bok's *Americanization.* Recently I read it again and found it no better than on first encounter. However, the Pulitzer judges cast their votes for it, in 1921 gave it the prize in the biography-autobiography category.

As far as I know, Harold Ross never wrote a book. There were acquaintances who said jocularly that he couldn't. I thought of him as a character in a book. Wolcott

Gibbs made him a character in a play, *Island in the Sun*. At one period, because we lived in Connecticut, we commuted to New York together. On the train one morning, after I borrowed a section of his New York *Times*, Ross, who must have been waiting days for such an opportunity, said, "I don't lend my paper to everybody. Now you owe me a favor, but it's not so big. I have a sister-in-law—she's a god-damned hell of a nuisance to me and I don't know what to do with her. She won't be of any use to you but you'll just have to give her a job." Naturally, I hired her. I remember why, but not for what purpose.

Slews of articles have been written about Ross, his talents and idiosyncrasies. Of the several books—*The Years with Ross* by James Thurber, *Ross, The New Yorker and Me* by Jane Grant (Ross's first wife), *Ross and The New Yorker* by Dale Kramer, and *Here at The New Yorker* by Brendan Gill—the Gill appealed to me as the most anecdotal and most fun to read. The essence of Ross's mannerisms, speech, memoranda, and dress have been exhaustively recounted; so much so that the general opinion of the man portrays him not only as founder of *The New Yorker* but still its heart and soul. He brought into being a new school of writers and cartoonists. He created a masterpiece, set the tone and style of the magazine. Every list of distinguished editors would have him at or near the top. Editors and writers who worked with him and are still on duty there are not likely to argue against his reputation. But those I know who have remained and been under the direction of William Shawn, Ross's successor, testify that the magazine's preserved stature is attributable to Shawn. No magazine I know of has stayed so steadfastly on course. It hasn't deviated from the policy of attracting and publishing the finest writers and writing; hasn't sought bigness, only quality, and the latter it has retained with no digressions.

I knew Ross well, had unmitigated fondness for him, played in the same poker game with him every week, in which we were equal losers. I haven't yet laid eyes on

Shawn and am not likely to. But I would say he is as superior an editor as Ross was. Some say better. I think *The New Yorker* the most consistently best general magazine published in the United States.

Ross's background hadn't been auspicious. In nine years he held nine different jobs on different newspapers. When the Army caught up with him in 1917 and sent him abroad there was an official American Expeditionary Force newspaper called *Stars and Stripes*, published every Friday. In the March 1, 1918, issue, Ross's name appeared for the first time as one of its editors. Two weeks later the staff was augmented by Alexander Woollcott, and by Franklin P. Adams one week after that.

The last issue of *Stars and Stripes* was published on June 13, 1919. Then Ross went with the *American Legion Monthly* and stuck with it, or vice versa, for five years. He went on to become editor of *Judge*, the weekly humor magazine that was tottering toward extinction. All the while Ross was dreaming of something that would be called *The New Yorker*.

On a Sunday when Ross phoned to ask that Mrs. Mayes and I and our daughters visit him, we drove over in the afternoon, to find him dozing on a cot by his Connecticut countryside pool. He sounded tired and seemed ill. How very ill we did not realize. A few weeks later came news of his death in the New England Baptist Hospital in Boston, and the telegram suggesting attendance at the funeral service. The country lost an editorial superman but gained another.

For a long time in the history of our journalism the editor held the central position on a magazine. It would have been unthinkable for publisher or management to interfere with Edna Woolman Chase when she was editor of *Vogue*, or with Betsy Blackwell, who always wore perky Sally Victor hats, when she was editor of *Mademoiselle*, or with Frank Crowninshield when he was editor of *Vanity*

Fair. These days I notice announcements of editorial programs being developed by magazines. They are issued by
the publishers, whose names are signed to them. No mention is made of the editors who designed the programs. I
notice business departments are asserting more authority,
and editors less, which bodes no good. When editors are
relegated to second place their enthusiasm wanes and innovations are fewer. In the women's field it seems possible
now to switch logos from one magazine to another with
readers being unable to see much difference. They are getting to be too much alike: same size, same price, largely
similar content.

Today's big-circulation magazine editors are very nice
men and women; too nice, most of them, entertainment-
world minded to a fault, nonliterary, their stature self-
measured by how often they can be interviewed on radio
and television and photographed in the company of "stars."
More often than necessary they associate themselves with
the culture of pap and pop, with a minimum of what's serious. They are not book readers, but skimmers. The demands of publishing management for appeasement of the
lowered public appetite and the appearance of the fast
buck has infected the editorial resource with the disease of
cheapness. As of the moment, the editor who would dis-
sociate from the prevailing trend must find a place on magazines of modest circulation.

Another thing: too many big-circulation magazine editors are too friendly with one another. They *mingle.* I hated
my competitors, had but one desire, which was to outguess
and outmaneuver them. There was more excitement when
the editors were enemies. They *dared* more. Playing it safe
has become the name of the game. But that will change. It
must. Somebody—by chance somebody who is going
through this book, man or woman—will get his/her dander
up. Maybe somebody not yet an editor. He/she will break
new ground. He/she may turn out to be a hero/heroine.

All I wish for editors is that they not tire of their jobs, ⎯⎯

that their enthusiasm not diminish. Here and there among the current crop I detect some sign of weariness, an attitude of, "Here's another issue to start on, I'm bored, I wish I were publisher instead of editor, part of management and administration." My personal good fortune is that such reaction did not, not once, not in all the decades I was at it, enter my mind. Every issue was a new adventure, another voyage on an uncharted course. This time, this day, I go through magazines still fairly new, *Working Woman, Quest, Self, Texas Monthly, New Jersey Monthly, Savvy, Mother Jones,* and envy the editors their opportunities. For that sense of anticipation I thank whatever gods there are.

If in this part of the century, in the area of mass-circulation magazines, there is less to claim of editorial excellence, there is an audience of lesser quality to serve. Editors need not be blamed. It may be the age we live in. If there were more of a discerning mass audience there would be editors to serve it. In my day I think editors may have been better only in the sense that they had a different function to perform.

I must seem to be assuming an adversary relationship to contemporary editorial talent, but I renounce derogatory intent and admit only to prejudiced perspective. The present editorial scene is manifestly under the control of management dedicated to profit and devoid of sense of propriety. There are contemporary magazines swollen with advertisements of taste, supplemented by vulgar pages touting obviously fraudulent claims for bust developers, the single purpose to squeeze the last available dollar for the management coffers, every vestige of decency unslyly and disgracefully put aside.

For a number of years Crowell-Collier was a thriving company, its encyclopedia business especially successful, but it was proudest of its magazines—*Woman's Home Companion, Collier's, The American.* The magazines began to run into trouble. Two men at the head of the company—

Albert "Cap" Winger and Clarence Stouch—paid too little attention to encroaching competition, not least from television. At first slowly, then like an avalanche, the magazines began to lose readers, advertisers, and prestige. Profit and loss statements got redder, and gloom blacker. The day came when money for the magazines was in short supply and the bosses worried. In fact, they panicked. But they hoped there'd be somebody around who'd know how to get everything back on the track and for the purpose they hired Paul Smith as their troubleshooter.

Before Smith accepted the proffered appointment, he consulted outsiders, of whom I was one of several. What did we think of the Crowell-Collier magazines and their editors? Undiplomatic questions to ask of competitors, but I doubt any one of us hedged when saying we felt the editors were being provided with editorial budgets too meager, and with limited independence. Nevertheless, I found Mr. Smith a zestful personality, confident of successful outcome. He had been known as a whiz kid; by age forty had been everywhere and met everybody. At one point he had made the San Francisco *Chronicle* into a successful newspaper. He had been daring and full of verve, knew how to get things done fast, obstacles hadn't fazed him.

Smith scarcely had accepted his appointment before he made himself president of the company. Before Stouch and Winger knew what hit them, Smith made himself chief executive officer. Plain power-mad, if there was a title he didn't yet have, Smith was bound to have it. So he also got himself made chairman of the board.

Three down and one to go. The company never had had an editor-in-chief. Smith made himself editor-in-chief of all three magazines. He fired all three publishers. He fired all three editors.

Before Smith knew what hit *him*, there was no money left to continue operating the magazines. He tried to sell the *Companion* to Norton Simon, already involved with *McCall's*. He went to Gardner Cowles with the idea of merging *Collier's* with *Look*. For all his scampering around the world, hobnobbing with Herbert Hoover and Hitler and Churchill and queens, kings, and crooks, and his intimacy with every admiral, general and politician and banker and labor-union leader, there was one thing Smith seemed not to have learned about magazines, something that had been known before he was born: it is not so much the survival of the fittest as the survival of the greatest capital.

He reached a point, it didn't take long, when the magazine division of Crowell-Collier was gasping for breath, without the wherewithal for producing even one more issue. Because of Smith's right-and-left chucking out of everybody who had been in his way, nobody anywhere would extend any credit.

The American was demolished first. Then, just in time for the employees to celebrate Christmas, *Collier's* and *Woman's Home Companion* were discontinued. There can be dignity in a magazine's passing. There was no dignity at Crowell-Collier that December in 1957.

Smith, who came in last, was last to disappear. Perhaps no measures taken by anybody would have saved the magazines; but their demise was foreordained once Smith decided he could be, as well as everything else, editor-in-chief.

They come and they go. *Collier's,* which originally had been called *Once a Week. The American,* whose first publisher was Noah Webster, had absorbed *Leslie's,* once a famous weekly. *The Saturday Evening Post,* which everybody in the country believed had been founded by Benjamin Franklin because it said so on the editorial page, though Franklin never had had anything to do with it. *Smith's,* the magazine originated not by anybody named Smith but so named because it was intended to satisfy the reading desires of the John Smiths of the country. *Success,* which in its twenty-seven-year history set a record for changes of ownership. The *New England Homestead,* which was the forerunner of sectional magazines like *Southern Living* and *Sunset,* the latter originally a house organ for the Southern Pacific Rail Road. *Encore* and *The Golden Book,* which had been marvelous reprint magazines. *Quick,* the first miniature-size—smaller than digest-size—magazine. *People Today,* as much a failure as today's *People* is a success.

The *Midland, Blue Book, The Reporter, Holland's, Woman's World, Yankee Blade, Munsey's, Lippincott's, The No Name Magazine, Reed's Isonomy, The Review of Reviews, People's Home Journal, The Black Cat, Black Mask, Belford's, Gunston's, The Dial*—a thousand other magazines have come and gone. Possibly five thousand. Possibly ten thousand.

Whatever the profession or business or racket, there are and always have been specific haunts for pursuing life's amenities; wining and dining, seeing and being seen. The food may be execrable, service shabby, decor tacky, but certain spots nevertheless acquire a cachet that sets them apart and makes appearance in them seem mandatory. They are a barometer of status, a form of identification like a duly registered passport. Who is seated where and why there is the preoccupying thought even while menus are being scanned. Are we being noticed, does that foursome sipping martinis and conversing quietly at the corner table know that we are here? Attention, please, we *are* here. The one-and-a-half hour lunch is a testing time, a probationary period, where one's ego can be shriveled and resolutions made then and there to do something about having it bolstered next time around.

So everybody knew Kenny's Steak Pub was for race-track habitués, Toots Shor's restaurant with the heavy smack-on-the-back greeting for football and baseball notables, Sardi's—after theater—for actors, producers, members of chorus lines; George Bye's Wednesday Culture

Club That Meets on Fridays for authors and editors. The Palm was magnet for cartoonists and caricaturists invited to paint their likenesses on the walls, the Coffee House for artists and writers, and Bleeck's Artists and Writers Club for guess who. And just as "21" for so long has been foremost among meccas for luminaries of stage, screen, and politics, for editors, publishers, and advertising big-shots, and where I still go regularly because I don't want to be thought dead, so once it was the Stork Club, in its era the most famous and gala of all nightclubs in America. It was sparkling and glamorous and at certain times wacky, with a mystique not normally expected from an altogether ordinary ex-bootlegger like Sherman Billingsley, who was its proprietor. Not a man to be satisfied with a velvet rope at the entrance beyond which only the privileged few were permitted to pass, he substituted a gold chain. A 14-karat gold chain. In the room reserved for music and dancing there were nights each week when the ceiling was festooned with colorful balloons which, when floated down, caused debutantes to shriek and leap and grab for them greedily, to discover if they had won an order for a gown from Bergdorf's, an all-expenses-paid jaunt to Paris, an evening on the town with a favorite friend, or a mere one of a dozen drifting hundred-dollar bills.

In the Cub Room, set aside for those who preferred an oasis of quiet, Billingsley would be on hand to greet every newspaper columnist. For Jack O'Brian there was a special table, as for Walter Winchell, Leonard Lyons, J. Edgar Hoover, James Farley, or the governor of the state. Outside at the curb was a chauffeured limousine waiting to take home a celebrity who had arrived without private transportation. If one was short of money, a packet of bills would be handed over discreetly. A patron was no sooner seated than a bucket of champagne was set beside the table. Did Mr. Billingsley come to stand at one's table to talk for a minute, did he sit down—the utmost in attention—for a little conversation? About such matters patrons wondered who never would have invited the host to their homes.

Cub Room regulars had an inviolable understanding with Billingsley: whatever they ordered, from caviar to cognac, they paid for. What largesse the host chose to throw in, that they conceded was his pleasure and on the house. The gifts he bestowed were costly, beginning with flacons of perfume—he was part owner of Le Gallion, the maker of Sortilège—and ending with small packages deftly deposited. A package might contain a watch, bracelet, or pin from Cartier's. Though I was far below middle in the pecking order, there would be conveyed to my home several times a year a dozen cases of assorted liquors and liqueurs. After I moved to a new home in Connecticut, waiting for me were gifts of a Welsh terrier and a Siamese kitten, a Winchester rifle and shotgun. As an afterthought there came a paper bag, not a neatly tied box, bulging with fifty identical blue neckties.

Each year in January, my wife and Ethel Merman celebrated their birthday together. After whatever play she was in at the time, Miss Merman arrived and we would have supper together around midnight. On one such occasion each woman was presented with a ridiculously extravagant handbag. Because it was not of shape, size, color, or material that Mrs. Mayes would use, I suggested she return it to Tiffany's for a credit. The next afternoon she did and with some embarrassment explained to the salesclerk how she had come by the gift. "No need to feel embarrassed," the clerk said, "Miss Merman returned hers this morning." We used to speculate about the benefactions distributed to other patrons. If we got a scarf from Sulka's, what was being handed to John Lindsay? Lindsay was New York's favorite congressman. Who cared? What was being handed to *Joan Crawford?*

Billingsley was tasteless but shrewd. He never spent a penny for advertising but got more advertising free than his money could have bought. His gifts, no matter how many or how costly, still came to less than the publicity he anticipated and never failed to get in newspapers and magazines. The novel by Vera Caspary, about a murder in the Stork Club, must have represented in terms of publicity a thousand times the value of the gifts I received. The story wasn't published to benefit Billingsley, but he shared the benefit.

That bustling, frivolous emporium, the showplace of showplaces, came to a dismal end. The waiters, maître d's, busboys, chefs—all highest paid in the restaurant trade—belonged to no union. When they were coerced into organizing, Billingsley was obdurate in refusing recognition. They picketed, picketed for two years, once sought to run over their boss with a car. Editors, publishers, writers, and Hollywood folk who could only afford to be seen where everybody else was, began to give their patronage elsewhere. Billingsley's fortune dwindled, shrank, vanished, there were no more balloons, dance bands, or gifts. The building on East Fifty-third Street that housed the Stork Club was owned by Billingsley. It had to be sold. The man died broke, and all the former patrons said, "Too bad," and forgot about him and found other places where they could be stared at and made much of.

The Book Table's members are a small group whose modest luncheon meetings take place the second Tuesday of every month. Charles Scribner, I think I remember correctly, resigned because of differences with a fellow member. Alfred Knopf is no longer active. Broadcaster Ben Grauer, literary critic Harry Hansen, and publisher Max Schuster have passed away. Still attending are Greystone Press's John Stevenson, Scanfax Systems' Walter Rohrer, Book-of-the-Month Club's Ralph Thompson,* Ridge Press's Jerry Mason, Harry Abrams' Andrew Stewart and Paul Gottlieb, *New York Times* Books's Arnold Zohn, Books & Arts Associates' Zachary Morfogen, Crown Publishing's Nat Wartels, printing entrepreneur Victor Davidson, author

* Whose death was recently announced.

Willard Espy, author Martin Mayer, Penguin Books's editor
Peter Mayer, Ruder & Finn's David Finn, book mail-order
specialist and author Aaron Sussman, publisher Harry
Abrams,† Dreyfus Corporation's Jerome Hardy, who used
to be publisher of *Life*, and myself. There is no agenda, discussions may be less than earth-shattering, about anything
from publishing to politics, from sports to the latest mug-
ging in Central Park. But we enjoy one another's company,
and nobody seeks to be a star or expects or gets special
attention.

The Dutch Treat Club, members recruited from all
communications and art fields, is genially presided over by
Lowell Thomas, now about to retire, and at each weekly
luncheon there appear one speaker and one entertainer. It
is a gathering that relaxes in an exchange of pleasantries
and gossip. It is another private, not public, group;
members sit where they choose, there is no rank and therefore no file.

There are other literary and semi-literary groups, flocks
of them, but I don't belong.

Writers, publishers, editors, actors, and producers in
New York had their favorite pastimes, one of which was
poker. Once a week, over the Barberry Room in the Berk-
shire Hotel, in two rooms thick with smoke from my pipe
and Franklin Adams' cigars, members of the Hoyle Club—
named after Edmund Hoyle, the English whist wizard ("If
in doubt, take the trick")—assembled after "Information
Please" in order that panelists on that radio program could
be counted in. In addition to FPA and myself, the members
were George Kaufman, Arthur Kober, Alfred de Liagre,
Harold Ross, Bernard Hart, Russel Crouse, and Howard
Lindsay. If there is any game at which I am less adept than
bridge, it is poker. Crouse, pitying me, pleaded that I give
it up and restrict myself to solitaire. Kober suggested that I
contribute a hundred dollars a week to the kitty and stay

† Whose death was recently announced.

home, saying he would arrange for a recording of the conversation for me and I would still save a hundred dollars. But I was enthralled by the conversation live, hung on until the end of every game, which usually went on until five in the morning. Except for Broadway producer de Liagre and myself, there are no surviving members. Between us we have all the memories.

I got into the Hoyle Club through FPA. He had been my guest at a session with Columbia students, in introducing him I said he would be glad to recite poems, in Greek and Latin if preferred, would in fact be happy to do anything but sing something from the *Mikado*. "I'll sing something from the *Mikado*," Adams interrupted, "or from *Pinafore* or *Iolanthe*. Which do you want?" One of the girls shouted, "Princess Ida." Adams got up from his chair, cleared his throat, and began, "If you give me your attention, I will tell you what I am—I'm a genuine philanthropist, all other kinds are sham." The class cheered.

At the end of the session, Adams went home with me and after dinner he asked, "You play poker?" I said I was a dreadful player, rarely held better than a pair of deuces and always lost. "We've been looking for you for years," Adams said. "Come along, we're going to the Hoyle. If you don't lose, I'll denounce you."

So I became a member, and lost.

Through my wife, and before we were married, I met Oscar Hammerstein. We were always guests at openings of plays he wrote with Richard Rodgers, the first being *Oklahoma!* In time, for nine years, we shared his house on Sixty-third Street, he occupying the lower three floors, we the upper two. Following the first performance of *Sound of Music* there was a party at the St. Regis Hotel, everybody waiting for the early newspaper notices to appear. When they did, they were not altogether favorable. Though leaving separately, Mr. and Mrs. Hammerstein and Mrs. Mayes and I returned from the party at the same time and entered our house together. All of us were depressed. It was to be Oscar's final effort in the theater. Despite some adverse criticism, the play proved to be a success, and the movie that was made from it was one of the most profitable in the history of Hollywood.

Our friendly neighbor-landlord had his study immediately below ours. It was where he did his writing, standing up before an old, high, long-legged bank clerk's desk. Anybody with that kind of desk would have no trouble producing the book and lyrics for an *Oklahoma!* or *Carousel,* and after I made that comment to Mrs. Hammerstein she graciously made me a gift of a replica. Just so I'd have a fair chance.

If I couldn't write like Oscar, I could write *something,* and did, but not on that desk and not at that time. Far back, in 1927, while still a newcomer with Hearst, I decided that in my spare time, at the suggestion of a friend, I would do a biography of Horatio Alger, Jr. The Alger name had long been legendary because of the more than a hundred books he had written about boys who rose from the ranks to achieve some modest fame and fortune. The sale of his books has been estimated by one person or another to have been as high as four hundred million copies,* a figure Frank Luther Mott, the magazine historian, said belonged to astronomy, not publishing.

From initial research it appeared that Alger, for all his stupendous output, was a dull man and had led a dull life. If he was dull, the story of his life would be dull and I lost interest. But when the idea was advanced that I might fabricate a biography, undertake a parody of the debunking vogue of the period, I took to it quickly. It seemed something I could dash off in a few months, or even weeks, during evenings and weekends, not interfering at all with my trade-paper job. Unencumbered by facts, I could make everything up. I did make everything up, to the extent of giving Alger mistresses he never knew, establishing him in Paris when actually he was still a student at Harvard, having him adopt a Chinese boy who never existed, crediting him as a child with essays and verses he did not write. I put in his mind the notion that someday he might be President of the United States. I had him acquire membership in clubs and societies he never joined. I attributed to him in early life a speech defect—a stutter—that was a figment of my imagination. With no basis for the statement, I had schoolmates taunting him with the nickname Holy Horatio. Occasionally I had him put on a wig he never owned. To a bibliography of books Alger had written I added a number of whatever titles came into my head at the moment.

All of it was fantasy, any element of fact having gotten in through carelessness or accident, rather like Mencken's

* A more realistic figure has been set at something like twenty million.

mythical history of the bathtub, published in the New York
Mail in 1917, that still is regarded in some quarters as bona
fide. Neither George Macy, president of the publishing
company,† nor any of the few other individuals involved,
thought it could be taken for anything but the spoof it was
intended to be. What happened was contrary to every ex-
pectation—the book was looked on as a true account of
Alger's life, was greeted with mixed reviews,‡ half of them
disparaging but with no critic at that time questioning authenticity. Since then, almost every biographical dictionary
and encyclopedia,* including the *Britannica,* has used my
Alger: A Biography Without a Hero as basic source material.

It seemed fair that a statement should be issued saying
the book had been written as a hoax. To this there was
some objection, one reason being that Macy was a friend of
Harry Hansen, book reviewer for the New York *World,*
who had praised the book highly. For another reason,
Macy was a comparatively new publisher and feared the
wrath of reviewers if the story of the hoax was revealed.
He was an erudite man, and ingenious, well rated as a writer
of light verse under the pseudonym of George Jester. He
was considered by almost everybody to be arrogant and
vain. Though a friend, his pretensions sometimes made one
want to say, "That's enough, George, stop acting like a
pundit."

More than thirty years after my Alger book was born,
four other Alger biographies were published, all to no small
extent repeating as fact what I had made up out of whole
cloth. In the interim, hundreds of articles about Alger also
had appeared in newspapers and magazines. How, one may
wonder, could so many writers, including eminent scholars,
have taken so much for granted? The plausible if not
wholly satisfactory answer was the one given by Mr. Han-

† Macy-Masius.
‡ See Appendix.
* Some new editions contain necessary corrections.

sen. If the book had been about a historical or literary figure—a Bismarck or Keats, for example—he said, he would have had some frame of reference for making a judgment; as no Alger biography had previously appeared, he took for granted that mine was a volume that could be relied on.

In 1973, while I was living in London, I wrote for *Newsboy*, official publication of the Horatio Alger Society, the story of my opus and how it had come about. As a result, there was suddenly a modest revival of interest in Alger; enough, apparently, to warrant a limited reprint of the original book with an introduction in which I set forth the details of its history. The new edition† sells for $31.50; the original sold for $3.50! As literary property my book is rubbish, its only value resting in the realm of curiosa. For whatever work I put in, from the very beginning until now, I received no royalties or any other kind of payment. What I did receive was an offer of honorary membership in the Horatio Alger Society, which I declined. In view of what I unwittingly did to Alger's reputation, I suggested a dishonorary membership might be more appropriate. Since then I have been an ordinary, regular dues-paying member.

"With hindsight, would you have undertaken the Alger biography?" It is a reasonable question. Given the same circumstances, the answer is unequivocally in the affirmative. Had I remotely suspected the book would be thought of as genuine and become the cause of so much controversy, neither I nor anybody else in his right mind would answer other than in the negative. Though the Alger venture began as a lark, I do not think back on it with any sense of satisfaction, and hardly with pride.

For me the Alger book rendered a definite disservice. Because of its acceptance as an authentic record of a life, it prevented me from ever again reading a biography or autobiography without speculating on its accuracy. A bi-

† Published by Gilbert K. Westgard II.

ographer has recourse to his subject's letters, diaries, memoranda, and exploits; and, if the subject is of recent years, to persons known to have known the subject. In their diaries and letters and conversations, however, some subjects have not been averse to exaggerating their virtues and disguising their faults, and sometimes making up, as I did with Alger, circumstances altogether spurious. It is one thing when an Emil Ludwig writes a biography in the present tense, as he did with his *Napoleon*, for then the reader knows it is a fictionalized biography. It is another thing altogether, though perhaps of no great significance, when a biographer tells us his subject looked distraught, or ate his dinner gustily, or hobbled down the stairs, or retorted angrily; or, obviously not having been present, presumes to quote verbatim conversations that may not have taken place, or describes a journey that may never have been embarked on. It is not that my enjoyment in reading biography has lessened but that my skepticism has increased. Writers of autobiographies recall romantic moments neither they nor anybody else ever experienced. Self-portraits can be notoriously biased, and even fabricated. I have become a little cynical about biographers' and autobiographers' sureness of their details, began to think of biography as names and dates, embroidered, and I keep remembering a statement made more than twenty years ago by Catherine Drinker Bowen,‡ herself a distinguished biographer. "In writing biography," she said, "fact and fiction should not be mixed. And if they are, facts should be written in black ink, and the fiction in red."

Because I know as little of what goes on in Wall Street as any of the people who have been ruined there, it seemed obvious I should write a book about it, but this was not to be an Alger-type hoax; instead, a heavily researched, thoroughly documented effort. Stories of the peculations and

‡ Author of biographies of Oliver Wendell Holmes, Tchaikovsky, and others.

speculations of the likes of Jay Gould and James Fisk, and their struggles for control of railroads, and their reckless bribing of public officials, have always intrigued me. What I had in mind had nothing to do with finance and cornered markets but with the social life of the robber barons, and I began to search into their histories and habits and over quite a period accumulated a closetful of background notes and anecdotes. Before writing a word or assembling an outline of chapters I thought it prudent to find a publisher willing to take it on, which brought me to breakfast with Kenneth McCormick, who was chief editor at Doubleday. I told him of my plan, said quickly that not a line had yet been written and that research was not nearly completed. And I added I had no intention of proceeding without an advance payment. McCormick asked how much I had in mind and I said $30,000.

McCormick said the idea sounded interesting, that he would talk it over with his associates and then would be in touch. He phoned a few hours later. "You have a deal," he said. "We'll draw up a contract and as soon as you sign it we'll send the check."

That evening I did what I should have done in the first place, which was to phone my tax accountant. "Don't be a fool," he said. "That money will have to be declared as part of earned income for the year, you'll be in a higher tax bracket, and the tax you'll have to pay is too much."

The next morning I put in a call to McCormick to ask that the advance be reduced to $10,000. The contract arrived in due course, I signed it, and the check from Doubleday followed. The book was to be completed in a year.

At the end of the first year I had not even finished my research. The more I dug, the more I needed to dig. "That's all right," was McCormick's solacing comment, "take another year."

At the end of the second year I walked into McCormick's office and handed him a check for $10,000. "What's it for?" he asked, and I said it was repayment of the advance, that I had researched so much and written so much and still needed to do so much more research that I knew the project never would be completed.

"This is only the second time in all the years I've been with this company," McCormick said, "that a prospective author has voluntarily returned an advance."

Anyway, I learned a bit about Wall Street.

George Macy had enough publishing ideas to have warranted a place for himself at the top of a very large publishing company but he preferred being his own boss and operating on a smaller scale. Nevertheless, he founded the Limited Editions Club, the Heritage Club, and in my opinion the most ingenious club of all—the Reader's Club. It was to offer its members books that, according to its judges, had literary value but had been ignored by both critics and public. The judges, it seemed to me, were the best that could have been found: Carl Van Doren was chairman, the other members Clifton Fadiman, Alexander Woollcott, and Sinclair Lewis. They were to take turns in selecting a book a month and in an introductory essay set forth the reasons for their choice. Because there was a wartime paper shortage, Macy could not get enough paper to meet his needs and the club had to go out of business, if I remember correctly, in about a year.

I thought the judges, because of their reputations, would be a desirable group to contribute regularly to *Good Housekeeping*. The first meeting to discuss arrangements was held in Mr. Macy's home, with all present except Mr. Fadiman. Lewis began by making a remark that offended Woollcott. Macy intervened by saying both men were out of order, and both men then turned on Macy. Van Doren sought to act as peacemaker and said that as a guest I was undoubtedly being embarrassed by the display of bad manners. In that case, Woollcott said, I certainly was to feel free to leave. We were in Macy's home, remember, but

Macy said that if I left he would have to leave too. Van Doren had the best suggestion of all—that the meeting be adjourned, which it was, and I never attended another for an understandable reason: Nobody invited me.

24

It is Saturday morning, August 11, 1979, and I wake up, quite proud of myself, knowing it marks the beginning of my eightieth year. That means I must be fairly close to the last stage of my life passage, though I'm in no rush about it, which also means I must be nearly through writing the memoir that concerns it, though "memoir" smacks of an importance I don't mean to imply. At this point, however, it is comforting to know who I am and what I am not, and to realize I have few ungratified ambitions and have had a good life, if that suggests I was able to do most of what I wanted to do, except perhaps try to breed miniature elephants as garden pets, a lunatic notion I have talked of but hardly believed in. I remember that *Advertising Age*—some *writer* in *Advertising Age*—in a squiffy moment once wrote of me, "He is a legend in his own time," and that I read the statement without batting an eye. "Legend," an easy-out word for lazy obituary writers, has come to embrace everybody who has been more than passably competent at anything. What has been unexaggeratedly commented on is a quick temper and a willingness to stand in combat, including physical, for what I believed in in publishing. I was known, and not ashamed for being known, as a tough nut for management to crack. As for accomplishments, a few of mine were important for a moment. Bruce Gould, Otis Wiese, William Bigelow, and I were good editors. Henry Luce, George Horace Lorimer,

Sam McClure, Harold Ross, Henry Mencken—*they* were *great* editors.

I regret having been obliged to use the first person singular in this narrative, would have preferred "we" if repetition didn't make it seem pretentious. I find it unseemly to be describing my jobs and myself in such terms as I have used and am using. However sincere a desire to be reasonably objective, every person in discoursing on a life's journey is inclined to self-dramatization. In effect, nobody is best or wisest, and when the words are self-applied they are not, it seems to me, self-believed. When Muhammad Ali crowed, "I am not only the greatest, I am the double-greatest," he was crowing it, I'm sure, impishly. Could he have said honestly he was greater than Jack Johnson or Jack Dempsey or John L. Sullivan? All of us in writing personally make ourselves out to be better than, deep down in our consciousness, we know ourselves to have been.

Of Bruce Gould, so long the editor of *Ladies' Home Journal,* I have said he was as great an editor as any and have no reason to modify the statement. But I well knew, along with others, that he was exceedingly vain and pompous. Following his abrupt departure from the *Journal,* I was asked by the *Herald Tribune* to write my impression of him. Undoubtedly the thought was that I would say something denigrating because we never had been friends. For all the times we had seen each other at meetings, Gould had pointedly ignored me. We never had shaken hands. But I knew he had been unexcelled in his job. That is what I said, and added there was no honor the publishing industry could tender him of which he was not deserving.

Shortly after the newspaper piece appeared, I had my first communication from Gould. He thanked me for what I had written. It was then time, I thought, that we should meet, have a nice luncheon and a chat about our experiences. I extended the invitation, we met, and if not a healing affair it was at least gentlemanly. Later in a note I received from Gould he explained he was writing his autobiography and asked if I would be good enough to answer one or two questions to refresh his memory. I thought I could quote from memory at least one sentence, and started to, but it didn't sound right, so I decided to get it from the file to be sure. "I had no idea how difficult it is," the note reads, "to write with the modesty required while at the same time giving yourself full credit for all the remarkable achievements you have done." Honest, that's the way the note reads.

I guess we all have those moments.

Other than the accomplishments I mentioned a few chapters earlier, who would remember anything of what Gould did? How "special" as I called them are editors? A man may run a race faster than any other before him, or sit longer on top of a flagpole, and thus records are set. But editors set no such records. How well remembered are leaders in any field, except for a time in their own time? Of the five men who served in succession before Lincoln as Presidents of the United States, nobody can say what they accomplished. Few people can name them. Baseball players live longer in public memory; one could start with Ty Cobb, Babe Ruth, Christy Mathewson.

I remember better than anybody else what I did as an editor that seemed constructive, but nobody else can or has reason to. I also remember better than anybody else how often I did and said preposterous things, the countless gaffes I made. Trivial and harmless enough, but in writing a narrative of which they were a part it may not be out of order to mention some of them. It would be out of order *not* to mention them.

On meeting Bernard De Voto for the first time I told him how very faithfully I followed his "Easy Chair" department in *The Atlantic;* actually I had been following it in *Harper's.* When Hervey Allen's twelve-hundred-page *Anthony Adverse* was made into a movie by Warner Brothers in 1936, Charles Einfeld, who handled publicity for it, said two young women in the picture were destined to become stars and asked if I'd be willing to meet one of them, maybe I'd be interested in having a story written about her. The pretty girl came first to my office, where we chatted, and then went on to the Algonquin for lunch. I liked Anita Louise very much. After lunch I walked her back to Einfeld's office. As we were saying goodbye she said sweetly, "By the way, Mr. Mayes, I'm not Anita Louise —I'm the other one, Olivia de Havilland." I did not have a story done about either girl then, but Miss de Havilland wrote her own for me some twenty years later when she was living in Paris. Also years later, when James Thurber was resident in the Bermuda house where Hervey Allen had written his opus, and was sitting at Allen's desk, he announced his intention of writing *Anthony Adverse* himself. But backwards!

In Hollywood when I thought I was being gallant to Hedy Lamarr she turned out to be Dorothy Lamour. Seated next to Mel Brooks at a party, I pointed to a woman I thought particularly interesting and asked if he knew her. "She's my wife," Mr. Brooks said, but didn't tell me she was Anne Bancroft; a few minutes later, when I spoke to Mrs. Brooks, I asked if she too was in the theater! Once I had a phone call from a Mr. Walter White, who said he wanted to talk with me about the National Association for the Advancement of Colored People. An appointment was made and during the conversation I said, "Mr. White, I'd like to know how a white man has managed to become spokesman for the country's most important society working for the cause of colored people." Apparently he'd heard the question many times before. "I'm often taken to be white," he said. "My name is White, but I am a colored man." After that it was not likely I'd decline his request to deliver a lecture at Shaw University, a college for colored boys and girls in North Carolina. In those days none of us had yet been asked to refer to blacks instead of coloreds.

At a luncheon following a Norton Simon stockholders' meeting I was talking with a stranger, a handsome and cultivated gentleman. Because I wanted to introduce him to somebody, I asked if I might know his name. He was most accommodating. "Grant," he said, "Cary Grant." When I told the story at home, both my children screamed, "You mean you didn't *recognize* him?" At another lunch, in London, with Sir John Wolfenden, then head of the British Museum, I said I supposed Greece always would hold it against the British for making off with the Elgin Marbles. "We didn't 'make off' with them," he said heatedly, "we bought and paid for them. And for your information, we pronounce Elgin with a hard 'g.'"

At a time when I was assiduously courting Margaret Truman, hoping to get her to write a book about her years as daughter of the White House,* we were on friendly enough terms so that on meeting I would kiss her cheek. On an evening when I called for her at the Carlyle Hotel to take her to dinner, she held her face away from me as I entered her suite, making it clear I was to refrain from any show of intimacy. She introduced me to a distinguished-looking gentleman, Mr. Clifton Daniel,† who had arrived before me. I stood for a while, then sat, wondering when and if ever the man intended to leave. At last I said, "Mr. Daniel, Miss Truman and I have a dinner engagement and I'm afraid we'll lose our reservation if we don't start now." He took the blunt hint graciously and departed. In the taxi on the way to the restaurant I said to Miss Truman, "I thought that guy was never going to get out, he sure was in no hurry," and she made no comment. Three days later Miss Truman's engagement to marry Mr. Daniel was announced.

Once on the Hutchinson River Parkway I was stopped for speeding. I protested I was going only seventy; the police officer said he'd been following me for fifteen miles. "Actually," he said, "you were going ninety." (Mrs. Mayes,

* Ultimately the book, *Souvenir*, was written, with Margaret Cousins collaborating.

† Then assistant to the managing editor of the New York *Times*.

a big help, later told me I was going ninety-five.) He asked for my driver's license, then inquired what I did for a living. When I told him I was editor of *Good Housekeeping*, he laughed, and said, "I suppose you print lots of stuff telling people to drive carefully and obey the law," and he was right. A man named Oliver Evans, an early American inventor, made a prediction. "The time will come," he wrote in 1813, "when people will travel in stages moved by steam engines, from one city to another, almost as fast as birds fly, fifteen or twenty miles an hour." Ninety miles an hour—ridiculous!

When Beatrice Lillie came to the office to talk over the autobiography she was planning, I was more than pleased to make her acquaintance but not that of the young man she brought along who was to be her ghost writer. Whenever Miss Lillie began to speak, the prospective writer interrupted, saying no, it would not be done in this manner but in another. When Miss Lillie said she would be glad to have my opinion about length, the man said that was a matter *he* would decide. By the end of a half hour I was sure Miss Lillie had had her fill and would be glad to see me usher the man out, which I stood up to do. I didn't expect the wonderful actress to follow, but she did. "He's my friend," she said angrily, "and if you don't want to listen to *him*, then I won't let him write for *you*." It was a short visit.

One day in Rome I had an appointment, or thought I had, with Orson Welles on the set where he was playing a part in *Upon This Rock*, a documentary about St. Peter's Church. I waited for the finish of a take and then walked over to him. "I'm here to write a piece about you and this picture," I said. He glared at me. "Write for *what?*" he asked, and I said *Saturday Review*. "I don't read it," he said. "Look," I tried again, "I was to meet you here, my name is Mayes—" "Don't believe I know you," Welles said. That too was a short visit. The picture had a short life.

A nicer reference may be made to Mary Martin. During a visit to her apartment when I was trying to induce her to write her autobiography, I noticed her collection of ornaments in the shape of clasped hands. Some weeks later during a promenade along Second Avenue, Mrs. Mayes insisted on doing a little business with Mr. Nerefsky, owner of a secondhand shop chockablock with hundreds, perhaps thousands, of small antiques and big pieces of junk. In such a place I see nothing but a blur, my wife can spot instantly some item she fancies. What she spotted among all the debris was a horseshoe to the narrow end of which was attached a pair of clasped hands. Embossed on the horseshoe were the words "Good luck to Mary." Nothing could have been more appropriate as a gift for Miss Martin. I retreated to the sidewalk, always being uncomfortable during a bargaining session. I knew there was going to be one because I know my wife.

Twenty minutes later my wife emerged, with the gift neatly wrapped. "He wanted five dollars," she announced triumphantly, "but I got it for three." Miss Martin was enchanted when she received the addition to her collection. I did not get the autobiography; but Mary Martin gave us for publication the magnificent needlepoint book I didn't know she was writing.

Not the least attractive aspect of the publishing business is that it gives an editor opportunities for doing almost anything, going anywhere, running into everybody. A list of people he meets and often works with can begin to sound like a compendium of names extracted from *Who's Who*. I am not overly sensitive about its sounding that way because I know people named Jones, Greene, Brown, and Smith. There would be James Jones, who wrote *From Here to Eternity*, whom I met in Paris; Jennifer Jones, star of many movies, recipient of an Oscar for her performance in *The Song of Bernadette*, whom I met only shortly before her marriage to Norton Simon; Harrison Jones, who was head of the Coca-Cola Company, whom I met in Atlanta when I went there to explain why *Good Housekeeping* had originally refused to accept Coca-Cola advertising; Gerald Greene, who wrote *The Last Angry Man* and *Holocaust* and was a student in my Columbia University journalism class; David Brown, who once worked with me on *Cosmopolitan* and deserted me, for which I forgave him, in order to produce such films as *The Sting* and *Jaws;* John Mason Brown, theater critic and author, who introduced me to the New York Society Library when he was a trustee; Cecil Brown, radio and television commentator, whom I first met when his book *Suez to Singapore* was published; and many Smiths including Walter Smith, who was head of Young & Rubicam's office in London and arranged my membership in the American Chamber of Commerce there; Betty Smith, who wrote *A Tree Grows in Brooklyn;* Lillian Smith, who wrote *Strange Fruit;* Margaret Chase Smith, who was a United States senator from Maine; to say nothing of the two wordsmiths H. Allen and Robert Paul.

I have figured that sixty years have gone by since I went into publishing in 1920. That comes to about three thousand weeks. At the modest rate for an editor of meeting only three new people a week, that comes to some nine thousand people. A portion of the time was taken up naturally by sleeping, and in murky conversation with railway porters (when they existed), income-tax examiners, panhandlers, and my mother-in-law. In any case, almost automatically, among an editor's acquaintances are men and women from the worlds of entertainment and politics. There's no wile or mystique about getting to know them, and it is one of the perquisites of the job if the editor likes that sort of thing. I have always liked that sort of thing, even though all of it is happenstance and none of it makes one an editor, not even Fleur Cowles, the world's champion celebrity collector, who created *Flair,* the magazine with the hole in the head, about which she said, "No publication ever excited the same stir or evoked more violent passions. . . . It was a phenomenon in American magazine publishing. . . . It was sold to the public for 50 cents—*365,000 copies each month!*" The exclamation point and italics are hers. However, according to the Audit Bureau of Circulations, *Flair* sold 245,000 copies at its peak (a third of which were sold for less than 50 cents a copy). "Whatever *Flair* lacked in longevity," Mrs. Cowles has said in print, "it made up for in publishing immortality."

Flair went out of business after its thirteenth issue.

In the realm of the theater no collaborators were better known than Richard Rodgers and Oscar Hammerstein. I had an idea for a collaboration between *Mrs.* Rodgers and *Mrs.* Hammerstein, both of them brilliant professional decorators. What I wanted was a book on their specialty that I hoped to announce as the newest of Rodgers and Hammerstein productions. The two women were intrigued, too busy to find time for it, but cooperated in preparation of a wonderful article about themselves that was written by Joe McCarthy.

In an office there are secretaries to keep files in order, at home there is no one and the time comes around for sifting and casting out. Besides the letters and memoranda flipped into folders, there are mounds of slips of paper, matchbook covers, backs of envelopes, all with a scribbled word or comment, that serve as reminders of days and events and people past. Daily my pockets would be emptied of the scraps, all of them saved because I have an aversion to tossing anything away.

My diaries and appointment calendars have as much luster as a laundry list. Some words recall incidents in detail, others have lost all meaning, little but luncheon reminders, somebody's birthday to remember, what time the train leaves for Scarsdale, meetings to attend. Now and then: "Henry Dreyfus—Rockefeller Center," "Sidney Kingsley, Detective Story, 8 p.m." Names—Mary Hastings Bradley, Rose Franken, Joy Chute, Mr. Morgenthau, Walter Thayer, Louis Nizer, Marya Mannes, Francis Drake —*Sir* Francis? No, I'm not *that* old.

I see "Eden—Pewsey, Wiltshire." Pewsey is the village in which Anthony Eden lived after retirement as prime minister, in Fyfield Manor, a pretty house with a garden that had a cote with accommodations for three hundred and sixty-five doves. I took Eden's word for it. He said that during the early nineteenth century the doves, one each day, would carry messages between England and France.

The man was not well during my visit, stood up to carve the roast the butler brought to the table, suddenly was seized with pain and couldn't move. His wife, Clarissa, rose to help him. After the depressing lunch, Eden asked me to join him in his library. "May I speak to you privately?" he asked. Because we were alone it seemed a strange question. Then I understood "privately" meant "in confidence." It wasn't much of a confidence.

An appointment book says "K Brush, 4 p.m." It is from March 12, 1946. Apparently I was to see the author of *Young Man of Manhattan* and *The Red-Headed Woman* at her home on East Fifty-seventh Street. She would be sitting behind her semicircular desk, which, if one could straighten the curve, would have been some twelve feet long. Herself petite, tidy, Katharine Brush never had on the desk anything but a small vase holding a single carnation. At the end of each evening she would go through newspapers and magazines that had been delivered, scan them all, and on small cards make her notations: which movies according to *Variety* were being best attended; which were the most popular phonograph records of the week. From *Vogue* she would copy details of the latest fashions—"Off-the-shoulder evening gowns, but only if they're for attractive shoulders," she said, the way women were dressing their hair and coloring their nails. She kept track of who scored the most touchdowns during a football season, when Tibbett first sang at the Metropolitan Opera, what sold for how much in the auction houses. Everything was on her cards: the baseball rookie of the year, what the President said at a press conference, after whom the sandwiches were named at Reuben's, what the taxi fares were in Pittsburgh— it was all there for her to use and in a series of articles she wrote for us she used, it used to seem, everything.

"Long, Glass, Cobb." Dated Friday, October 3, 1930. The first time I had been invited to the Central Park West home of *Cosmopolitan*'s Ray Long. Glass would have been Montague, and Cobb, Irvin. Honest-to-God authors. Somebody might not think that worth writing home about. I thought it sensational.

"Dinner—Billy Rose." From Thursday, May 4, 1961, the occasion a party in the baronial Rose home for Bernard Baruch, who was already in his nineties, still tall, erect, handsome, and despite his hearing aid very deaf. The then Mrs. Rose had been Joyce Mathews. She had been Mrs. Rose twice, once divorced from Billy, then married to him again. She didn't appear at dinner—was taking a nap. She was still napping when we left. Two years after that evening I was soliciting Billy Rose's interest in writing a monthly column. He became obsessed with the idea, talked of little else for a while, then wrote for us "A Girl Named Fanny," about Miss Brice, who had been the first of his wives.

"Carmel Snow, 4 p.m." The date, November 6, 1959. Carmel Snow had been fashion editor of *Vogue* when she was lured to *Harper's Bazaar* where, when appointed overall editor, she served brilliantly, becoming a vital—some said the most vital—character in the world of fashion. In 1957, after long service, Carmel Snow, to her chagrin, was involuntarily retired. More to her chagrin, Nancy White, her niece, who had been my own fashion editor on *Good Housekeeping*, was chosen to take her place. No longer queen bee in New York and Paris, but proud and buoyant, Mrs. Snow swallowed her pride and phoned for an appointment.

What she wanted was a job. She had money enough, needed no job, but *McCall's* had become, in effect, at least for the moment, the talk of the town. If I had in mind taking on a new fashion editor, Carmel was willing to take over. She wanted the chance to prove what she still could do.

One had to admire her. If the job had been available I would have offered it to her, though already she must have been seventy years of age. She understood the situation.

Was quite majestic as she said so. "Anyway, you've been kind," she said.

"Edith Oliver, 5 p.m." The date is February 17, 1976. An old, very close mutual friend had died and the deceased's family had elected to dispense with the usual funeral service. Miss Oliver, for many years and still *The New Yorker*'s "Off Broadway" theater critic, phoned. "We can hold our own service," she said. "Let me come to your apartment and we can touch hands." She came, and my wife and I and our two daughters stood with her and we touched hands. It would have pleased the man we were remembering.

Dated February 19, 1970, the appointment book says "Bob Jastrow." Director of the Goddard Institute Space studies, he has come to London with a copy of *Red Giants and White Dwarfs*, his wonderful book about astronomy. Jastrow said he had written it for his mother. If she could understand, he felt I might.

The next day, February 20: A meeting in a hotel private dining room with four Americans, a German, a Frenchman, and several Englishmen. Lord Ivor Evans has something to say, is interrupted by one of his countrymen. Lord Evans is angry. "When a lord speaks," he says, "commoners listen." I repeat this to my wife later in the evening. "I don't believe it," she says, "it's too disgusting." A week later we are the guests of Lord Evans at the Atheneum. In the course of conversation he makes a remark that gives me my chance. "That sounds just like your 'When a lord speaks, commoners listen.'" His wife says, "Ivor, you *didn't* say that?" He replies, "I did, and I meant it." I was glad to have my wife know I hadn't made it up.

"Monday, November 12th—Guaralnik, lunch." It was 1946. David Guaralnik had sent a copy of his newly edited *Webster's Dictionary*. I asked why some words are accented on one syllable rather than another. (I have forgotten the explanation.) I remember Maxwell Nurnberg, who was a teacher in New York City high schools and whose articles in *Good Housekeeping* ended up as a book called *How to Build a Better Vocabulary*. Nurnberg teased me about differences between words like "complacent" and "complaisant," "prone" and "supine"; trapped me with "nectar" and "ambrosia," on the pronunciation of "schism" and "grimace." When I told my wife the correct pronunciation of "grimace" she said she would refuse ever to use the word again. Nurnberg assured me "antidisestablishmentarianism" was not the longest word in the language but I've forgotten which one is. Also forgotten is the definition he said was Samuel Johnson's for "network," but I have looked it up for this paragraph and don't believe it: "Anything reticulated or decussated at equal distances, with interstices between the intersections."

Vocabulary is enlarged most of all by general reading. For a person who's had little more than grade school education, I'd guess as good a way as any to become familiar with the use of language is to pick up two or three of the dozens of books on the subject. I found Isaac Goldberg's *The Wonder of Words* useful but pedantic; liked Robert Hall's *Leave Your Language Alone* and Henry Alexander's *The Story of Our Language*. Israel Shanker's *Words and Their Masters* is excellent, and Willard Espy's *The Game of Words* enchanting. For me the most fascinating book about English as a world language is Lincoln Barnett's *The Treasure of Our Tongue*. A note I have says a dictionary is a book above all other books—all other books are in it, it's only a matter of sorting them out. In its issue for January 1945 the *Reader's Digest* inaugurated a feature called "It Pays to Increase Your Word Power" and in no issue since then has it failed to appear.

"Partridge, Savile, 1 p.m." The appointment was canceled, Mr. Partridge couldn't keep it. No lexicographer has been more deserving of honor than Eric Partridge, and none has received less for his labors in the way of worldly goods. Several times in England I inquired why this man, whose dictionaries and language guides are standards of their kind, never was recognized by the Crown; why in his old age, ill and with an ill wife to care for, no knighthood was bestowed on him, why he never was accorded the gift of a grace-and-favor cottage. I was told his Dictionary of Slang and Unconventional English, with its necessary résumé of vulgarities, though familiar to every adult, may have been considered offensive. Yet that book alone seemed to many of his countrymen to entitle him to plaudits and grants no less than those given to actors, politicians and their mistresses, and cricket players, to say nothing of the Beatles.

"Shap, new women's mag." Dated April 5, 1977. S. O. Shapiro, dean of circulation directors, relayed a rumor: Time-Life planning a magazine for the women's field. Everybody's expectations were high, everybody's expectations disappointed. The Luce group's first issue of *Woman* was undistinguished, the first issue also the last. Because of women's insatiable interest in medicine, I would have included "Medical Update," probably a 12-page section, the feature to run in every issue, the largest, most comprehensive, promoting it extensively; the section to cover worldwide developments in medicine, surgical procedures, all that's going on in hospitals, clinics, pharmaceutical laboratories. I thought it would be recognized immediately as something constructively different. Good idea? Apparently not. I have suggested it to several editors, found none interested.

My concept of a good diary is the one that Samuel Pepys kept. He wrote personal history and spared no detail. "To my Lord's in the morning," says the entry for October 13, 1660, "where I met with Captain Cuttance, but my Lord not being up I went out to Charing Cross, to see Major-General Harrison hanged, drawn and quartered, which was done there, he looking as cheerful as any man could do in that condition. He was presently cut down, and his head and heart shown to the people, at which there was great shouts of joy." *That* I regard as useful information.

Some of my notes are undated. One, obviously from the early 1960's, says, "Meeting—Mrs. Kennedy." About a year after President Kennedy's death, Norman Cousins and I and another colleague called on Mrs. Kennedy in her New York home. We invited her to join *McCall's* as an associate editor; offered a salary of $75,000, an office in New York, an office in Washington, and a personal secretary of her choosing to be in each office. It was an interesting meeting, with Mrs. Kennedy, for her part wisely, deciding not to accept the proffered appointment.

"Star of Hope." Undated. I remember only that it was the name of a "house organ" published by inmates of Sing Sing, articles written for it signed not with inmates' names but with their prison numbers.

On various slips of paper: "Joe—walk." "Joe—10 p.m." "Joe—dinner." The name appears far back, very far back, and continues to appear to this day. It is Joseph Leigh, oldest of old friends. We came together in PS 5 in 1909, have been as close as friends can be, for so many years, seventy of them, with never a cross word between us.

"Lunch, Woollcott." December 17, 1942. Alexander Woollcott brought the article he had finished for us (it was the last he wrote) about a young man, formerly a newspaper office assistant, who happened to be a real British earl. The article was called "My Seventh Assistant." Somewhat unfortunately, Woollcott brought himself along, his face as owlish as so often caricatured. He seemed out of sorts. Our lunch date was at the Plaza. Apparently not feeling well, he nevertheless placed an order large enough to awe the waiter taking care of us. "It's all right," I said, trying to bring a little gaiety to the table, "he's been on a diet since breakfast and wants to make up for lost time." "That's a snotty remark," Woollcott said, "and if you don't have enough money to pay, it can be charged to my account." He didn't have a charge account there. "What are *you* having?" he asked, and I said my usual fried eggs and bacon, toast and coffee. "I wouldn't order that for a dog,"

Woollcott said, and I said I wouldn't either, that my dog always liked his eggs scrambled. In literary circles that goes under the name of repartee.

Woollcott had for over so many years a reputation, like Dorothy Parker, for being about the quickest and most withering wit in the city. Friends loved his bon mots. I wasn't one of his friends. His radio broadcasts that he gave as "The Town Crier" always had an enormous audience. Once upon a time his recommendation could send a book's sales soaring. On this day all I wanted was his manuscript.

For no reason except to alleviate the boredom of my company, he started a quiz session. As he talked, his spirits rose. "Tell me," he said, "which of our states is the Valentine State?" I hadn't known there was such a one. "Oh, yes —Arizona, because it came into the Union on February 14, 1912." Fascinating, but, according to the *World Almanac* which I consulted later, not true. "Tell me," Woollcott said, "what is the shortest verse in the Bible." To my don't-know shrug he exclaimed, as though it were a fact any imbecile would have at the tip of his tongue, "Jesus wept." Bully for you, was my unexpressed reaction, but I was to be further enlightened: "The gospel according to St. John." "The New Testament, I assume," was all I could think of to say, to prove I wasn't totally ignorant. "Hardly would be the *Old* Testament," was what I got in return. "What's Mike Todd's real name?" he asked, and I stared at him blankly. "Aaron Hirsch Goldbogen," he said grimly. Normally I enjoy conveying such a piece of vital information myself.

The manuscript was handed over. Woollcott got into a cab. To my surprise, he waved what seemed a friendly farewell. I wasn't sure.

"I can't understand," Woollcott had said on an earlier occasion, when he had come to my office, "why magazines like yours must use the stupidities you call blurbs, telling people how wonderful the stories are, when you must know they're pretty stinking. Are your readers such cretins that everything must be spelled out for them?" There the man had a point. Every magazine story is "the best," "the most rapturous," "truly fantastic." Readers are not cretins, but editors continue to do the rhapsodizing under every title. The practice embarrasses me, not merely to see those blurbs but to remember I wrote so many of them myself. It can't be left to a reader to discover he's about to be introduced to a romance or murder mystery, one is obliged to say "The greatest novel since *Of Time and the River*." A majority of stories so fulsomely exploited are out of mind by breakfast the next morning.

As much by magazine blurbs, irritation can be aroused by publishers' announcements for their books. One need only glance through the ads. "The most terrifying epic of the 20th century," "A narrative never to be forgotten," "Most brilliant novel since *Rebecca*." Everything has to be overwhelming, a masterpiece. I remember still with rising blood pressure the ad for Bernard Malamud's *The Fixer*: "Will last as long as books are read," it said. Imagine! Another overworked phrase is "In the tradition of . . ." No harm is done; but if a book is promoted as "in the tradition of *The Naked and the Dead*," shouldn't Norman Mailer get a slice of the royalty?

The blurbs on book jackets, like the advertisements for new movies, are bombastic. Everybody reads them. Not everybody believes them.

Another common practice is that of having books reviewed by people who already have written books on the same subject. Oscar Levant could become livid about it, asking why a new biography of Beethoven, for example, had to be reviewed by somebody who himself had written such a biography, or why a book about the Crimean War had to be covered by somebody who already had written one. He pointed out that all too often such a reviewer, no matter how otherwise favorable his notice, managed to end by emphasizing some minor inconsistency—an incorrect date, or the misspelling of a name. Levant said the better the book, the bigger the chance another author would find fault with it. "A book about nuclear weapons can't be re-viewed by somebody whose specialty is Burmese table eti-quette," critic George Oppenheimer said, "but there are nuclear weapon specialists who have not written about them and are competent to give an objective, independent, unbiased point of view without carping."

When somebody points out the extraordinary gift a writer shows for insight into the mind of another writer, I'm not convinced he had any insight at all or that the au-thor pretended to have any. When somebody says this is the most beautifully integrated suspense novel written in ten years, I wonder how many suspense novels that some-body has read in the ten years. Twenty, fifty, maybe a hun-dred out of a thousand? There are times when I wonder about the search for hidden meanings in the simplest of narratives. When a critic referred to the Freudian approach I had taken to the tenth-rate biography I had written about Horatio Alger, mentioned some chapters earlier, he rather surprised me because I didn't once think of Freud while writing it.

June 17, 1970. "V. Royster." Vermont Royster, for a long while editor of the *Wall Street Journal*, in London with his wife, has come to dinner. His visit reminds me that the columns he wrote were among my regular and favorite reading. He could write about people, politics, travel, eco-nomics, always clearly, sprightly. I thought his style a model for journalism students to study, recommended it often, and still would. I wish I had known him earlier and better.

August 1947. No date. "James Farrell, dinner." I had been a fan of Farrell's Studs Lonigan books, but ours was a desultory relationship, mostly through letters. His son Kevin and my daughters were enrolled in the same idiot-ically progressive Walt Whitman School where an hour each week in learning Chinese was compulsory. My main interest in the evening was in meeting Hortense Alden, his second and beautiful wife, with whom I had fallen in love when she was on Broadway performing in *Lysistrata*.

May 27, 1971. "Norton—Jennifer—Dorchester." It's in London, Norton Simon and Jennifer Jones in town, my wife and I join them and other guests at the hotel for late supper.

May 30, 1971. "Norton—Jennifer—Heathrow." Reporters, photographers, crowds outside the Dorchester, waiting to see Norton Simon and Jennifer Jones, suddenly, on the spur of the moment, married yesterday. I go with the newly wedded couple to the airport to see them off. A happy, wild, whirling dervish of a bank-holiday weekend. Mr. Simon still owes me forty dollars that he forgot to pay the two chauffeurs who drove the wedding party to the airport. He's embarrassed about the money, keeps wanting to repay it so that I'll stop telling the story, but I like the story as is.

May 25, 1953. "Dinner—G. Marek." Thomas Mann was the other guest. I said if he were writing his masterpiece *The Magic Mountain* today instead of 1924 the novel would have to be much different, tubercular patients now curing in the climate where they normally live and not being sent off to mountains and sanitariums. Mann, a humorless man, was not inclined to discuss it. Did say Shakespeare sounded better in German than in English. Really? Marek read passages from *Othello,* Mann followed, reading them in German. Mann seemed to be right.

"Barney, around 3." That would have been Bernard Gallagher, whose weekly newsletter *The Gallagher Report* was read and feared by the publishing and advertising industries. He had been trying to get me to answer business questions I thought none of his business. But I told him I would be glad to answer any he asked, on one condition: if I said it was off the record, it had to be off the record. "But suppose I then get the same information from some other source?" he asked. I said I would trust him. Thereafter we must have met anywhere between thirty and fifty times. He asked many questions, I answered most of them and can testify that he never violated a confidence.

"Get Dubuque poem." It meant I wanted a copy of a

four-line verse I had written, the only one, and sent to *The New Yorker* during its very early era. The quatrain was a "rebuque" about the little old lady in Dubuque. Signed only with my initials, given no return address, it could not be acknowledged. But it was printed, probably because the editor had space for a one-inch filler. I still don't have a copy.

"Dinner for Cooke." The date is May 23, 1973. The Cooke was Alistair. Six or seven other guests. In London. I asked that we discuss anything—anything but President Nixon and what was going on at home. During the first course, Cooke asked for a show of hands: How many thought Nixon innocent? Ah, well. Later there was talk about American and British English. I mentioned a book by Norman Schur that dealt with the subject. It was a distraction. I gave Cooke my copy. I suppose he still has it.

"Order car, Bemelmans, dinner." Date mutilated, but I was to drive to the town in Connecticut where Ludwig Bemelmans had opened a restaurant called, I think, the White Turkey Inn. Over the years Bemelmans had done some special features for us, about Genevive the pup, Miss Clavel, the house in Paris covered with vines "where lived twelve little girls in two straight lines." Somewhere in somebody's house there should be one of the original *Madeleine* illustrations he gave me.

November 3, 1959, "Lunch, Cowan." Lou Cowan, remembering the success of the old Phil Baker "$64 Question" on radio, revived it on television in the form of the "$64,000 Question." Few programs equaled it in popularity. Evidence came to light indicating it had been rigged, contestants being given in advance clues to forthcoming questions. President of CBS at the time, Cowan, without documentation to justify the action, was forced to resign. His bitterness was uncontrollable. I asked if he would do the whole story for *McCall's*, from first thinking of the idea to the end. He promised to think about it; may have thought, but didn't write.

27

There's a note that goes back to 1937. It says, "Lunch, Burton." That had to be Harry Payne Burton, who succeeded Ray Long as editor of *Cosmopolitan*. Long, finally ousted by the Hearst business management, tried his hand at book publishing, then in Hollywood. Failing in both, he killed himself. It came Burton's turn to be dismissed. He took an overdose of sleeping pills. Succeeded by his assistant, Frances Whiting, she was deposed in short order—nothing happened to her, a lucky woman. Her assistant (can't think of her name) hoped for the job, didn't get it, and hanged herself. Holly Roth, in charge of the magazine's editorial production, jumped or fell off a ship in the Atlantic and was never seen again. *Cosmopolitan* holds the world's record for that sort of thing. I myself ran *Cosmopolitan* on several occasions, always managed to come off unscathed. That too was a record.

Who can say what it is about editors and writers that leads so often to a violent end? During a period when he was engaged in research for me, I asked Wallace Brockway to recall as many instances as he could of lives strangely terminated. In his report he included W. C. Brann, notorious editor of *The Iconoclast*, who died in a pistol duel in Waco, Texas; Margaret Mitchell, who was killed by a speeding car; Ken Purdy, once editor of *True*, who shot himself; Jack London, who imitated the hero in his novel *Martin Eden* by taking an overdose of sleeping tablets;

Vachel Lindsay, poet, took poison; Hart Crane, his poetic gift exhausted, threw himself off the deck of a ship in the Gulf of Mexico; Lewis Browne, author of *This Believing World,* preferred self-inflicted death to blindness; Logan Clendenning, author of *The Human Body,* severed his jugular vein; Constance Fenimore Cooper, an early regional novelist, killed herself in Venice; Mrs. Malcolm Nicholson, who wrote, under the name Laurence Hope, "Kashmiri Song" ("Pale hands I love beside the Shalimar"), took a dose of poison; F. O. Matthiessen, who wrote biographies of Henry James and Theodore Dreiser, committed suicide on his forty-eighth birthday; Paul Leicester Ford, an editor, biographer, and author of novels including *The Honorable Peter Stirling,* was shot by his brother; Maxwell Bodenheim, poet, for many years pointed out as one of the "sights" of New York's bohemia, was shot with his third wife in a hovel off the Bowery; David Graham Phillips, whose *Susan Lenox: Her Fall and Rise* was a spectacular success, was shot by a man who thought his family had been defamed in one of Phillips' novels; Edgar Allan Poe drank himself to death; Stephen Foster fell on a piece of glass during a brawl, cut himself, died in Bellevue Hospital; Philip Freneau, one of the important poets before Bryant, slipped into a bog and died of exposure; MacDonald Clarke, known as the "mad" poet, was drowned; Thomas William Parsons, famous for his translation of Dante's *Inferno,* tumbled down a well; Richard Halliburton, explorer and writer, whose best-known books were *The Royal Road to Romance* and *The Glorious Adventure,* was lost at sea in a Chinese junk while sailing from Hong Kong to San Francisco; Donn Byrne, author of *Messer Marco Polo,* drove through a seawall and was drowned; Pulitzer Prize-winning playwright Sidney Howard died when a tractor pinned him to a wall; poet and critic Randall Jarrell was walking along a road when struck down by a truck; Marguerite Wilkinson, author of *The Great Dream,* drowned. Gene Stratton-Porter was killed in an automobile crash; the death of Louis Adamic, noted author of the 1930's, remained a puzzle though officially listed as suicide; Margaret Fuller, author and one of the noted critics in the nineteenth century, died in the wreck of a ship off Fire Island; Elbert Hubbard went down with the *Lusitania*. Perhaps Ambrose Bierce should be mentioned, though nobody ever found out what happened to him. At age seventy-two, in 1914, he disappeared in Mexico. If still alive, he is a hundred and thirty-seven years old.

Wallace Brockway's compilation, though he claimed it to be nowhere complete, contains only names of Americans. A rundown of foreign editors and writers who perished prematurely would take a separate chapter.

"Mrs. Kathryn Murray—2:30." In *Good Housekeeping* we had published an article poking fun at claims made by dancing schools. No specific mention was made of the Arthur Murray Dance Studio on Fifth Avenue but there was no doubt it was the studio being ridiculed. From Mrs. Murray I received a letter so sweet and earnest, asking for an appointment, it seemed only decent to let her come and make what obviously would be a personal protest. She did. She spoke eloquently. Then I said I had been one of her studio's beginners, had given a check for four hundred dollars in order to be taught everything from a one-step to a tango. After seven or eight lessons I quit, never went back, still can't dance. "Please stand up," Mrs. Murray said, "I'm going to give you a lesson right here and now." In my office! "All right," she said, "if you won't do it here I'll go to your home and teach you there. Where do you live?" When I said that was strictly private, she smiled and left.

A week later when I arrived home for dinner, my wife told me there had been a call from Mrs. Murray. "Did you get rid of her?" I asked.

Another week later I was given a similar message. "You got rid of her again?" I asked.

But there came an evening when my wife said we were

having surprise guests—a special treat for me. Who? Mr. and Mrs. Arthur Murray, in the flesh, the two of them. My wife had gotten sick and tired, she said, of making excuses for me.

The Murrays arrived carrying a stack of records and I was surrounded. Mrs. Murray danced with me, then Mr. Murray danced with me. They danced with each other so I could see how easy it was. At the end of the evening they decided I was impossible.

On a later occasion Mr. Murray tried to pay back the four hundred dollars. To this day the Murrays, though they live in Hawaii now, have remained our friends. Kathryn Murray addresses me as "My dear delinquent pupil."

"Sullivan, 4 p.m." It is Thursday, November 25, 1948. Frank Sullivan was always one of our guests on Thanksgiving, and we always wondered whether he would make it in time, or at all, from his home in Saratoga. He hated to travel anywhere, had a morbid fear of travel that lasted throughout his life; but he did arrive, the sweet, loved-by-everybody homely man hugged my daughters, they returned the compliment, and merriment, as they say, was unconfined. "Don't be a square worrier in a round dilemma," Sullivan was wont to say, but the wont didn't keep me from being a pretty habitual worrier.

"To My Adopted Daughter—I Wish I Hadn't Told You" was an article several members of the staff were strongly opposed to publishing. To me it seemed one woman's honestly expressed personal experience. We were submerged in a cataract of angry protest, particularly from adoption agency officials. On the other hand, staff members were favorably disposed toward "How to Stay Married Though Unhappy," written by Bishop Fulton Sheen, which to me seemed sappy. Another wave of protest, from as many Catholics as Protestants. So I worried about editorial judgment.

Instead of using ordinary common sense and dismissing the idea, I let a writer be assigned to do a piece about the way packages were inspected that were sent to the White House for the attention of the President. A Secret Service representative called on me, said the article would give cranks too much dangerous information and that we could not publish it. After the "could not" I mumbled some inanity about freedom of the press and said we'd go ahead regardless. We didn't, however, not after a call from Jim Hagerty, Eisenhower's press secretary, who asked if I was in favor of having the White House blown up.

I worried because my gums were bleeding when I brushed my teeth after coming home from an all-night session at poker. Had I brushed too strenuously? No, it was a hemorrhage and I learned I had TB. Nothing serious, a mild case, caught at the beginning. But "you'll have to stay in bed for several months," the doctor said. I worried about my work—how would it get done? Did anybody in the office miss me? Was the staff speculating on when and if ever I'd be able to return? Meanwhile, I followed the doctor's instructions. It was a nice rest. In three months I was back on the job. I returned to the poker game.

Where were the illustrations long past due from John Gannam and Saul Tepper, the tardiest of all our illustrators? How could we go to press without those pictures? Would Thyra Samter Winslow ever finish the story about the British shopkeeper whose birthday fell on the same day as the Queen's? Would Robert Kennedy ever send us an okay on the statement we attributed to him? Would Katharine Graham show up for the appointment set with Norton Simon and me to discuss our purchase of *Art News*? Where was Maggie Cousins—still at lunch after three hours? Had she forgotten we had an appointment with Irwin Edman?

I worried about the increasing volume of advertising pages. We closed one issue of *Good Housekeeping* that ran to four hundred pages. How would readers react—resent the endless breaks of editorial columns needed to accommodate the advertising? There was a time—a blessed time—

when magazines kept all editorial content together, in one chunk, so to speak, with no advertising interruptions; when advertising pages were bunched together at the beginning of the magazine, or at the back. I solved our problem: We would divide the issue in two—run two hundred pages with editorial and advertising pages in normal sequence, then have the reader turn the issue around and begin from the other end, with another two hundred pages of editorial and advertising. All we had to do was duplicate the front cover on the back cover! We would lose the back-cover ad but would gain double the positions preferred by advertisers. It was a grand, unique concept, with one drawback: couldn't be done, insuperable mechanical problems. So I worried as much about too much advertising as too little. Now and then I thought wistfully of an era before mine when magazines like *Collier's* and *Harper's Monthly* ran ads only for books published by their own companies, and when a magazine like *Scribner's* carried no advertising at all.

28

When Abbott Lawrence Lowell succeeded Charles W. Eliot as president of Harvard, he observed that universities are full of knowledge. "Freshmen bring in a little," he said, "and seniors take none away, and thus knowledge accumulates." The men and women who worked with me—most of them—had been through college, but half of them weren't educated at all. What they'd had in college was a social experience. Even a good college education has little relevance to vocational reality. I am not sure the overall situation is better today, what with passing grades being given to students who haven't passed, and a growing emphasis in the belief that no one has a right to anything, including education, that isn't available to everybody else.

The elective system inaugurated by Dr. Eliot during his forty years at Harvard was imitated by other institutions of higher learning, enabling students to take cinch courses that provided more pleasure or leisure than knowledge. Regardless of credentials and experience, every person who came to me for a job was asked to write a critique of whatever magazine I had charge of and suggest what might be done to improve it; as fair a procedure as one could think of for gauging a candidate's usefulness. If not taken on, at least there would be a check tendered for time and effort expended.

I suppose I have made clear that I had no college background. What made up for it was a good—really better than good, rather freakish—memory and a passion for the printed page. Reading was an obsession. I took to books not because of subject matter but because they were printed. I took to them as indiscriminately as voraciously, gulped them down without rhyme or reason, nibbling bits and pieces of some, battening on chunks of others, swallowing some whole. A book called *The Five Basic Philosophies,* written by a man who was a professor at Bowdoin College, whetted my appetite for that subject. In time I lost most of my early craving for scholastic precocity, but about what I wanted to know I hoped to know as much as anybody. An ambition, needless to say, unfulfilled.

An editor's job is to edit. He is under no compulsion to be a peerless writer or conversationalist or entertainer. I was none of those. Yet most of the time as I grew up in literary company I rarely felt myself at a disadvantage. A wide reading background can provide a wide general education and conceal a multitude of learning deficiencies. In circles where a topic under discussion was as unfamiliar to me as the quantum theory, which wasn't broached every day, the wise course was to say nothing. I regarded myself wisest when I was quietest. Like a yogi, I could concentrate—there was nothing else to do—on what the participants looked like, wonder how they ate, played, prayed, fought, brought up their children, traveled, toiled, made love. We meet a general bedecked with ribbons and medals, then a common soldier who has served in exemplary fashion for a dozen years and never risen above the rank of corporal. We wonder what accidents of fate brought the one so high and left the other so low. I was curious about what notions passed through people's minds; what their fantasies were and might have been. I learned only recently that my wife was mystified as a child because men and women married to each other had by the strangest coincidence the same surname. And that my younger daughter was ten years old before making the extraordinary discovery that eggs marked with an "X" did not come hard-boiled straight from the hens that laid them.

The greatest knowledge is to know what one doesn't know. All one needs to know is where to look for what one needs to know.

My predilection was for using books, not for preserving them. A third of those I collected I marked up without remorse, tearing out for future reference pages with meaningful passages. My once extensive library was sometimes called the most mutilated. When Harold Ross saw it for the first time he uttered his favorite expletive: "Jesus!" It was a pleasant experience quite recently while rummaging through long-stored odds and ends to come across Dinah Maria Craik's *Little Lame Prince,* all in one piece, all pages perfect, with the pseudonym Miss Mulock on the title page and my HRM initials drawn in pencil, back in 1906, on the inside back cover.

I don't know of a truly educated person—what one would describe as a scholar—who was editor of a magazine of the kind with which I have been associated. What would such a person have done with a *Better Homes & Gardens* or *Household?* Would a man like Herbert Croly, who had been editor of *The New Republic,* or Van Wyck Brooks of *The Freeman,* have been attracted to such domestic subjects as child care and the arrangement of kitchens? I have wondered if, had I the education I craved, I'd have been able to do what was required on *Good Housekeeping.* All I possessed was knowledge that came from reading, which sometimes made me discontented with the circumscribed focus of my work, solace coming from the specious thought that a classical background might have been a hindrance.

Books have been an all-embracing pleasure. In whatever limited space I had for a study, I gathered books, kept them row on row, never in alphabetical order of author or subject matter, but always where I could lay hands on any I wanted to reach for. Once I covered a wall at home with book jackets. The wall was disfigured but the montage seemed colorful. Some books I can't resist rereading, though no fiction, except to verify descriptions of characters or elements of style. I couldn't bear the thought of going through *Ivanhoe* again, or *The Newcomes* or *David Copperfield,* or *A Study in Scarlet,* and finding them less absorbing than the first time around. History is what I read over again, and biography and autobiography most of all.

An editor can never be sufficiently grateful for whatever started him on reading at an early age, for making acquaintance with Madame Defarge, D'Artagnan, Maggie Tolliver, Jean Valjean, Mr. Toots, Raskolnikov, because once established in editorship so much of his time must be given to books of the moment. Unless he has a rigid program for filling in the gaps, reserving a portion of every week for getting to know authors whose work has stood up well, his literary horizons remain restricted.

If it had not been for the need to earn a living, if I had been born to wealth, I could have forgone editorship and given my life over to books. Not to studying, simply to reading, to becoming a literary person, a literatus. I could have been, and would have been with never a qualm of conscience, a reading bum.

On an occasion when Jack O'Connell was trying to talk Wolcott Gibbs into writing for us a piece about people who had made good without benefit of a college education, Gibbs claimed the three most important people he could think of in that category were Jesus Christ, Eleanor Roosevelt, and Abraham Lincoln. It must be obvious that Gibbs had not yet heard of me.

As it is, I am well read without being educated, uneducated without being uninformed; have become more experienced with the passing of years but do not know that I am much wiser. Because I was competent in the world of the printed word I sometimes thought I might have been more pleased with myself in working for a *Harper's* or *At-*

lantic. Oddly enough, one day when Frederick Lewis Allen and I were having a late breakfast, Allen, who was editor of *Harper's,* said *he* might have been happier running a *Good Housekeeping* because of its vaster audience. He didn't really mean it.

Outside our own shop there was no editor to whom I felt a close attachment, but in the advertising milieu a number of warm friendships developed. Raymond Rubicam, co-founder of Young & Rubicam, was a friend, and one day he and I had lunch with his son-in-law in the latter's imposing production studio for radio and television commercials, where we were unnerved by the bands of musicians, groups of actors, camera crews, and equipment that looked like contraptions from Mars or the inventive mind of Rube Goldberg, all of this at the cost of a fortune for nine seconds on television with a line like "My mommy says Yimmies are yummy." In a prior era, advertising was more an art than a disease, and Rubicam could say pensively, "Ah, me, all I had to work with was a pencil and a pad of yellow paper."

Rubicam's time was the time he wrote Squibb's "The Priceless Ingredient" ("A thing that is bought or sold has no value unless it contains that which cannot be bought or sold"); when Theodore MacManus wrote Cadillac's "The Penalty of Leadership" ("That which is good or great makes itself known, no matter how loud the clamor of denial; that which deserves to live, lives"); when F. R. Feland wrote "Brown's Job" ("What does Brown say? What does Brown say? What the hell does Brown say? Well, why don't you do it, then?"). Once a month I had lunch with Gordon Seagrove, whose "Always a bridesmaid but never a bride" and "Even your best friend won't tell you" were Listerine classics. Occasionally at the Dutch Treat Club I still sit next to John Caples, who wrote for the U. S. School of Music the time-honored "They laughed when I sat down at the piano" ("As the last notes of the Moonlight Sonata died away, the room resounded with a sudden roar of applause"). Who that read it would not remember the International Correspondence School's "University of the Night" ("Up from the mines, down from the masts of ships, from behind counters and plows, from chauffeurs' seats and engine cabs—from all the places where men work they will go home and pick up their books because they yearn to grow").

Most of the ads I remember were soft-sell, more literary than product-pushing, but they sold. On any basis it wasn't just a good copy era, it was a fabulous one.

I had many an afternoon and evening good talk with advertising men and women. Once a year I made it my business to drop in on every major agency in the country, often without appointment. The people there were usually flattered when I visited them, as they would be about almost any editor, and as I always felt flattered to be received. We discussed anything but advertising for my magazine. It's the only way for an editor to help his magazine get advertising.

Contemporaries continue to enjoy quoting me as having said my office door was always open to a magazine's salesmen provided they came in on their knees. Invariably omitted—they think it makes a better story that way—is that I said it with a smile, in fun. Of all the salesmen on our magazines I think it can be said honestly that they found me more than willing to see them, spend time with them, give whatever help I could. A man selling space has a rugged job; it seems rugged to me, I know I couldn't handle it. With a rate card and perhaps a copy of *Newsweek* in his hand he must convince media departments that his magazine represents a better buy than *Time*. The salesman who needs one more order that will earn him a bonus may have a mortgage payment coming due, an unexpected medical bill, an income tax installment—all the personal problems that beset a car salesman, department store general manager, bookkeeper, bookie, or editor. Such a man may find helpful word from the editor of a feature already scheduled that could be of importance to a prospective advertiser. I knew of no reason why the information should not be passed along to every advertiser who might want to know. If a prospective advertiser could be set on the right track by having the editor clarify editorial policy, there was no reason—in my opinion but by no means universally shared—the editor shouldn't make the call. I knew editors who did not make any calls at all, who considered it beneath their dignity. That's what they said. I didn't consider a salesman's need any less important than my dignity.

When Sigmund Larmon was head of Young & Rubicam he demanded that every employee from lowest to highest position be in the office no later than 9 A.M. and report to the reception desk so that time of arrival could be noted. It was a self-defeating regulation because employees who knew they were going to be late simply phoned in and reported sick and didn't show up at all. I never cared when our editorial people came in or went home—only for stenographic and clerical help was there a specified schedule. Nevertheless, every office must have some rules. We had a few. There was one about skiing accidents. Anybody who suffered an injury was to go off the payroll for the duration of the absence, or so I announced. I had no doubt skiing would be done away with. It wasn't, and however long absent everybody with splinted arm or leg stayed on the payroll. Some chance of taking anybody off! An enforced rule, however, was that we must never save or space ideas; instead, to use them profligately and immediately—ideas give rise to more ideas, they breed, hatch, the more there are, the more there are likely to be. A seriously observed rule was not to buy a manuscript without knowing in which issue it was to be used, and if in doubt about a manuscript never to buy it. By building inventory, future choices are limited, and some ideas without the full endorsement of the editor at the beginning are vulnerable to his total loss of interest and are junked into cold storage.

It was not necessary to have rules about office dress. In my day, editorial people, even the younger men in the art department, could have passed for junior executives in a bank. The women were a trim and tidy bunch, none overfussy about clothes but definitely not a slattern in the lot. To some extent this has all changed, though "to some extent," as it applies to men, may be an understatement.

There must be senior citizens other than me who remember horses and when there used to be blankets for covering them in cold weather. Late last fall I beheld a spectacle wrapped in a horse blanket tied around the middle by two neckties knotted together. There were ropes of beads around its neck. Its shoulder-length hair was pulled together in the back by a ribbon. On one foot was a boot, on the other a white sock. It was stretched out on the floor, "relaxing."

I had stopped in to pick up an old agency friend. "What is that gargoyle I just saw in one of your offices down the hall?" I asked. Just about the best "conceptualizer" in the business, I was told. Would I like to meet him? Not at all.

I don't understand what induces grown men to get themselves up in such attire. Because the conceptualizer was no longer in his office, my friend and I stepped into it before taking off for lunch. The walls were covered with certificates of award for excellence in the visual arts. Laid out on a table were specimens of work that had earned them. The specimens were stunning. Given the opportunity, I would have been tempted to lure that art director away and sign him to a long contract. But not in that getup.

We had a rule about Christmas office parties. There were none. Verboten. At *McCall's*, we took over a hotel ballroom, invited employees to bring all the children they could muster, who could watch magicians, acrobats, and clowns, disport themselves on seesaws, slides, and merry-go-rounds, be gorged with sandwiches and milk and ice cream, receive gifts from a Santa Claus. No liquor for the adults, and nobody seemed to miss it, and all the girls could go home no less virginal than when they came.

We did have another rule, not taken seriously though sometimes I wished it could have been: anybody heard saying "dias" when intending "dais" or "apprise" intending "appraise" or writing "alright" instead of "all right" was to be subject to instant dismissal. Had the rule been binding, we would have lost half our secretarial pool.

In connection with the above I have a copy of a delightful memorandum once written by Marie Longyear, manager of editing services at McGraw-Hill. "A forceful type of expression," she wrote, "is what the writer can be able to achieve following perusal of the following rules as to good usage and grammer."

> Subject and verb always has to agree . . . Being bad grammar, the writer will not use dangling participles . . . Parallel construction with coordinate conjunctions is not only an aid to clarity but also is the mark of a good writer . . . Do not use a foreign term when there is an adequate *quid pro quo* . . . If you must use a foreign term, it is *de rigor* to use it correctly . . . It behooves the writer to avoid archaic expressions . . . Do not use hyperbole; not one writer in a million can use it effectively . . . Avoid clichés like the plague . . . Mixed metaphors are a pain in the neck and ought to be thrown out the window . . . In scholarly writing, don't use contractions . . . A truly good writer is always especially careful to practically eliminate the too-frequent use

of adverbs . . . Use a comma before nonrestrictive clauses which are a common source of difficulty . . . Placing a comma between subject and predicate, is not correct . . . Parenthetical words however should be enclosed in commas . . . Consult the dictionary frequently to avoid mispelling.

30

On ordinary days the editor's office may run into a crisis, but the publisher's office is a prefecture of perpetual panic because a competitive magazine has unexpectedly announced a change in circulation base, or reduced its cost per thousand, or had the biggest increase in linage, or according to the latest survey has more readers under the age of puberty.

The publishers and advertising directors I knew—worked with—were a polyglot lot. Jack Creaver of *American Druggist* was the soul of propriety, a model of sobriety, and couldn't sell space. He was followed by Tom Greeley, who had a fondness for late hours and developments therein and the consequences thereof, was seldom sober, and never came back from a call without an order in his pocket. John "Bill" Buckley of *Good Housekeeping* and *Cosmopolitan* had a fondness for being important. He liked to *look* important, and did. I didn't care for him, he cared less for me. Nevertheless, he was competent in his way and our differences were subordinated to the magazines' general welfare. Almost always.

Robert Davidson of *Pictorial Review* was always a pleasure to be with. No workday really got started until he came to my office. "Just a few throws, kid," he would say. Then for fifteen minutes we pitched quarters. He was a splendid salesman. A one-call salesman, that is, meaning he made a great sale by promising an advertiser editorial favors impossible to provide. Thus he did not dare make a second call on that advertiser for at least a year. One afternoon he bustled into my office, shut the door behind him, sat down, and hung his head in pretended shame. "Kid," he said, "I've done an awful thing. I'm in terrible trouble and you're the only person who can help me." "Cut out the guff," I said, "and tell me your trouble." "I'm embarrassed." "You've got plenty to be embarrassed about already, but what now?" It was in the *Pictorial Review* period when I was using little girls as models for our photographic covers. "Kid, I've just sold a page to Wrigley." "Good for you," I said, "but what's the trouble?" "Well, I had to offer P.K. something—you know, it ain't easy getting an order these days." "What did you offer?" I asked. "Well," Bob Davidson said, "I had to promise that on one of your next covers you'd show a girl holding a package of Wrigley gum."

It was impossible to throw him out. For one thing, he was too big. For another, he was too likable. "I'm going to do you a big favor, Bob," I said. He jumped up from his chair, grabbed me and kissed me. "You'll do it?" he asked. "No, that's not the favor," I said, "but I'm going to let you get out of here without killing you."

For a few seconds he remained morose. "Tell you what, kid," he said then, "let's pitch a few quarters."

There was Tom Buck, for a while but not long on *McCall's*. Buck had lost a leg in an airplane accident. Shortly after he joined us we went off together to a convention and shared a bungalow. That night while he was preparing for bed I sat with a bundle of manuscripts I had brought along to read. I saw the man remove his trousers. Then I saw him unscrew a wooden leg. Anybody never privy to such a sight has my word that it is not worth seeing. Buck had eleven children.

There was Arthur Stein, first with *Redbook*, then *McCall's*. I could always tell it was *Arthur*—we had several Steins around—because each morning he took off his jacket on arriving at the office and sat behind his desk in the gleamingest of white shirts. He seemed to prefer not making calls on advertisers. It was generally supposed he expected advertisers to call on *him*. Not many did. Not *any* did.

There was Harry Dunlap, part of the time on *Cosmopolitan*, part on *Good Housekeeping* (publishers got shunted around). Dunlap was very genial, very proper. Darien, Connecticut, and all that. To me rather disconcerting because he had a visible terror of editors. He *trembled*.

There was Warren Agry, way back, on *Good Housekeeping*. A good man and a fiercely proud· son of Dartmouth. Knew everybody in the publishing business who had been to Dartmouth. Felt obliged to hire as salesman anybody who'd been to Dartmouth. We certainly got a lot of linage from advertising agency men who also had been to Dartmouth. But Agry was *good*. There was no better publisher. Any editor would have profited by being associated with him.

There was A. Edward Miller. Strictly *McCall's*. Looked and dressed less like a publisher than any other publisher; was the most literate and well informed. Knew how to build a sales staff and in his understated way command its respect. He understood editorial, circulation, promotion, was wise in every aspect of publishing.

There was T. W. "Bill" Towler. Of *Town & Country*. How he got there would be hard to explain. He must have had the Indian sign on somebody. He was as poorly equipped to be a publisher as Steve Kelly, whom I had brought from *Sports Illustrated* to *McCall's*.

There were other publishers in my life, including Frank Thomas of *Good Looks Merchandising*, but most of them had short shrift. As for Thomas, he was unquestionably as impressive a man in speech and appearance as anyone could hope to meet. Even more impressive-looking than any editor. He was tall and handsome and had beautiful white hair. His clothes were made by the best tailors. He had a weakness for forging checks and landed in the penitentiary.

All the publishers, even those I held inept, must have been better than I have indicated them to be. Some of them, Agry and Miller in particular, were extraordinary. They were great publishers. They were also gentlemen and scholars.

Who has the last word on a magazine—editor or publisher? We have to get to that sooner or later. The answer is incontrovertible: usually it is neither. Usually it is management, in the person of the company's chief executive officer. Even he is not always boss because he may be subject to decisions of the company's board of directors, the board of directors subject to decisions of the stockholders. The real boss may be a person never in evidence and not at all active in the magazine's affairs—he may be the sole owner.

In general, the publisher is held accountable for a magazine's performance in terms of dollars and cents—profit or loss; the editor, for the magazine's editorial content. If the publisher's record for bringing in advertising revenue during a given interval is viewed as more important than the editor's for attracting readers, he may be considered more indispensable than the editor. If the editor's record for attracting readers is viewed as more important, he may be thought the more indispensable. Except in instances of magazines that generate a substantial revenue from newsstand sales, the publisher brings in the revenue—the advertising revenue—that keeps a magazine afloat, from which circumstance has come the traditional notion that publisher outranks editor. A cockeyed tradition, not easy to lick.

There is a fundamental difference between a publisher's philosophy and an editor's. The editor assumes that when a magazine accepts payment for a subscription or newsstand sale there is a commitment to give the reader what has been paid for, that the magazine can't arbitrarily reduce ratio of editorial pages or cheapen paper stock because advertising has fallen off. The editor thinks first of the reader. Most publishers think first of profit and loss statement; if they can't make profit quotas except by shortchanging the reader, they are inclined to shortchange. It takes a strong editor to stand up for the readers, a strong publisher to stand up for the editor, a wise management to decide in favor of readers and editors, and a wise editor to recognize there are special times when temporary compromises and sacrifices can't be avoided.

When a magazine is flourishing, when circulation and advertising are satisfactory, when management has nothing to complain about, editor and publisher may have equal status and shine in equal glory. It happens now and then.

In ideal circumstances, should any develop, publisher and editor participate in basic decisions: what circulation objectives should be, what advertisements accepted or rejected, which agency should handle the magazine's account, the quality of paper to be used, the choice of printer, and together with the circulation director the size of each issue's print order. They join in determining the magazine's goals, immediate and long-range. The experienced editor has sense enough to listen to the circulation director's suggestions about cover lines.

Who occupies which office? Don't fool yourself that it's not important. If the offices are on the same floor, perceptive management sees that the editor's office and the publisher's are of equal size, with the same number of windows and an equally favorable outlook. If on different floors, the offices are of similar dimensions and amenities.

It sounds petty. It is, but not to either editor or publisher.

Who gets the higher salary? Usually the publisher, because that's the way it's always been. If the editor is important enough, his may be the higher salary, but it's an unusual circumstance. Most editors are willing to settle for less money because they are beneficiaries of a prestige that submerges the publisher's. To most editors prestige and influence are of greater consequence than income. Now and then an editor emerges who has highest power *and* income. Helen Gurley Brown is such a one. She never worked on a magazine in her life before 1965, when she took over *Cosmopolitan,* then about to fold, and made it the most profitable women's publication in the world. Her annual income, based largely on circulation achievement, is estimated at $350,000. Too much? Too little. The Hearst Corporation is a private company, its earnings not made public. But I am not bad at figuring these things out, and my conservative guess is that before taxes *Cosmopolitan* brings close to $25 million a year to the company. All due to Mrs. Brown. During a period when I was running the magazine, with David Brown (before his marriage to Helen Gurley), Jack O'Connell, A. E. Hotchner, and young Johnny Marquand as chief associates, I think we represented quite a consortium of editorial brains. Among us we turned out a brilliant magazine. It was so brilliant that it dipped to the lowest circulation level in its history. We were editing the magazine for a general-magazine dual audience that no longer existed and we were not smart enough to be aware of it. Nobody knew what to do with *Cosmopolitan* until Helen Gurley Brown came along.

One evening when Mr. and Mrs. Brown were with me, I said, "David, for all your success in Hollywood, when the history of our time is written you will be a footnote. But Helen will be a whole chapter." *Cosmopolitan* may not be everybody's cup of tea (I don't know of a magazine that is), but with the formula devised for it by Helen Gurley Brown, it has, more than anything else, made for women's current freedom of mental and sexual expression.

It's true that $350,000 is a big chunk of money. A man like Henry Mencken would have said it doesn't exist. When he was editor of *The American Mercury* his salary was $9,000.

Profit and loss details are generally unavailable to editors, who are not regarded as financially astute, which makes little sense, the infantile theory being that if the editor is told how much money his company is making he may demand more for himself. As though he couldn't do his own calculating.

The publisher editors despise is one who in conversation refers to "my editor," as though he held some proprietary right. "I'll tell my editor to take care of that," or "I'll have my editor see to it." It's an obnoxious phrase.

The person who aspires to a combined title—editor *and* publisher—is treading on dangerous ground, inviting trouble, a personal opinion, of course. An advertiser may ask for editorial favors, and because the publisher's task is to get advertising orders he is on the horns of a dilemma; he runs the risk of subordinating his scruples as editor to his desire to bring in as much linage as possible. No editor-publisher I ever met was altogether immune to advertisers' pressures.

On a few magazines the experiment was made to keep editorial and advertising departments wholly divorced from each other. Theoretically, separation is to be commended; from a practical standpoint it doesn't work. A magazine's advertising department has good reason to know what the editor is doing and planning. The editor has good reason to know what the publisher is doing and planning. To suppose differently is unrealistic.

The kind of promotion undertaken by a magazine's advertising agency is something with which editor and publisher both need to be involved. Now and then they become involved too late. As when *Good Housekeeping*'s agency ran a page of advertising promoting the magazine's then current splash about food. The advertising appeared in New York and other metropolitan cities—on Yom Kippur, the Day of Atonement, the most important religious holiday observed by Jews, the day they don't touch food and when the orthodox don't even buy papers.

Editors who make a direct pitch to sell advertising in

order to ingratiate themselves with management, or for any other reason, demean themselves.

At a time when *Good Housekeeping* had no slogan, I created the one it still uses: "The Magazine America Lives By." After it appeared for the first time, the publisher came to my office. "It's a good slogan," he said, "but don't you think you might have discussed it with me first?" I thought about the question for a while, because I wanted to give a sensible answer. Finally it came to me. I said, "No." But the publisher was right; I should have discussed it with him. He was entitled to that courtesy.

31

From an objective standpoint I can't say what an editor should do beyond supervising his staff and selecting the material that becomes a magazine. I got into a lot of things, or had editorial associates get into them, that weren't strictly in the editorial sphere. An editor acquires as much authority as he is willing to risk assuming. A candid recital of my activities would make me out, and fairly so, an interrupting presence in territory usually designated as the publisher's, or the promotion or circulation manager's. I could not deny an unsqueamish impulse to be involved in a magazine's every area. With a fierce passion for my own independence that demanded isolation of a business department from editorial affairs, I was always vulnerable to the charge that I rode roughshod over protests and was intransigent in not always recognizing the independence of the publishing department. There are no laurels to be placed on the head of an editor who writes copy that is the function of the promotion department to write, or who usurps the function of a magazine's advertising agency and insists it is his own copy that must fill a page in tomorrow's newspaper. For overstepping editorial department boundaries I had no choice but to plead guilty. But I found it hard to accept second-rate copy and had a compulsion to get what I thought the best in our promotion and circulation efforts, which meant that toes were stepped on, and egos bruised; but I was part of a tough business and not interested in winning a popularity contest.

Excursions into other than editorial realms may seem to have reduced the amount of attention that should have been applied to editorial content. But the hours I put in were unusual. I took the time because it seemed worthwhile. Some of the activities could have been skipped and often enough were without meaning. No good purpose was served (I'm not sure there was one), except for a squib in the papers by roaming the city at night in a police car; or, at the behest of the War Department, in touring the country's plants engaged in the manufacture of armaments and munitions; or in escorting the "teacher of the year" to Washington to present her to the President. One year I took time to edit *Dateline*, the magazine published annually by the Overseas Press Club. As a friend of the *Christian Science Monitor*, I undertook an analysis of that newspaper's editorial formula, as at the request of Basil O'Connor, then head of the American Red Cross, I prepared a report on the two dozen periodicals sponsored by that organization. I spent several hours a day for a week with the owners of *Paris-Match*, talking about publishing procedures in the United States. I took on the task, several years in a row, of choosing the winners in the annual story contest conducted under the auspices of the Catholic Writers' Association; served as a judge in the J. C. Penney–University of Missouri Awards, and the National Magazine Awards; and it hurt to hear my wife say once in a while, "Do you think you could take a few minutes off tonight to talk with me?"

Some of the outside engagements were silly though not unpleasant, as when I served as one of the judges in the Atlantic City Miss America pageant. The important publicity activities were more directly tied to the magazine. Many New York residents will recall the entrance to *McCall's* Park Avenue building, with the two huge glass-enclosed areas with their displays of puppies, kittens, and birds, all related to features in the magazine. Every available space for posters in Grand Central Station was filled with blow-ups of *McCall's* covers, and no ad agency commuter could escape seeing them. At *Good Housekeeping* I sponsored the NBC radio network program called "College Quiz Bowl," with Allen Ludden master of the quiz. It cost us the pitiful sum of five hundred dollars a week, which we awarded to the winning college. Stupidly, because our advertising agency stupidly claimed it was too intellectual, I let myself be talked into dropping it. General Electric took over as sponsor and was pleased to pay five thousand dollars a week for the privilege. Then the program was transferred to television and continued on its successful course.

In all such efforts as the above, and others, though not so designated on an organization chart, I did not hesitate to immerse myself. Promotion of any kind, I felt, was part of editing, and editing is part of anything that concerns a magazine's welfare. A publisher also is part of anything that concerns a magazine's welfare, with the exception of editing. The publisher is not part of that because he isn't an editor, which may have a belittling implication I do not intend. Like anybody else, he may say what he likes and doesn't, but no more than that. Most editors stay as far away as possible from anything that is not strictly editorial. Some are unwarrantably excluded.

An editor who can make a good speech possesses an invaluable asset. The better the speaker, the greater the demand for him, and the shrewder the editor, the fewer invitations he accepts, three a year being, I thought, the desirable quota. If he isn't splendid at it, the editor does best who makes no speeches at all.

Bruce Gould's peregrinations, whether to India for an interview with Gandhi (or was it Nehru?) or to Spain to have a breezy chat with the king, always gave him effective anecdotes he could draw on. *Look's* image was enhanced when its Leo Rosten could be induced to deliver a talk, *Fortune's* when articulate Eric Hodgins could be gotten on a platform, *Reader's Digest's* when its spellbinding Charles

Ferguson could be trapped. *The Atlantic's* Ted Weeks, successor to Ellery Sedgwick, could charm any audience anywhere. Ring Lardner, when asked to make a speech, always had a standard excuse for not accepting: "Sorry, but that's the baby's night out and I must stay at home with the nurse."

It doesn't take a canny mind to know that no speech is wholly bad if it is short enough. I have made a fair number of speeches myself and rated them as of rare vintage. Peculiarly, nobody ever invited me back to make another one. (That's not strictly true. This year I was invited to return to the University of Stanford to repeat a lecture I had given there in 1978. Apparently some of the students and members of the faculty, having heard me describe myself as adorable and enchanting, wanted to hear how I would describe myself the second time around.) My longest speech—the Harold L. Cross Memorial Lecture—was given at the University of Missouri. It took a full hour. Not all of the audience lasted as long as I did. The second-longest was made at the University of Tennessee, where I was the Commencement speaker. It was the only time in my life I had worn cap and gown, which had been rented for the occasion.

Working for *McCall's* was a public relations character named Gene Shalit. For circulation sales he dreamed up ideas, stunts, contrivances, machinery, schemes, plots, subplots, gadgets, and, for all I know, weapons. They worked. One look at him and you knew they *had* to work. I found out he could play the bassoon and the clarinet. But *good*. He could conduct a symphony orchestra. After a while he decided he should be a writer. He began by writing an article for *McCall's*, recommending books to buy for children. He said that if children didn't like the books he recommended, parents should send the children back, not the books. I sent a short note to Shalit saying I liked the piece. Now it's about seventeen years later and he still thanks me for it.

After still another while Shalit began to do radio broadcasting. Then television. Anybody who has seen the "Today" show on NBC knows Gene Shalit. He's a special person.

I suppose what I have been saying is that a magazine is part show and that the editor is, or should be, part showman; and if he isn't part showman he is only part editor. DeWitt Wallace, however, has been complete editor and showman by virtue of never doing anything in public at all.

The most impressive of all promotion events that I remember was the Waldorf dinner sponsored in 1963 by Henry Luce when he had on the dais about two hundred notables whose portraits had appeared on the covers of *Time*. There was another promotion effort I remember in which all of the country's magazines participated. Conceived by Paul MacNamara, one of the brightest of Hearst executives, it resulted in July 1942 in having every magazine substitute for its normal cover a photograph or art rendering of the American flag. Even *Reader's Digest* switched its front cover index of articles to the back cover.

A hero sandwich is not the sort of thing to inspire a chorus of praise, but I will mention one because it did inspire such praise. I had asked our food department at *McCall's* to make the most heroic of such sandwiches. It came out fifteen inches long and almost three inches high, the biggest damned thing of the kind I'd ever seen. We photographed it and ran it straight across two facing pages of the magazine. We called it "McCall's Magnifique." I assumed our readers would be pleased and amused, but I also wanted advertisers to be. So starting at five in the morning, in Chicago and New York, people worked to make a hundred such sandwiches, and two dozen Western Union messengers were engaged to see that one hero sandwich, promptly at noon on the day the issue came out, would be delivered to the receptionist in every top advertising agency in the two cities. It was a good stunt and I gave myself a gold star for it.

Quite a few advertising executives play bridge. During my *Pictorial Review* days I arranged for a series of matches to be played for the husband-wife championship of the world. Mr. and Mrs. Ely Culbertson and Mr. and Mrs. Hal Sims, at that time the best-known bridge players, were to be the contestants, and advertising executives the audience. The trouble was that there were not then any means for having an audience see the play of the hands. So the whole thing was a failure.

All of us live in a world that's constantly promoting something. Some promotion efforts work out fine. Some of mine worked out awful. An editor can do peculiar things. So can a writer. A man named E. V. Wright once wrote a fifty-thousand-word novel called *Gadsay,* and he wrote it without once using the letter "e." I wasn't all that peculiar.

I *was* peculiar enough to sit in the reading room of the Forty-second Street library and start and finish that book. It's terrible.

32

Anybody who has stayed the course this far is entitled to know how I was regarded by my editorial associates. It can be put this way: sweet, lovable, and kind. The Illustrators Society once presented me with a sketch of myself, and it hangs not far from the desk at which I now sit. Looking at it, I can see I am, or was, pipe in hand, reflective. Contemplative. Gentle. As nice a fellow as anybody could want to have in charge of a magazine.

I was congenial. Always ready with a cheerful word. Everybody's friend.

What mystifies me still is why nobody in the office ever called me by my first name. I'd say, "Good morning, Henry," or "You look like an angel, Elizabeth," and get back: "Morning, Mr. Mayes," "It's kind of you to say so, Mr. Mayes."

Forget the formality, I'd say, call me by my first name. Nobody did.

"May we barge in on you, Mr. Mayes?" It would be Maggie Cousins. Never in the decades we were so tied together did Maggie ever address me in the office by my given name. Today, for all our ages of working together, there are editors I meet who address me similarly. After twenty years of most intimate association with Dr. Watson, Sherlock Holmes always called him Dr. Watson. That seems to have no relevance here, but it just came to mind.

"You looked so stern," Celia Mendelssohn, the art agent,

said. "You didn't bite, but we always thought you were on the verge." Gene Davis, our capable art director, used to go for a walk when he heard my voice raised. "I'm the nervous type," he would say. "Mitch," the building bootblack, told one of the secretaries he always crossed himself before coming in to polish my shoes; what Mitch said, however, could not always be accepted as gospel. We engaged a copy assistant who during her first two days with us went through a few manuscripts and changed every "said" in "he said" and "she said" to *stated, mumbled, murmured, muttered, asserted, asseverated, declared, cried, remarked, purred, roared, howled, simpered,* or *snarled.* That's a bit much, as anybody would agree. I always preferred the simple "said," and when I yelled, screamed, or boomed that we'd have to dispense with her services, she called me a heartless monster. My few words to her had been: "Please get your things together and get out of here quick." I said "please."

A monster! Was I even a martinet? I put the question to our winsome copy chief. "Why, no, not at all, Mr. Mayes," she said, "we think of you as an ogre." Of course, I knew she was joking.

Printers' Ink, when it said I ate an editor and a writer every morning for breakfast, must also have been joking.

"Mayes," said *Time,* "is bellowing, belligerent, brilliant." To the brilliant part I took no exception. Then: "He brooked no interference." True enough. And then, quoting a free lance writer, it added, "he ran *Good Housekeeping* like the overseer of a chain gang."

Can anyone imagine that? I invite anybody interested to come here and take a look at the Illustrators Society likeness of me. It's scheduled, I'm told, to adorn the jacket of this book.

Poker and membership in men's clubs notwithstanding, I lived in a women's world. The top magazines in my care were *Pictorial Review, Good Housekeeping,* and

McCall's. On each the staff was composed largely of women. About 90 percent women. With one or two there was a drinking problem. With Dorothy Draper, our famous decorating editor, there was a sense-of-proportion problem: for families inching along on fifteen thousand dollars a year she designed rooms in white—off white, light white, bright white, creamy white, whiter than white, always dotted with roses—lovely to look at and impractical to live with. She adored her work but not people who weren't rich. "You'll have to tone down these ideas of yours," I would say. "Oh, Mr. Mayes, please—just this once. Can't we raise our sights a little?" "Yes, Dorothy," I would say, "but not to the hundred-thousand-dollar level—you're way out of line." Then: "But just see how heavenly this bedroom is," she would go on. And I would say, "Dorothy, take this damned stuff out of here. I don't want to see it again." Then, taking another squint at the photographs she brought in, my gorge would rise. "Dorothy, get rid of this goddamned stuff. Our readers aren't paupers, but they're not Rockefellers. Get out!"

As nice a person as anybody could want to have in charge of a magazine.

Then there was Willie Mae Rodgers. When the incomparable Katherine Fisher retired as head of the Good Housekeeping Institute, I brought Miss Rodgers in to replace her. Miss Rodgers idolized almost everybody. "Do you know how very much I love you?" she would ask, and her eyes would glisten and a couple of tears would be squeezed out and trickle down her cheeks. She asked the question of me, and of anybody who seemed to have, or about to have, any degree of authority. She was known by members of the staff as Madam Crocodile Tears.

I lived in a women's world not only in the office but also in my home. There I had a wife, two daughters, maid or cook or somebody else female. No men. Once a month I took home the batches of cartoons that had come to the office. In peace and quiet I would be able to go through them, except when my daughters, then in their mid-teens, would join me, uninvited. They would do their own examining. "Dad, how can anybody think this one is funny?" one would ask. "Dad, this is terrible," the other would fume. "Dad," both of them would groan, "you're crazy to waste your time looking at this mess." They meant well.

The world is full of women. The majority seemed to be working or living with me. Yet I am not a misogynist. I do happen to like to smoke my pipe and watch prizefights and wrestling matches. I have been a member of various clubs—the Dutch Treat, the Hoyle, the Column; in London the Savile, the Reform, the American, and the Paternosters. Membership in all of them was restricted to men. It just happened that way. If it happened any other way I wouldn't be fool enough to admit it.

My wife is an editor. My two daughters are editors. My two sons-in-law are editors. All of them, I'm sure, believe they are better editors than I ever was. Knowing on which side my happiness is buttered, I am not inclined to argue.

My one and only grandchild is not an editor. His tenth birthday is coming up, and who knows?

33

There isn't an editor who's been around for any length of time who hasn't known and done business with every writer mentioned in this narrative and whose experiences, good and bad, haven't been like my own. We shared a fund of sympathetic and antipathetic memories; have the same tales to tell, the same bank of names to draw on. If I have a fuller store of anecdotes than some others it is because I was born long before them, my editorial life began long before theirs. "You mean you actually *knew* Kathleen Norris?" an acquaintance exclaimed a few years ago. Knew her? Good grief, I *published* her. I am a Methuselah in the trade.

It's been a long time and a long way back since I said anything of *Good Looks Merchandising* and the Lon Chaney story. I did not mean to leave things up in the air there, but because the beginning and the end of a special relationship took place in one place and with the same people, all of it seems most of all to belong in one place for the telling.

When I left the cosmetics magazine and three days later, on the morning of Monday, February 7, 1927, went to work for William Randolph Hearst, his magazines were called International Publications, Inc., the offices located on West Fortieth Street in New York—a few years were to pass before the company's name was changed to Hearst Magazines, Inc., and it moved to Fifty-seventh Street and Eighth

Avenue, to the grotesque building designed by the Viennese architect Joseph Urban. The company had just acquired *American Druggist,* a trade paper, and with it I
began my long, strange, and ultimately disastrous Hearst
journey.

The youngish Richard E. Berlin was then an advertising
space salesman on Mr. Hearst's *Motor Boating,* not what
anybody would rate an auspicious jumping-off place for the
position of power he was to reach. But for future prospects
he had in his favor a slight acquaintanceship with Millicent
Hearst, the wife of William Randolph, who passed word to
her estranged but nevertheless attentive husband that
something about Berlin struck her as intelligent and that he
might be worth keeping an eye on. Berlin was not without
other assets: a commanding physical presence to begin
with. He had business acumen, consummate political reflex,
insatiable ambition, and luck. *Irish* luck, he would emphasize with a grin, never quite comfortable with the knowledge that some people might think him related to another
kind of Berlin, like Irving.

He had an exquisite instinct for gauging the present
place and future prospects of those in higher authority. His
moves were cautious but not timid. He stood well with
those on the way up without losing touch with those on the
way down. His sense of timing was impeccable. He absorbed statistics and the intricacies of finance as naturally
as he walked. His friends were legion.

Without a false move, his ascent to the summit was
nothing short of miraculous. He swept the Hearst landscape of obstacles, becoming the single dominating figure
in the hierarchy, with plenary control irrespective of executive committees, boards of directors, and trustees, all of
which and whom he jostled dexterously, manipulated and
maneuvered, contriving always to be at the peak. In the
1930's—when the dynasty had been on the verge of economic collapse, actually in receivership due to Mr. Hearst's
unbridled extravagances and his stubbornness in clinging

to newspapers that were losing millions of dollars every year—it was primarily Berlin's grinding drive, his relentless pounding, his iron nerve, that compelled the paper suppliers to reduce the company's obligations to them, that restored the confidence of the banks, and that in time brought order out of devastating chaos. There were individuals who advised and made constructive contributions, among them Clarence Shearn, Thomas J. White, Martin Huberth, and John Hanes, formerly Undersecretary of the Treasury, who hoped to share in the final success; there were lawyers and financiers—most important of all the Boston banker Serge Semenenko—who were engaged in the restructuring; but the return to solvency, the mind-boggling wealth and solidity of the organization today can be attributed almost exclusively to Omaha-born, little-educated Richard E. Berlin. Long years after the reorganization, during a festive dinner attended by dozens of the company's executives, William Randolph Hearst, Jr., spoke a few words. "I'd like to remind all of you," he said graciously at the end, "that if it weren't for this fellow Dick we wouldn't have even enough money today to pay for this meal." It was true.

It didn't take many years to get there, but Berlin got there. His first post of whopping power was as head of the magazine division, of Hearst divisions the steadiest profit producer of all. In that division were men themselves no slouches in the aspirations department—at one time or another the able assistant general manager Arthur Moore, great circulation director Tom Buttikofer, brilliant sales manager Earle McHugh; robust John "Bill" Buckley, the handsome, energetic Ray Petersen, the gentlemanly Fred Drake, all of whom were publishers; the physically big, mentally unastute Jack Herbert, who agilely hopped from one periodical to another; William Fine, publisher, who when striving to be most elegant would proudly toss off "between you and I." All of them had a great deal more than average ability. They are listed in my personal *Who's*

Not Who because in the Hearst merry-go-round they just weren't lucky enough to grab the brass ring.

Elsewhere, in other Hearst offices, were Joe Connolly, supervising both King Features Syndicate and International News Service; rough-and-tumble scrapper, no pushover for anybody, Connolly while he lived fought valiantly for the crown; and in Boston, "Hap" Kern; in Chicago and Baltimore and Los Angeles, half a dozen others. . . . But Berlin, employing a classic ploy, neatly kept all off balance, nicely pitting the potential challengers for his position one against another, murmuring a subtle promise to this one and when necessary implementing a promise to that one, allegiance, with some fingers crossed, being sworn to him by all. The fantasy of all of them was that someday— someday, when Mr. Hearst chose it—the mantle of leadership would be draped on *their* shoulders. Berlin, impassive, knowing but unconcerned, watched those who thought themselves favorites tangle among themselves for position and authority; saw them scheme one against another, team up—first this twosome and then that twosome against another twosome. Pairings shifted, depending on who was where and what and when. Overtly all of them were Berlin henchmen, praised him publicly, a few covertly hoping he would make some irreparable mistake and be gone.

Among the covey of the ambitious was one who, for reasons that had to do with me, my position, my future, my life, must be mentioned separately.

I mention him separately: Richard E. Deems.

No matter how frenzied the gallop, Deems, who had started as an advertising salesman for *Harper's Bazaar* and then moved up to be its advertising manager, seemed among the business associates always to be closest to Berlin; some steps behind him but at least half a step ahead of everybody else. Amazingly, the initials—REB and RED— had a euphonious ring. More amazingly, Berlin's middle name was Emmett, and Deems's middle name was Emmet, the difference being only in an extra "t." When Berlin became supreme ruler of everything in the Hearst empire, it was Deems that Berlin anointed head of the magazine group, the beachhead from which Berlin had catapulted himself to the top of the Hearst heap. Deems was very much on the move, trying hard always to be affable, as Berlin was. The general feeling was that he tried too hard. When he was given a new office, it was immediately adjacent to Berlin's. Right next door. So it seemed that in time, maybe a long time though it had to come, Deems would take the place of Berlin as president.

Two men, progressing inauspiciously in position and authority, held apart in the contest for succession. Neither deigned to enter the fray. One was Frank Massi, gentle, quiet, conscientious bookkeeper on *Pictorial Review* back in 1934. The other was John Miller, who came in soon thereafter as a bright young man to learn the subscription business, starting at the bottom. Massi and Miller took no sides, formed no alliances, became nobody's partisan. To neither one did any of the others pay attention. There was no reason to. Massi and Miller were never in contention and everybody knew it.

So there they were, the cluster of contestants, Massi and Miller excepted, with their jockeying. Waiting. Working hard while waiting. Writhing while working hard and waiting. And wondering. They waited and wondered until Berlin was past sixty, getting on to sixty-five. They waited until he was seventy. Then seventy-five. Had the man no intention of ever stepping down?

At last Berlin began to repeat himself, telling the same story over again that he had told twenty minutes earlier. He was beginning to forget things—names, numbers, places, days and dates.

But he looked great, only his hair thinning, and he hung in there, the arm a little erratic but still pitching. Soon Berlin would be eighty—threescore years and ten plus ten— himself running the show, seemingly indestructible.

Any one of the five Hearst sons could have taken over.

Bill, Jr., or Randy might have had the job for the asking. They were shrewd enough to know they had no need to. Who ran the company made no matter, so long as it was run well, and Berlin ran it well. He ran it better than well. Thus the Hearst boys could have the maximum of benefits with a minimum of cares, their stance benign apartness. After all, it was *their* business, and their descendants'. They were the heirs. It *belonged* to them. And they could find ample satisfaction in the thought that someday one of the grandsons, or perhaps a great-grandson of William Randolph Hearst, would decide to emulate the Lord of San Simeon and be the nominal and functioning head, so that the name of Hearst would be a monumental name again. The empire would still be there, because Richard Berlin had rescued it from oblivion.

Early in our association Berlin had begun to look on me as a chap who might be of some use to him, somebody he could depend on, one of those romancy screwballs, a think-up-things nut, with no pipe dreams about administrative precedence. In a publishing shop editors can be a confounded nuisance with all their crazy talk about creativity and that sort of stuff, but somebody's got to get out the magazines. No? Yes. Berlin would need editors. He would, maybe, need me. So I became a sort of editorial acolyte. "Good fellow—no inhibitions about talking up. He's smart—flippy, but smart."

In making use of me Berlin was no different, nor should he have been, from executives in any industry who gather around them individuals credited with some general or specific aptitude. What brought me to notice was what he called flippy—brashness, I suppose, a contempt for routine and red tape and "regular" hours. If he came to the office at eight in the morning, or on a Saturday, I was there and he'd sit down to talk. I got to know a lot about him. He got to know a lot about me. In November of the year I became part of the *American Druggist* staff, Berlin knew I had senselessly trudged in hip-high boots through ankle-high mud from Burlington, Vermont, to Waterbury, which had been destroyed by the flood of the Winooski River. A few hours before my arrival the town had been placed under martial law, with troops from Fort Ethan Allen in command. The whole point of the foolhardy venture was to get hold of a druggist who for a story in *American Druggist* would describe the services he performed during a local disaster. There was no trouble in finding the druggist. Of more importance was the fact that no news service man had yet gotten into Waterbury. Early the next morning a sergeant arranged to get me back to Burlington by truck, where I filed a story about what had happened in Waterbury. Though I had no connection with Hearst's New York *American,* the paper printed it, by-line and all. The escapade made me a wunderkind in the shop. For a whole half day.

While editing *American Druggist* I began to issue a weekly newsletter called *The Drug Whirl.* In one particular issue I reported how a Dr. F. Donald Coster was planning to make himself the most powerful factor in the distribution area of the pharmaceutical industry. I was able to name the banks and Wall Street brokers involved with Dr. Coster, and what the financial setup of the projected enterprise was to be, how many shares of stock were to be issued and who was to get how many, who the officers of the new McKesson & Robbins company would be. I had every detail that until then was known only to Dr. Coster and, as far as he knew, sealed away in his personal safe.

It was a very special story. It stunned the industry. The impact of it stunned me.

The story became more special when it developed later that the man I thought to be Dr. Coster was an impostor. A smuggler, forger, embezzler, and swindler. Who had served two terms in prison. Whose real name was Phillip Musica.

Richard Berlin was well aware of the commotion caused by the McKesson story; and that *American Druggist* itself was being favorably talked about. Ray Long, most visible and indomitable editor in the Hearst magazine framework, paid the magazine some particular attention; referred to me as "the young maverick." To Berlin that sounded like a compliment.

The Hearst organization had a think-tank committee that met irregularly to exchange ideas about future projects. All branches of the company were represented, including the trade paper division, which was how I got scrounged in as a member. Being the least important person on the committee was no deterrent. I arrived at meetings always with a dossier. Never stopped submitting ideas. Talked out of turn. Nobody seemed to mind. Not much, anyway.

Mr. Hearst was in the motion picture business, had his own production company; owned the endless, frenetic *Perils of Pauline.* Because he was also owner of International News Reel Company and had partial ownership of Metrotone News, I suggested we begin to buy up all rights to all similar newsreel companies—Pathé, Paramount, Universal, etc.—so that someday we would have a monopoly of the newsreel field. It was obvious that with the passage of time old newsreels would become increasingly valuable and be worth a huge fortune. I pressed hard on that one. And lost.

Nothing was needed but a ruler for measuring to see the whole editorial content of *Time,* which was very much thinner in those days, could be contained on two facing pages of Hearst's then full-size non-tabloid New York *American.* To be written curtly and concisely, *Time*-style, the spread would give readers in a hurry a capsule review of news under headings similar to *Time*'s "Law," "National," "Medicine," "Sports," "Education," etc. General manager Tom White said the idea was exactly what he had been looking for. He had dummy pages set in type. Mr. Hearst when he saw them said they weren't what *he* had been looking for.

Because the company's monthly *Town & Country* was getting nowhere, I thought it might be changed to a very glossy biweekly fashion and society tabloid, with debutantes in metropolitan centers serving as local reporters. Berlin was sufficiently impressed to take the notion to California to recommend to Mr. Hearst. Mr. Hearst preferred the status quo and losing money.

Along the way, over the months, more and more through the years, I began to be identified as Berlin's editorial alter ego; once a week went to his bachelor apartment on Park Avenue for breakfast. Once a week we had lunch together in his office. Affection developed early and was mutual. Whatever he referred to me I took care of, or tried to, promptly. His appreciation was profuse and freely forthcoming. What ought to be done with the Cosmopolitan Book Corporation, which was faring poorly? I thought it should be sold (and so did everybody else). It was sold. Did I think John Anderson on Hearst's New York *Evening Journal* rated as high as other theater critics? As high as any (until he gave an unfavorable notice to Thornton Wilder's *Our Town*). Was there anybody in the Curtis or Luce shops Berlin should be talking with? I didn't know. Mr. Hearst owned a sprawling medieval castle—St. Donat's, on a 150-acre estate near Llantwit Major in Wales. It was a white elephant, one of Mr. Hearst's three or four white elephant castles. Had I any idea what might be done with it? After a visit to Wales I recommended it be made into a summer camp for children, so that it would generate some revenue. The suggestion was tabled. (Later it became the United World College of the Atlantic.) Would I attend in Berlin's stead a dinner in honor of his friend Eddie Rickenbacker and say a few nice words? I did.

A serious problem confronted *Puck, the Comic Weekly,* the company's Sunday collation of comics. "Take a few days off," Berlin directed, "and give me some thoughts." I recommended it be changed to a supplement presenting in comic-strip form the same kind of editorial content that ap-

peared in home-service magazines. Berlin took to the idea
with unrestrained enthusiasm. "That'll *work*," he said, and
wrote to Mr. Hearst for approval of the new formula. He
received a telegram from Joe Willicombe, Mr. Hearst's per-
ennial secretary: "The Chief says no."
It was a good idea. Berlin thought Hearst shortsighted
in turning it down. So did I.

Undoubtedly I was of value to Berlin. He was of
inestimable value to me. From nowhere and nothing and
being nobody I was being introduced to areas and given
responsibilities of which I had not dared dream. Berlin
seemed more than fond of me. I was more than fond of
him.

When *Pictorial Review* entered the company's orbit on
a lend-lease basis from one of the large printing companies
—Hearst never really owned it—Berlin decided it was time
for me to head a consumer publication. With Mr. Hearst
consenting, I was appointed editor. Of the then "Big Six"*
women's magazines, *Pictorial Review* was in last place.
Moribund. Something needed to be done in a hurry to
breathe it back to life.

These days who has any recollection of *Pictorial Review?* But in its time it had been a women's magazine of
stature, its title belying its content. Like other magazines in
the field, it published fiction that earned good marks as
American literature. Arthur Vance, *Pictorial*'s editor at its
zenith, was a man of discerning taste who, like every other
editor, sooner or later became tormented by his magazine's
financial morass. He had chosen to publish Edith Wharton's *Age of Innocence*, found it necessary to shorten some
of the installments, was dismayed to receive a letter from
Mrs. Wharton saying, "I cannot consent to have my work
treated as prose by the yard." Mrs. Wharton, a disciple of
Henry James, was a proud and defiant woman, cared little

* *Ladies' Home Journal, Good Housekeeping, Woman's Home
Companion, McCall's, The Delineator, Pictorial Review.*

about the magazine's dollar deficit and the need for conserving space due to a falling off of advertising revenue. Editor and author compromised, the installments ran longer than originally planned. When the novel emerged as a book, it was awarded the Pulitzer Prize, the first time a woman author had been so honored.

Editor of *Pictorial Review!* Much of its glory gone, it had a remembered past, and I was puffed up to be chosen to head it. The magazine seemed to call for a new look, so I engaged T. M. Cleland, a famous typographer and designer, to redesign it. I wished I hadn't; it was a bungled job. But introduced in the magazine was the so-called complete-in-one-issue book-length novel, not then appearing in any of the competitive magazines. Shirley Temple was all of six years old when the time seemed exactly right for her autobiography! I had it written†—*My Life and Times*—and it was an enormous success. It was an era when magazines were held in high esteem whose short stories were selected for inclusion in the annual *Best Stories* anthology compiled by Edward J. O'Brien. I engaged O'Brien as a consultant to *Pictorial* with the understanding he would find for us each month at least one story that then automatically would be starred in his collection—a sure way of not being left out.

From Caroline Miller, whose *Lamb in His Bosom* had just won the Pulitzer Prize, I acquired a first short story. Margaret Ayer Barnes, very big in Chicago society and very rich, had done a dramatization of Edith Wharton's *Age of Innocence* that ran well on Broadway. She decided then to try a novel, her first, which appeared as *Years of Grace* and won the Pulitzer Prize. I asked her to write a sequel. It came in as *Within This Present* (in book form I think it was called *Modern Instance*). That was in 1934 or maybe as late as 1936. We were good friends for a while but I dropped out of her circle when she said it wouldn't

† By Max Trell, later a Hollywood writer and author of a fantasy novel called *The Small Gods and Mr. Barnum.*

matter what Hitler might do, she didn't want us involved in any war that could demand the services of her sons.

The assassination of the chancellor of Austria prompted me to send a cable to his widow, Alwine Dollfuss, who responded surprisingly with a graphic account of the tragedy. Arthur Brisbane wrote a piece, only insisting he be billed as "The World's Greatest Journalist." A contest for the best popular song‡—words and music—to be written by a person who had not previously had a song published, received favorable attention. The prize of a thousand dollars was presented to the winner; and then columnist Walter Winchell discovered and reported, correctly, that the song had been submitted by a professional under an assumed name. Ida Tarbell, the early-in-the-century grand dame of muckrakers, who once had written the exposé of John D. Rockefeller and his Standard Oil Company, was prevailed on to relive the experience for our readers. An ineffectual effort. "I don't feel bitter any more," she told me, "I can only think of Mr. Rockefeller now as a lovable old pirate."

We published Sylvia Thompson's "The Lilacs Are in Bloom," a fictionalized version of the King Edward–Wallis Simpson affair, for which she foretold a melancholy end. The new story brought Miss Thompson, already famous for her novel *The Hounds of Spring*, fame of a different kind, negative, and brought the magazine subscription cancellations from unhappy readers.

The like of it all strikes one now as ordinary editorial formula. What then seemed so very special to me was no more special than what also appeared in competitive magazines. We were able to boast, however, that the previous year "*Pictorial Review* gained as many new newsstand buyers as all its distinguished contemporaries put together, plus 50,000," which provided some personal satisfaction, but advertising in that depression period was sluggish and we were losing money. We absorbed *The Delineator*,

‡ The judges were Deems Taylor, George Marek, Paul Whiteman, and Rudy Vallee.

which was no longer a great bargain, and I grew convinced we could not long survive.*

Jake Wilk, head of the Warner Brothers office in New York, was constantly trying to think of novels in public domain that could be made into films. We were friends, I recommended several, particularly George Moore's A *Mummer's Wife* and Mrs. Craik's *John Halifax, Gentleman,* writing a synopsis of each and presuming to suggest casts. From Warner Brothers, unexpectedly, came an invitation to join the company as an "idea" man. Little as I wished to give up editing, it seemed an offer hard to refuse and I was sorely tempted.

Berlin brushed aside the temptation; said that *Good Housekeeping,* the company's major magazine, was being viewed as old-fashioned and he intended I should give up *Pictorial* and take on the other. Not as editor, as managing editor—responsibility without authority—but with assurance that within two years William Frederick Bigelow would relinquish the more important title in my favor. Bigelow had been imposing as an editor, had made the magazine a power in publishing. However much he could be faulted for taking success too much for granted, his reputation for splendid editorship must be part of the record. Unfortunately, with the passage of years, he had begun to show evidence of fatigue and the magazine was beginning to reflect it. It was said he still believed nice girls did not kiss boys unless they were engaged. He was remembering the world as he had grown up in it, as he was living in it in his small Roselle Park community in New Jersey. He had developed an aversion to change. Of all this, however, Mr. Hearst, who only glanced at his magazines but didn't read them, had not been told. Harnessed with Bigelow, I suggested innovations, conservative and of no great consequence; but because I had been thrust on him he viewed me, with good reason, as an unwelcome interloper. At last, my mere pres-

---

* *Pictorial Review* was discontinued a year later.

ence offensive to him, he protested to Mr. Hearst, who promptly ordered Berlin to get me out of the way.

With a directive from Mr. Hearst, Berlin had no alternative. Neither had he any intention of getting me so far out that he wouldn't have me available. I was sent, in a fashion, into reposeful exile, for almost a full year appeared every day in the new office given me and from arriving time to leaving reread Shakespeare from beginning to end, except that also in the interval, by persuading my dearest friend George Marek† to collaborate, I completed an outline for a screenplay to be made of the life of Tony Pastor, the "father" of vaudeville in the United States, which was purchased from us by Warner Brothers.‡ By which time Mr. Hearst at Berlin's urging had taken a good look at *Good Housekeeping*'s situation. And also by which time Marek and I, with the Tony Pastor bounty, had taken off for France, Switzerland, and England. On the night of the first trial blackout in London in August 1939, Berlin cabled, asking for my immediate return. I took passage on the *Champlain* to New York.

Berlin and I had lunch at the Plaza. Staff disturbances on *Good Housekeeping* were getting out of hand, he stated. And he gave me then, with Mr. Hearst's blessing, full authority as well as responsibility for editing the magazine. I could not fairly object when told that for a reasonable period Mr. Bigelow would continue to write his editorial page, just so long as that was to be—as it was—his only editorial participation.

† Later to be head of RCA Victor, and author of biographies of Beethoven, Mendelssohn, Toscanini, Puccini, Chopin, and others.

‡ The outline was sold by Warner Brothers to Samuel Goldwyn, who incorporated it in a film about Lillian Russell.

34

For all of the time in most of the years, Richard Berlin and I were in intimate, happy association; he the fun-loving fraternal boss, I an aide who had the privilege of being around him. He had the power, I was permitted to bask in a little of the glory. Within the editorial precincts he granted me unrestricted initiative. When publishers and promotion managers and circulation directors complained I was intruding on their territory, he said if they couldn't take care of themselves it was just their tough luck and he wasn't going to run interference.

When editorial tribulations on any of the company's magazines arose to plague him, Berlin delegated me to "fix things up," which meant going to other editors' offices and one way or another trying to help them spruce up their magazines and suggesting what might be done to achieve the sprucing up. It is the most malignant of ordeals. Editors find meddling, no matter how well-intentioned and diplomatically undertaken, repugnant. No one could blame them.

Berlin was unfailingly flattering about the manner in which my editorial chores were discharged. To build a magazine's circulation, he used a phrase that summed up his philosophy of what an editor was supposed to do: "Just put something between the covers." The idiocy of it used to drive me frantic, but I knew what he meant and he expected me to know what he meant.

I marveled at the man's perfected skills in the management of a realm that enveloped a newspaper and magazine complex, radio and television stations, forest lands, mines, and hotels. Richard Berlin, who had no training for any of it, became master of all of it.

If my domain was limited, at least it was conspicuous because magazines are conspicuous. I was his magazine handyman. Except to be an editor I had no ambition, and he was aware of it. I was not interested in being a general manager, publisher, or president. Being editor, I have always believed, is the best and highest magazine post of all. If he is good enough, the editor is more than president, general manager, or publisher. When I became editor of *McCall's*, I was more important and had infinitely greater influence than Governor Langlie, who was president. When I succeeded Langlie as president, I felt I was less important than any editor in the shop.

There was little Berlin didn't do to encourage me and make me feel wanted and needed. There were times when for suggestions submitted he rewarded me with very special gifts. For his confidence and generosity I was grateful.

At one point Berlin felt I ought to have a weekend house in the country. "Got to keep this fellow in condition," he said to my wife, and had the company buy a country house for us to live in. House? It was a manor, with six acres of land to romp around in. When my wife was to undergo serious surgery, Berlin was at the hospital at eight in the morning and stayed through the day. During another family illness he forwarded a munificent check, "for contingencies." When he thought I was exhausted from overwork, he ordered me off to Palm Beach to rest.

Good Housekeeping was doing well.

Berlin took me to the Ritz Tower in New York for my first meeting with Mr. Hearst, who held a dachshund in his lap while he talked for a full five and a half minutes and I sat in awe and listened. Berlin took me to his home in Purchase to meet Mrs. Hearst; to the Warwick Hotel in

New York to meet Marion Davies. Representing him, I escorted Arthur Gordon to the Santa Monica beach house to introduce him to Mr. Hearst as one of our new editors. Berlin made me a person. His kindnesses would make a catalogue.

Today's generation might not know why I was awed by the name of Hearst, the bearer of which had first seen the light of day during the Civil War and lived to be eighty-eight. He was a publishing lord. Born to millions, he made many millions more, and borrowed and spent hundreds of millions. He was a titan. He lived like a king-emperor.

35

My first immediate superior in the Hearst setup was Ray Sherman, who headed the trade magazine division. When he was a very old man and ill he asked that I call and spend a few minutes with him. His days were coming to a close. "I wanted a last look at you," he said kindly, and held on to my hand. "I hoped you'd make it," he said, "and I think you have. I hope everything continues to go well."

In the end, I could feel that all did go well. I think the good part of my story is the end. My mother would have liked it.

Everybody wants recognition for work well done, I wanted it no less than anybody else and from Richard Berlin I had been receiving a more than bountiful share. His favors so often bestowed, I tried the harder to please him. Publishers, advertising directors, promotion managers, and salesmen under his aegis knew that for tasks capably performed there would be a ready compliment, a boost in salary, a bonus. He had been liked by almost everybody. Those who did not like him at least admired him. Even those impatient for his retirement and hoping to succeed him admired him.

Midstream in his regime, the breezy, beaming Berlin of the 1920's, 1930's, and 1940's got to be a different person. What normally would have been a request from him became a brusque command. A few minutes of bantering small talk could be followed by an unreasonably sharp criticism. His normally temperate temper grew noticeably intemperate. His language, normally inoffensive, became vulgar. Associates, long congenial drinking companions, began to feel the bite of his tongue and grew increasingly ill at ease in his presence. They feared him. To some extent they always had feared him. Now they feared him more than ever. For a minor indiscretion the company's overall circulation director, Tom Buttikofer, was banished to a pointless post in England. Among subordinates, office politics became a full-time occupation. All businesses are rife with politics, from lowest levels of personnel to the highest, but publishing can claim the championship.

It is not possible to pinpoint exactly when, but it was as though Berlin had wakened one morning to realize the magnitude of his power, the wide scope of his authority and control in the Hearst organization, of which he had long since become president and chief executive officer and where his word was law; as though waking that morning he knew he could utter the name of any banker, politician, tycoon industrialist, and have instant attention; could call judges and senators and governors and address them by their given names, as they addressed him by his. He could call the White House and have Dwight Eisenhower respond, or John Kennedy, or Lyndon Johnson.

It was not a certain month, no one now can say it was in a certain year. He changed, and it was that of which everyone was aware. There were personal reasons that were to some extent behind the change; special problems, which he spoke of freely, with his children. They were constantly on his mind. He could be holding a conference; recollection of an incident with a child that morning would surface and the business at hand would be forgotten for the moment and the morning's anger vented on men gathered to meet with him.

No less than anybody else was I exempt from Berlin's altered attitudes and stormy moods. To me it seemed that evidences of anger were with himself at first; perhaps he had gone too far and granted me too wide a range of independence; there might be those who thought that in editorial areas he could not do as well without me. Called on so often, seen in his presence so much, I might begin to think myself indispensable. Thus there would be a belittling remark, a word of deprecation. "Since when are you such a genius you know you're going to pass the *Companion* in circulation?" Or: "How dared you change art directors on *Town & Country* without talking to me first—you don't own this company, you know." As though, with his knowledge, I hadn't been changing editorial personnel for years. Long after Franklin Roosevelt had died, and knowing I had been a fervent follower (though I did not vote for him the fourth time around), he burst out with "I remember when you used to be in love with that paralytic son of a bitch."

On the subject of Roosevelt, Berlin never ceased being apoplectic, convinced not only that Roosevelt had been intent on destroying the country but, more important, Berlin personally. What right had that man to clamp such rigid restrictions on paper supplies? The war would have been over sooner if he hadn't been so palsy-walsy with Churchill. The British offices of Hearst magazines need not have been so depleted of personnel. "There must have been a streak of Jew in Rosenfeldt," Berlin would say.

From the time I first met Berlin he counted a number of Jews among his intimate friends. The number grew as he grew older, which made even stranger his newly sporadic and startling anti-Semitic remarks. I never knew him to be anti-Semitic, any more than Mr. Hearst, who as far as my knowledge of the latter was concerned was without a trace of bigotry, though often reputed to be otherwise because he had had an interview with Hitler. I would myself have been eager to interview Hitler, Mussolini, Al Capone, or Bluebeard. But the magazine *Liberty* had printed excerpts from the diary of William E. Dodd when he was United States ambassador to Germany. Dodd made Hearst out to be pro-Nazi. Following demand for retraction, it was discovered that portions of Dodd's diary had been fabricated; the charge was found unfounded, *Liberty* released a statement saying it regretted the injustice done Mr. Hearst.

More fervid in denouncing Bolsheviks than Nazis, Hearst was never equivocal about the latter's persecution of Jews. On his part there was no religious bias of any kind. He had none. On that I will stand up and be counted. The properties he owned were staffed by as many Catholics as Protestants. As for Jews, the general manager of his newspapers was Jacob Gordotowsky, and before him Solomon Carvalho. Moses Koenigsberg had been head of Hearst's King Features Syndicate, Clarence Lindner of the San Francisco *Examiner*, Seymour Berkson of the New York *Journal-American*, Jack Lait of the New York *Daily Mirror*, Mortimer Berkowitz of the Sunday supplement *American Weekly*, Edmund Coblentz, Victor Polachek, Albert Kobler, among others. All Jews.

In the magazine division the situation was somewhat different. There was no Jew other than myself as editor of the magazines during Berlin's time and only one or two Jews in any other positions of consequence. It just happened that way. I never believed Berlin planned it that way or suspected for a moment that he would turn away from any person for a religious reason. That didn't stop him from being occasionally blindly sadistic. While sitting alongside of him in his office with Benjamin Epstein, an official of the Anti-Defamation League of B'nai B'rith, I heard him say to Epstein, "Is it true you fellows look after niggers as well as Jews?"

Generous as he often could be, and was, so often could Berlin be mingy. Unpredictable. A year following a verbal agreement that I would be entitled to a bonus for increased newsstand sales on *Good Housekeeping* he reneged, maintained the sum, some $35,000, was exorbitant and offered to settle for half. I refused and settled for a modest increase in salary.

The man who for so long had been moderate in all things was now in one moment the epitome of gentleness and in the next satanically wrathful. Outraged because I refused to discharge an assistant he heard was a "Commie," he threw a book at me. I threw it back. Both of us missed, deliberately.

The country house that had been so generously bought by the company for me to live in, I was then obliged to pay for.

Unaccountable exasperations and fitful sarcasms were frequent. "Watch out, my friend," Berlin said to me one day, "you're only a small fish in this fry." I wasn't, and he knew it. But he could say it and he said it. I was neither alarmed nor frightened by him, not then or ever was stampeded into fear of losing a job. Early in our marriage my wife and I had reached a clear understanding—I was never to stay in a place I didn't like, somehow or other we knew we'd be able to get along.

We came to an ugly dispute, Berlin and I, over the continuing presence of John Aloysius Clements. Known as "Honest John" because there wasn't an honest bone in his body, Clements, the magazine company's undercover man, snooper, spy, sneak, reported on company employees, with whom they associated, where they went, what they did. Just before I was appointed to *Good Housekeeping*, the magazine had been under attack by Rex Tugwell, a leading "consumer advocate," who had seized on the Good Housekeeping Guaranty Seal as a particular target, asserting the magazine did not in fact "test and approve" every product advertised in the magazine. The magazine made no such claim. It claimed to test and approve every product that was permitted to carry its guaranty seal. It had no facilities, for example, for testing automobiles; accepted automotive advertising, but automobiles were not granted the guaranty. Not once, however, as far as I know—and I would have known—did the magazine refuse to honor a claim made by a consumer against any product that failed to live up to its advertised performance. The crusade by Tugwell against advertising in general resulted in an attempt to have Congress enact a law that in effect would make the government responsible for grading and labeling all products. The attempt failed, but in the meantime the Federal Trade Commission had brought charges against the magazine. Clements, ruthless and stupid, undertook one night to break into the offices of the Commission in Washington to discover what its plans in connection with the magazine might be. He was caught in the preposterous act.

In years when manufacturers were not as scrupulous as they are now about the quality of their products, the Good Housekeeping Seal with its little star in the oval trademark was the most significant independent endorsement that consumers knew. The phrase "Guaranteed by Good Housekeeping" became part of the American idiom. *The New Yorker* carried a cartoon in which a little boy looks up at the night sky, sees a single star there, and says to his mother, "Look, Mom, God has approved Good Housekeeping!"

It should be remembered that Dr. Harvey W. Wiley, who had combined a crusading spirit with his scientific background, who had been chief chemist of the U.S. Department of Agriculture for thirty years and led the campaign against food adulteration, who was sponsor of the Pure Food and Drugs Act, resigned from government service in 1912 and assumed direction of the Good Housekeeping Bureau of Foods, Sanitation and Health. He remained in that post until his death in 1930. He set the magazine's laboratory standards, and they never varied.

The seal does not have the same weight today because virtually all manufacturers have their own extensive testing laboratories, and government regulations are more strictly enforced, but the seal served a public need in its time and there are countless consumers who still look for it and are guided by it.

After Clements' Washington misadventure I felt, like

others, he should and would be thrown out of the company. He wasn't. A few years later, with a man whose name I believe was J. B. Matthews, a reformed Communist, Clements set up, in the Hearst building itself, an espionage network, digging into the private lives of decent men and women around the country who had done no more than attend anti-fascist meetings. In his files were collections of faked facts.* He was a natural-born mudslinger and had his minions everywhere. "I hear you had lunch yesterday with Dexter Masters," he said to me once. I had indeed had lunch yesterday with Mr. Masters, who was an editor or officer with Consumers Union or Consumers Research and as honest as Clements was not. Ergo, I was keeping dangerous company! I protested to Berlin. "He's doing good work," Berlin said of Clements. I denied it, we shouted at each other, it was a sickening episode. For a while, depressed, I sought refuge in a cottage in East Hampton to regain some peace of mind; wasn't there a week when Berlin, as though nothing had happened, forwarded a note to say *Cosmopolitan* was in trouble again, he was sorry to interrupt my "holiday" but would appreciate my early attention.

Following another acrimonious dispute over what he considered an extravagant salary I had promised to pay an art director, he came jauntily to my office to say that John Cuneo, our printer, had acquired control of *Liberty,* was now eager to dispose of it, and would I dream up a program for bringing it into the Hearst orbit.† Such a program I did dream up, so much to Berlin's pleasure that he asked if I would be interested in a new bonus arrangement. I would not be.

How frequently large principles can be tested by

* Right-wing members of Congress received much of their propaganda material from Clements.

† In the end, Cuneo sold the magazine to Floyd Odum, head of the Atlas Corporation.

small incidents! An unresolvable clash came out of what seemed an implausible situation, a circumstance ludicrously petty. In an issue of *Good Housekeeping* I had published a poem by Sara Henderson Hay, a writer of verse highly popular and everywhere respected. This was it:

THE NEIGHBORS‡

But Jesus said unto them, A prophet is not without honour, but in his own country, and among his own kin, and in his own house. —Mark, 6:4

News of the trouble in Jerusalem,
His trial and the manner of his death,
Came to his own village and to his neighbors,
The people of Nazareth.

They talked: "His mother'll take it pretty hard.
She set great store by him, though I must say
He treated her, at least to my way of thinkin',
In a mighty highhanded way."

"Why, you remember the time, he was just a boy,
He give 'em such a scare?
Lost himself for three days in the city,
And never turned a hair

"When they found him, but answered, as cool as
you please,
He was doing his father's business, or some such
truck!
As if most of us hadn't known his father, Joseph,
Since he was knee high to a duck,

"And his business was carpentry, not talking back to
priests!"
But Mary, she always remembered it. Some claim

‡ Reprinted by permission.

She was a little mite teched (had visions and all)
Before he came."

"She was always partial to him; but if you ask me,
He'd 'a' been a better son
If he'd stayed home and raised a family,
Like his brothers done."

"The trouble was, he didn't use his judgment,
He was forever speakin' out,
Though many's the time I've told him: 'There's *some*
       wrong things
People just don't talk about.'"

"They say, though, in some parts of the country,
He drawed great crowds—five thousand or more. I
       don't know.
Here in Nazareth nobody'd walked two blocks to
       hear him,
And it probably ain't so."

"It's hard on his family, the disgrace and all,
And I'm sorry about him. I was his friend.
I liked him, you understand. But I always said
He'd come to a bad end."

Patrick Scanlon, reactionary editor of *The Tablet*, a periodical with wide distribution in the country's largest Catholic diocese, wrote to Berlin to denounce the poem as sacrilegious and demand that a public apology be issued.

Though a Roman Catholic, Berlin had no more understanding than I of the alleged offense. The biblical "a prophet is not without honour" made the point of the poem crystal clear. But I wanted a cleric's opinion and went to the Union Theological Seminary to consult Reinhold Niebuhr, who was professor of applied Christianity. Dr. Niebuhr assured me my interpretation could not be chal-

lenged. On his part, however, Berlin thought it prudent to consult Francis Cardinal Spellman, who declared the poem's reference to brothers of Jesus could not be tolerated; that according to Catholic theology Jesus had no brothers. "You mean," I said to Berlin, "that only Catholic beliefs are to prevail in this country? When was that decided?" Berlin said both the Cardinal and the editor were being narrow-minded, the best thing to do was write a short note of apology and get the matter over with. I said I was hardly likely to apologize for something I felt any magazine had every right to publish. "Then why not pay Scanlon a little visit," Berlin suggested, "just for a talk—you'll be able to handle him." I said if I called on Scanlon it would only be to *man*handle him.

Nothing was done. Not until subscription cancellations began to dribble in. Scanlon had printed an editorial in *The Tablet* telling his readers that *Good Housekeeping* had perpetrated an unpardonable transgression.

Berlin then not only asked but insisted an apology be written, and immediately. To stay calm was not easy, but I managed, and refused. "In that case," Berlin said, "I'll have to have one written anyway. I'll sign it myself." "Write that letter," I replied, "or have it written by somebody else, and I'll quit."

The letter was written, but because he had his own doubts Berlin had it sent to me before being mailed. I gathered my personal possessions and closed my desk. Having heard the commotion from her office next to mine, Margaret Cousins looked in, took in the situation, got her own things together, and we waved farewell to the Hearst building.

Next morning, Raymond McCauley, head of the magazines' legal department, phoned to say Berlin had changed his mind, the letter had been destroyed. On the day following, Miss Cousins and I returned to our desks.

In justice to Berlin it should be stated that several years later, when I decided to publish serially a novel—*The Car-*

dinal—by Henry Morton Robinson, and word of it reached Cardinal Spellman's office, Berlin was advised that Spellman was asking for publishing plans to be withdrawn. Berlin read the manuscript, concluded as I had there was nothing in it that could be construed as objectionable but on the contrary it could well be taken as a valid and favorable exposition of what goes on in Catholic ecclesiastical circles. Berlin so advised the Cardinal, adding that he could not be dictated to by the Church.

As a serial, as a book, as a film, the Robinson novel was a stupendous success, with never a disapproving word from anybody.

For more than a year following our publication of the novel, Cardinal Spellman and Berlin were not on speaking terms. As for myself, with Spellman I was a pariah. At length, however, he asked me to have lunch with him at the Residence. In the course of it I said, "Your Eminence, I have become convinced you would rather be an editor than a cardinal, whereas I—I would rather be a cardinal than an editor." Spellman chortled. "The difference is this," he said, "I could be an editor, but you—you could not be a cardinal!" We parted amicably and remained on friendly terms.

Some time after cordial relations were reestablished we learned Cardinal Spellman never had read a word of the story. A copy of the manuscript had been sent to him by Simon & Schuster, who were to publish the book. He confided to us that an overzealous secretary had read it for him.

From being an outspoken supporter of Charles Edward Coughlin, the pro-fascist "radio priest,"* Berlin became an outspoken advocate of the preachings of Wisconsin's Senator Joseph McCarthy. As his rightist enthusiasms developed, so did my resolution to be less closely tied to

---

* Coughlin was finally silenced by his Church superiors.

him. Except for special editorial quandaries he directed to my attention, we were no longer often together. The once intimate personal relationship was on the way to total disintegration.

After his original support of Franklin Roosevelt in the early 1930's, Mr. Hearst himself had become fiercely anti-New Deal. His newspapers, which not merely reflected his opinions but were under his constant surveillance, expressed no editorial opinion that was not dictated by him. His attitude toward the magazines was diametrically opposite—all he asked was that they be the best of their kind and that the editors be left to carry on their jobs without interference. Not once in all thirty-two years with the company did I ever receive a word of instruction from Mr. Hearst. The nearest thing to a directive I heard only as a statement attributed to him: "I do not expect my editors to support or even agree with my political views. I would only wish that in the magazines they would not openly oppose them." As the magazines were not of a nature to be politically involved, there was no problem.

But Berlin began to formulate his own ideas. "That fellow Hutchins in Chicago is a red," he said to me one day. "I think it would be a good idea if you ran an article saying so." I explained I'd never met Dr. Hutchins but knew a great deal about him, that he was no more a Communist than Berlin himself. In good conscience, I said, I could not commission anybody to write an article attacking the University of Chicago chancellor. Within a matter of weeks I was jolted to receive from Berlin a maniacally anti-Hutchins manuscript. On his own, something unprecedented in our years together, he had gone over my head in this manner. Through John Clements he had delegated Irene Corbally Kuhn, a free-lance writer, to produce the article. I read it, found it laden with unsupportable accusations, returned it to Berlin, saying it was not publishable.

Berlin sent it back to me. "Would very much appreciate

your cooperation," his memorandum said. "Please run this, either in *Cosmo* or *Good House*." I tore it up.

McCauley came to my office. "The boss wants you to use the Hutchins piece," he said, "he's made up his mind."

I told McCauley the manuscript was no longer in existence. "The boss has a copy," McCauley said, "and you have no choice. It's got to run."

"Not a chance," I responded, "and it won't be put into print by anybody. It's libelous, as a lawyer you know it's libelous. But I'm not waiting around to see—I'm getting out of here now." I closed my desk and started for home. Having heard the commotion, as once before, Maggie Cousins looked in. "I'm going home, too," she said.

Two days later I was called by Martin Huberth, who headed Hearst real estate transactions, was one of Mr. Hearst's oldest and closest friends, and the exceptional individual of whom Berlin stood in some awe. Huberth asked me to visit his office. "You know as well as I do," he said, "that Dick is irrational about Communism. He's made a poor judgment here. I've talked with him and the Hutchins thing is out. Come along with me and see him, we'll shake hands and make up."

Berlin and I shook hands. But between us from then on the alliance had to be considered abrogated. I had defied him again, and Maggie Cousins and McCauley were once again witness. But now Martin Huberth also had been a witness.

36

In the Hearst magazine firmament *Good House-keeping* was the bright star, in circulation and profits biggest by millions. It was never brighter than in mid-October 1958, when, after having served as its editor for twenty years and during that spell also on occasion had complete editorial supervision* of *Cosmopolitan* and *Town & Country*—after a total of thirty-two years with the company —I was summarily discharged and ordered to be out of my office by the end of the week. I had been summoned to Richard Deems's office. "You've wanted to know who's boss around here," he said, "and now I'll show you. You're through."

I walked the few steps to Richard Berlin's office, stalked past Lou Eden and Nan Murray, his startled secretaries. Berlin seemed not to be expecting me quite so soon. "I'm disappointed you didn't have the guts to do the job yourself," I said, "but had to leave it to a flunky." Berlin was no coward. At that moment he was. All he said was, "Herb, it wasn't my idea at all, but you have nothing to worry about, you'll be taken care of as long as you live." In that instant I hated him more than Deems.

An hour later, from I. S. Young, the company's chief accountant, I received a note he had been directed to write.

* Though functioning with full editorial authority for specific periods, I did not use the title editor, generally did not have my name appear in those magazines at all.

"I enclose herewith a check for one-half month's salary," it still reads. "Your name is being eliminated from the company's group life insurance coverage."

Beyond the half month's salary there was to be no severance payment.

No pension.

My employment contract would not expire for another year; nothing of what was due me was paid. Not then. Not since then.

Against the advice of my attorney, emphatic in his opinion a suit could not be lost, I refused to press my claim in court. A matter of pointless pride.

I was fifty-eight years old.

That no love was lost at that time between the Berlin-Deems axis and me may go without saying. For them I had been too much of a loner. There had been no intimation of impending action. When it came, it took even members of the Hearst family, as well as all segments of the publishing industry, by surprise.

William Randolph Hearst had died seven years before. Bill Hearst—William Randolph Hearst, Jr.—phoned me. "What's going on around here?" he asked. His brother Randolph flew from the West Coast to make inquiries. Both of them had always been kind to me.

Three years earlier Berlin had selected Deems, who started with the company on *Harper's Bazaar,* to be executive vice-president of all Hearst magazines. To relieve Berlin of miscellaneous pressures, Deems was now the individual to whom at least theoretically—theoretically in my opinion—the editors would report. Deems and I knew each other little more than casually but my independence was not less well known to him than to any other person. He considered it important to let me know he rather than Berlin was now my superior. I was as determined to have none of him as he was determined to have some of me.

It had been established procedure for editors to bring or send dummies of their new issues to Berlin. Henceforth

they were to go to Deems. My own custom had been to send them to Berlin's office. For Deems it was not going to change. There came a day when his secretary asked me to go to his office. "Just wanted to check through this dummy with you," Deems said, warmly enough. As I sat by his desk, he turned the pages. "I like this layout," he said. "I like this one, too. Now, over here—well, don't you think the title should have been on the right-hand page? Could look better that way. This next spread—say, it's nice, I like it. But this one here—I don't know, I think you might have—"

He got to the last spread. He looked at me. "What do you think?" he asked.

I might have said his comments made some sense. Or that I would give thought to them. Or that I agreed with one or two but not with others. I might have smiled and said nothing.

Berlin had usually returned dummies to me with a brief "Good job" scribbled on the cover, or "Would like to talk when you have a minute." His comments during a discussion were invariably pertinent. Though he possessed even less formal education than I and had scarcely ever read a book, his editorial intuition was extraordinary. He sensed quickly when a magazine was off course, could spot a weakness in a schedule. He knew when a magazine needed to be "fixed up." However offhandedly I might jibe at his comments, when I returned to my office I would mull them over, generally was guided by them.

But Deems? To me it was as though a minor-league coach were passing judgment on Reggie Jackson's stance at the plate; as though a bit player from the Borscht Circuit were dissecting the performance of Richard Burton in *Equus*. The callousness of it, I thought, the bumptiousness, the gall.

I do not believe an editor is vested with any divine right. When I have talked of editorial freedom I have had in mind a presumptive independence, which must be asserted within bounds and exercised with fastidiousness.

The editor is not inherently an opposition factor and has no grounds for chronic resistance to criticism or suggestion. What he must have is latitude for the expression of a personal sense of direction, the direction in which he believes a magazine should go. Management may be obtuse in demanding that a scheduled editorial feature be withdrawn; it has the right to make the demand. It may request that something be printed; it has no right to demand that it be printed. To make such a demand is to deprive the editor of his presumptive independence.

Where Deems was concerned with the dummy he examined, no political problem was at issue. It was a problem of understanding a human element—*my* human element. An editor's belief in himself is not much different from believing in the hereafter. The belief is in his bones.

So when Deems asked what I thought, I said, "I'll tell you what I think—I think you don't know your ass from your elbow."

There is no law that says an editor must be logical. If I expected my editorial authority to be recognized and respected, Deems had the same reason to expect his managerial authority should be recognized and respected, whether I cared for it or not. With me he must have experienced as many frustrations as I with him. But there were more substantial reasons for pique than those that had to do with the dummy. Under Berlin, budgets were conservatively established but never chintzy. Under Deems, when that task devolved on him and the ultraconservative company treasurer Fred Lewis, every item from postage stamp allowances to messenger services had to be scrutinized, analyzed, debated, necessary to be argued over. To get a paltry increase in salary for a secretary became a tortuous experience. "But she had a raise only a year ago—you're trying to knock the hell out of our whole salary structure."

A professional, experienced management knows that editorial budgets must be of a size consonant with a magazine's needs, but once a budget is set, the editor is under

the absolute necessity of staying within it. Whether with a trade paper's minuscule budget or a consumer magazine's munificent one, I paid well and was often accused by competitors, and management also, of overpaying and "spoiling" the market. But I had too much respect for writers not to pay the maximum of what I had available, in which way I was serving my company well because generous remuneration is almost the last thing an author will forget and it helps ensure loyalty where his future work is concerned. I was responsible to management but partial to writers.

To keep *Good Housekeeping* the unquestioned leader in service to readers, wanting the Institute to be constantly expanded, I had added kitchens to the original ones, built an engineering department; had designed and built a chemistry laboratory, a textile laboratory, a children's center, a sewing and needlework department. Among magazines, *Good Housekeeping* always had the best service departments. During my administration they were kept the best and made the largest.

Everybody knows when a magazine is losing steam, growing stale. The screams come from all directions. The time to be concerned is when everything is going beautifully, when circulation and advertising are satisfactory; it is then one must conceive a novelty, diversify, modify, substitute, surprise and startle. Previously unheard of, the introduction in *Good Housekeeping* of "take-outs"—special sections given over to a single subject—was one of that special nature: a thirty-six-page cake cookbook, a twenty-four-page sewing manual, a complete home course in manicuring, a complete home course in interior decorating. From twenty-five new hairdos to redoing a dozen living rooms, from transforming attics into playrooms on to a manual of table settings—such features were innovative at the time, invariably practical, of immediate benefit. The sound philosophy is never to let a reader take a magazine for granted; to have him or her wait hungrily for the next issue, to rejoice in the pages. When ideas cease to flow

freely, then is the time for the editor to lay off for a spell, go fishing, get lost in the woods, take on a mistress or get divorced, seek inspiration in drink, see a psychiatrist. Or be replaced.

The absolutely most important meeting a publishing shop can call is when its magazine has climbed to a new high level of excellence and prosperity. The two questions to ask are: What do we do now? Where do we go from here?

I was a confirmed reader of the comparatively new *Changing Times,* a monthly magazine issued by Austin Kiplinger's organization in Washington. For fifty cents a copy one received forty-eight pages of extremely useful information about taxes, education, insurance, banking, every subject that might be helpful to any household. The magazine carried no advertising.† Such a magazine, if made an integral part of *Good Housekeeping*—a supplement, in effect—would be a handsome bonus for readers and one which with *Good Housekeeping's* enormous profit picture it could well afford. By using smaller type and narrower margins I knew we would be able to get everything in *Changing Times's* forty-eight pages into sixteen of our own smaller-size pages. From the moment the concept occurred to me it seemed as constructive as any I'd ever had. It still seems so. I decided to call the supplement "The Better Way" and find a few youngsters fresh out of college to produce it every month.

In the sixteen pages the plan was to present an average of twelve separate tightly written short articles. A person whose interest might be in working for magazines like *Daedalus, American Scholar,* or *The Nation*—all of a special nature and small circulation—would not find absorbing what appeared in "The Better Way." But one interested in mass-circulation magazines would have a greater appreciation and for such I have selected a group of typical articles that

† At this writing the magazine is considering the acceptance of advertising.

we published, titles of which are self-explanatory: "When the Doctor Tests Your Metabolism," "Does Title Insurance Really Guarantee Title?," "Inside the Library of Congress," "Bargain Buys from the Salvation Army," "Osteopaths and Chiropractors Are Not the Same," "The Power of Power of Attorney," "Rating Bridge Players by Master Points," "How to Apply for a Fulbright Scholarship," "Who Gets the Rhodes Scholarships?," "When the Bank Bounces Your Check," "What Is a Mexican Divorce?," "If You Have a Joint Checking Account," "How to Set Up a Thrift Shop," "Etiquette for Eating Artichokes and Other Awkward Foods," "Landlord versus Tenant on Moving Day," "Good Jobs for Women in the Foreign Service," "The Assessed Value and the Real Value of Your Home," "20/20 Vision— What It Really Means," "Just What Is an Honorary Degree?," "Being a Co-maker Means You Owe the Money, Too," "When Your Insurance Policy Reads $50 Deductible."

At least three or four such articles appearing in each issue of the magazine were bound to attract attention. Most of them were timeless in appeal and could, if brought up to date, be valid today. At first the young editors Margo and Richard Marek began to think up ideas, joined later by Marjorie Fatt and Ben Srere, all supervised by Bart Sheridan.

It never ceased to surprise me that Deems did not instantly recognize the value of the proposed supplement; he expressed no enthusiasm for it. In any case, for the project an increase in budget would have to be forthcoming. I sought the increase, was rebuffed, but by consultation with staff found it practicable to reduce regular departments by the needed sixteen pages. "The Better Way" proved to be as precious an innovation as any in the magazine's long history, excepting only the Institute and the Guaranty Seal. It has been imitated under various titles by a dozen other magazines. It still appears in *Good Housekeeping*, though now reduced to half its original size. To this day, *Good Housekeeping*'s subscription drives are predicated prima-

rily on material that appears in "The Better Way." Deems
did finally find a way to express his appreciation. "That
wasn't a new idea you had," he said, "you cribbed it from
Changing Times."

What is no less important to know about editing than
the inevitable need for change and surprise is that few
ideas are ever original. Almost always they are and must
be adaptations, with new twists and turns, different and
changing angles.

From a friend returning from Puerto Rico I learned
there was in progress in that Commonwealth an experiment
with an oral contraceptive that was showing signs of success. I assigned our medical reporter, Maxine Davis, to investigate. The facts she collected in Puerto Rico were
astonishing. Here was an improbable development, something that would change the lives of women everywhere;
that could change the world. I was elated by the thought
that our magazine would be first to publish the story.

Management could not tell me what to print. It could
tell me what not to print. Deems ordered the article removed from the schedule, holding it would be found objectionable by the Church.

The Pill, still undergoing clinical tests, was years from
being made available to the public; but often since I have
thought that Miss Davis's article, had it been published, all
by itself would have entitled *Good Housekeeping* to a ped-
estal in some publishing Hall of Fame.

For all my differences with him, it should not be assumed that I saw Richard Deems without some surfeit of
talent, which was in the advertising area from which he
came. In those days he simply had no talent for understanding, much less inspiring, editors. About editors and
editing he had only superficial comprehension. He thought
he had what Berlin had. He hadn't.

The Pill episode was by no means the first in which
Deems had thwarted me. There never was a time, however,
when I did not recognize management's right to make the

ultimate decision—not, as I have said, about what to print but about what not to. Yet even in the latter context there are limits. I expected management to recognize those limits. If I did not suit management, management always had a prerogative: it could dismiss me.

Management exercised that prerogative.

Meanwhile, simultaneously, there was trouble brewing, big trouble, in the McCall Corporation.

It was quite a week for gossip and speculation in the magazine industry.

For thirty-two years Otis Wiese‡ had been editor of *McCall's*, the same number of years I had been with Hearst. After sixty-four years between us, both of us were at liberty. Out of jobs.

Norton Simon, generally referred to in the press as "the West Coast financier, industrialist, and art collector," had recognized in 1952 an opportunity to purchase in the open market enough McCall shares that might give him control of the company. Basically a manufacturer of food products, there was no reason why he should not also be in publishing, as later he was in steel, glass, and railroads.

Already in control of Hunt Foods, a heavy user of print advertising, Simon believed more manufacturers could and should be using more advertising in magazines despite the growing popularity and influence of television. After several years of trying without success to persuade the McCall management to become more publishing- than print-oriented—to be less in love with the giant printing plant in Dayton than with *McCall's* and *Redbook*, even though the printing plant produced the greater share of the company's profit—Simon decided to make a management change. In his opinion Marvin Pierce, president of the company, was too determined to keep putting most of the company's dollars and investments into the printing area. In place of

‡ He had become editor of the magazine when he was only twenty-three years old.

Pierce, Simon chose Arthur B. Langlie, who had been several times governor of the state of Washington. In Simon's judgment, particularly after inquiry about and meetings with Langlie, if Langlie could run effectively the affairs of a state as earlier as mayor of Seattle he had run the affairs of that city, it seemed reasonable that communications would be a natural for him even though he was without prior experience in the periodical field.

Wiese had been the beneficiary of all the emoluments and perquisites that attach to his kind of executive position. He was held in high esteem by the publishing community, and no less so by Mr. Simon. He was better known than Pierce and in fact had more power and prestige. But he wished also to be president and felt slighted when the Langlie appointment was announced—to some of his friends an understandable emotional reaction. Less understandable to all of them was his quick decision to make an issue of it. He resigned precipitously; in a forthright exhibition of personal loyalty, a dozen principal editorial associates resigned with him, along with the advertising director. Wiese had no other position in view and was not thinking of any. Believing the McCall organization likely to be in disarray without him, with nobody in it in his opinion of sufficient stature to run its biggest magazine, he guessed Simon would quickly reverse himself, pay off Langlie, and install Wiese as president.

Everybody makes a wrong guess now and then and on Wiese's part this was a fatal one. Simon was not a man to be threatened, positively not one to buckle under pressure. He let the resignations stand.

I received a phone call from Stanley Frankel, personal assistant to Langlie. It resulted in a luncheon during which Frankel inquired about my plans. Perhaps, he reasoned, I could fill in on *McCall's*, if only temporarily. Informed there scarcely had been time to think about my future, if any, much less to reach a decision about it, Frankel asked that I meet with Langlie.

The publishing and advertising trade press as well as the daily newspapers and *Time* and *Newsweek* had been reporting on the McCall situation with gusto—editors and staffs do not nonchalantly relinquish high income and job security. Langlie did not seek to minimize his problems; said he needed at once somebody who could pull the pieces together; preferred the editorship, and substantially larger income than I'd been getting from Hearst.

I inquired about editorial autonomy, was assured it would be absolute. "Does that mean absolute, or absolutely absolute?" I asked. Langlie said it meant absolutely absolute, positively absolute, whatever I wanted it to mean. As to editorial budgets, I was told there'd be no less money available than at *Good Housekeeping*. "You can set your own budget," Langlie said. My final question caused him to blink. "Does the magazine have a dining room?" I asked. It hadn't, and I said it would be nice if one could be installed, for the entertainment of authors and advertisers. "But isn't that awfully costly," the governor asked, "and much more expensive than taking them out to a restaurant?" I explained there was a superb dining room at *Good Housekeeping*, that I'd grown accustomed to it, that it was the best possible means for private conversation. There were few important authors and advertisers not familiar with the *Good Housekeeping* amenities. "Well, if that would make you happy," Langlie said, "I suppose we could manage it. But are you ready to say you'll join up with us?" I promised to give him an answer before the end of the day.

Because of the editors who had resigned with Otis
Wiese, there were positions on *McCall's* that had to be
filled. From *Good Housekeeping* came half a dozen of my
former chief associates, Margaret Cousins the first, then
Nathan Mandelbaum, the decorating editor, with arrangements made for others ready to follow. Which prompted an
evening visit to my home by the Hearst legal department's
head, Raymond McCauley, who handed me this letter:

> In appreciation of and in consideration for your
> 32 years of able and diligent service on behalf of The
> Hearst Corporation and its subsidiaries, The Hearst
> Corporation extends the following offer for your
> consideration and acceptance:
> If at any time in the future your annual income
> from gainful employment or employee retirement
> benefits from sources other than The Hearst Corpo-
> ration should not exceed $25,000, The Hearst Corpo-
> ration hereby agrees, after thirty days actual notice
> of such condition, to employ your services as a con-
> sultant at an annual salary of $15,000.

It continued:

> Under the terms of this agreement and in consid-
> eration of the obligations herein undertaken by The

Hearst Corporation, you agree that you will not now or in the future, without the prior written consent of an Executive Officer of The Hearst Corporation, directly or indirectly solicit the services of, or in any other manner cooperate in the hiring of, agents or employees of The Hearst Corporation or its various subsidiaries where such action on your part may result in their accepting employment for another publishing enterprise.

You will please indicate your intent to accept the benefits and obligations hereinabove described by signing below in the space indicated. Such signing will cause the contents of this letter to become a binding contract between yourself and The Hearst Corporation and will also serve as a release of all rights or claims of whatever nature which either party hereto had or now may have against the other except those contained in this agreement. It is furthermore expressly understood that each and every convenant herein contained is essential to the entire agreement and that, should any covenant for any reason fail to be performed, this entire agreement shall become null and void.

In the preceding hereunto, whereas, and wherefore manner did the great, powerful Hearst magazine management of that time seek to forestall further decimation of its staffs. It was tendering a bribe. Reference to "release of all rights or claims" was blatant sophistry; the company had no claims against me, it was I who had claims against the company for violation of employment contract. Aside from the impropriety of the letter, mention of an annual consulting fee of the size specified was insulting. If the amount had been five times the size, it was preposterous to assume I would dishonor my new agreement with the McCall Corporation.

It did not take me long to respond:

My interest is wholly and exclusively in *McCall's,* and I would be remiss in duty and obligation if I did not directly or indirectly make available to it—which I intend to do—every resource, including personnel, anywhere, at any time, on which I might draw. This includes all areas of the Hearst organization and its subsidiaries.

My position on *Good Housekeeping* was given by Richard Deems to Wade Nichols, who had been editor of *Redbook.* He proved not to be the happiest choice. From being the company's most prosperous magazine, *Good Housekeeping* under Nichols went deeply into the red.

If the manner of my removal seemed crude to me, only its timing was incomprehensible. No organization is big enough to accommodate two such diverse personalities as Deems and myself, each equal in determination, one to dominate, the other not to be dominated. There had to be a day when one or the other would have to go. But the loss of position was not the real affront, which did not occur until two years later when the Hearst organization published the *Good Housekeeping Treasury—75 Years of Its Best Stories, Articles and Poetry.**

Chosen for the anthology were 95 separate features, of which 10 had appeared during the tenure of Clark Bryan and Eaton Tower, the first editors of the magazine; 27 during the tenure of William Frederick Bigelow, my predecessor; 56 during my own tenure; and 2 (one of which I had left in inventory) during the tenure of Nichols.

In the introduction to the book, gratitude is expressed to Nichols (not yet two years as editor!) and to Bigelow. My name is nowhere mentioned. Not once. Not anywhere. I had been made, they thought, a non-person. As far as *Good Housekeeping* and my thirty-two years with the com-

---

* It was distributed by Simon & Schuster.

pany were concerned, I never had existed, though there I had spent and devoted most of my working life.

How many times have I looked at the *Treasury?* A hundred? I do not know. I still reach for it. I see "My Aunt Lavinia" by James Hilton, the first fiction I bought for *Good Housekeeping* even before I had full authority to do so; "A Trip to the Moon," the first story I acquired from John Cheever; "The Man Who Waited," the first short story written by Ketti Frings; "The Blazing Star" by MacKinlay Kantor. I see also the names of Shirley Jackson and Howard Fast, Santha Rama Rau and Edna St. Vincent Millay, A. A. Milne, James Thurber and Margery Sharp; Irving Stone, Philip Wylie, Rumer Godden—and the others whose work Maggie Cousins and I brought to the magazine.

Maggie Cousins' name? It isn't mentioned either. Not anywhere.

Regardless of disputes with management, every hour of every day as editor I gave to the company all of whatever good was in me. Publication of the book without reference to my name or Maggie's was the ultimate in shabbiness and indignities. It was published with the blessing of Richard Deems. Omission of my name and Maggie's was authorized by him. It was a tinhorn trick. Despicable. He will have to continue to live with that recollection.

It has been intimated a number of times—I have made no secret of it—that I have a quick temper, am not possessed of an equable disposition, never suffered from delusions of humility. One could say I had been crass in snapping at Deems as I did; that had I been more flexible I would have tolerated or laughed at his exercise at being boss, kept quiet, gone about my business, and given no further thought to his editorial inanities. Perhaps. Perhaps one could also say that Deems, had he been more flexible, might have lived with the knowledge that I was a cantankerous person, made up his mind that come hell or high water he would wear me out or win me over, thought that time might resolve our differences, and made peace between us.

Was Richard Berlin going to reign forever? Not quite. At eighty, his memory erratic and failing badly, the time had come at last for him to step aside. Which meant the day had come for Richard Deems to take over. To become president and chief executive officer.

In London I received a cable. It was from the new president and chief executive officer. "What do you think now," it read, "of your old Italian friend?" It was signed by Frank Massi, always my most intimate business confidant in the Hearst organization, who never had been in the running. It was Massi who got the votes that enabled him to succeed Richard E. Berlin.

After three years in office, his health and family entitled to more of his attention, Massi relinquished the title. He retired in favor of John Miller,† the other dark horse and my friend who had not been in the running. I was not likely to be displeased that Deems had lost. After all, the *Good Housekeeping Treasury* is in libraries around the country and Deems saw to it that my name shouldn't be in it.

In recent years Mr. Deems and I have come to social terms. We lunch together, we dine together, he has gone out of his way to extend courtesies. We talk about old times but not about old differences. We tell stories, gossip, laugh. And I wonder, and I wonder if he wonders, how things might have turned out, if . . .

However rancorous the circumstances that prevented rapport between management and me, there were full measures of compensation; the men and women who shared my daily editorial tasks were a gallant lot, proud of their magazine and their enormous contribution to its monthly production. I was a demanding and often quirky

† Miller chose to retire in 1979 and was succeeded as president by Frank A. Bennack, Jr.

boss. But most of the time there was badinage, joking, enthusiasm, a sense of excitement, an atmosphere of well-being. If I have placed stress on my angry moments, I should not forget they were followed quickly with an embrace and a gentle word. There was no reason for the staff to be concerned with or be privy to my wrangles with management. That was my affair and knowledge of it to the best of my ability I kept to myself, only in Maggie Cousins confiding evidences of friction.

The people in charge of the editorial departments were so capable they could function without being watched over or prodded; professionals, all of them, deserving of the peace that pervaded the copy room, the reading room, the production and art departments, the service departments and laboratories. On those fifth and sixth floors of the building there was an aura of contentment.

Of the men and women who were my co-workers I looked on all as friends and trusted them implicitly. Aside from my respect for them, they would be pleased by visits when they were ill, by small bouquets that reached them on Valentine's Day, and the little gifts distributed on birthdays and Christmas. They confided in me, many of them, their personal problems, marital and otherwise. Even now there are those who send holiday greetings, and snapshots of their families and pets. Each year, still, on my birthday, there are those who prepare a luncheon observance.

There is infinite kindness in the world and I have known much of it. Messages sent to my home following my dismissal soothed an injured ego. On the evening of the Hearst crisis day I was visited by Ralph Delahaye Paine, then one of the more intimate colleagues of Henry Luce. "Harry feels you should come over with us," he said. "Don't know in what spot but we're big enough to find something that will keep you happy." The same evening there were calls from two major advertising agencies, and on the following day calls from Max Schuster of Simon & Schuster and from DeWitt Wallace of *Reader's Digest*. Each call brought with it an invitation to an assignment.

Also on that day came a luncheon invitation from an old, very personal family friend. "I don't know what your financial situation is," he said when we met, "but in the meantime I'd like you to have this. It isn't a loan, it's a present with no strings attached. Keep in mind there'll always be another when you can use it." What he was trying to hand me was a check for $25,000.

During the week after my separation from Hearst, I received a scroll, and on it was inscribed:

To Herbert R. Mayes, whose dedication and loyalty to a great ideal has informed us all; whose recognition of the potential in each of us has given us new inspiration; whose leadership has inspired us to heights we would not otherwise have known. With us he shared his spirit, his heart and his dream. With love and gratitude—

There had been 121 members of the *Good Housekeeping* editorial staff. There were 121 signatures.

I didn't need to be told, but I knew Maggie Cousins had written the inscription.

If success makes even a fool seem wise, the success of men and women who once worked with me proves me very wise indeed. The fact that they would have achieved their goals regardless of any personal association with me is beside the point. They shared the responsibility for the magazines of which I was editor and I was the beneficiary of their skills. Wherever and with whomever they began they would have moored in the end in the same hoped-for harbors. Elizabeth Gordon became editor of *House Beautiful*, Arthur Gordon of *Cosmopolitan*, John J. O'Connell executive editor of the Hearst newspapers, John Mack Carter editor of *Good Housekeeping*, Geraldine Rhoads editor of *Woman's Day*, Nancy White editor of *Harper's Bazaar*, Martha Stout editor of *Junior Bazaar*, Lenore Hershey editor of *Ladies' Home Journal*. Richard Marek is head of the book company that carries his name. David Brown is one of

Hollywood's most successful film producers. A dozen men and women who were mere boys and girls when we were first associated have gone on to eminently successful, best-selling authorship. My pride is in what they have done on their own, my pleasure in remembering that once they were my editorial partners.

More than once I have been asked why I didn't leave the Hearst shop of my own volition; why, the understanding with my wife still valid that I was always to feel free to quit a job that didn't fit, I didn't hand my resignation to Berlin and Deems years before. There had been offers of positions with Field Enterprises. With *Esquire*. I may have been the tenth person to turn it down, but Huntington Hartford had asked me to become editor of *Show*. The editorship of the New York *Herald Tribune* had been tendered.

Elsewhere I could have earned more money, but my love affair was with *Good Housekeeping*. I felt married to it, needed no other magazine for mistress. It was not a church, had no pulpit, I was no preacher. We were not a citadel of higher learning, I had no academic credentials, and was no scholar. For me for two decades it was a multi-classroomed public school, with a roster of just under ten dozen resident teachers, and countless consultants, advisers, and contributors, and a syllabus that accommodated every subject under the sun, and I was principal of the school. We had millions on millions of pupils, some starting with us young and coming back term after term, finding us deserving of their attendance and attention. That was my beat.

If I could have been divorced from all other Hearst magazines, perhaps my days might have been altogether fulfilling. *Good Housekeeping* presented opportunities and challenges enough. There was no need for more. Among other reasons, I stayed because there was a special relationship with members of the staff. I sought no greener pastures. I knew of none.

On the other hand, why didn't Berlin get rid of me earlier? However useful to him, I was expendable. In business, everybody is. Perhaps he kept me on for deep-down sentimental reasons, recollections of long-past evenings when we sat alone in his house in Purchase and the one in Smithtown, where we talked endlessly of shop; in the Cub Room of the Stork Club, where we dreamed about new projects. Perhaps because of recollections of his early romances and the confidences he reposed in me. Not least, perhaps, because of my great fondness for the woman he married.

Of the innumerable executives reporting to him I know of no other who presumed to stand up to him so often, refused to be intimidated. From the beginning I think he had some grudging respect for my independence, a worker who sometimes caused him to have second thoughts. He may have felt the need for at least one occasional dissenting voice.

Well, one does not know. And one might wish sometimes that the final dissolution of the friendship, when it came, could have been avoided.

Two years ago, when I was dining in "21," Richard Berlin left his table and came to where I was sitting with Judges Irving Kaufman and Milton Pollack. He placed his hands on my head. "Just imagine," he said, "this is the best editor I ever had. He was my boy, you know, and then you know what he did? He upped and deserted me, just to go and live in London." Poor Berlin. His memory was in sad confusion.

But I was beholden to that man for so much, and loved and loathed him for so much. Even without him I would not have ended up editing a small trade journal. I'd have done all right. But what I will remember and be grateful for as long as I live is that he was first to open for me the doors to a world of which I longed to be a part.

38

The McCall editors who had resigned with Otis Wiese scattered, went on to other jobs, none comparable to those they'd had. "We were loyal to Otis," a fashion editor told me long after the event, "and we didn't feel we had much choice. As things turned out, it wasn't very good for any of us. If we had stayed, we could have managed—it wouldn't have been bad and might have been very good. Otis would have had Mr. Simon's support—too bad that he walked out and that we all followed him blindly."

Wiese himself waited around for editorial offers that should have come but didn't. He was too good to be marking time, but there seemed to be no major editorial spaces open. In time he joined an advertising agency in Chicago. He was not fortunate, later, in trying to be a literary agent. His hundreds of friends seemed in no position to help, or perhaps thought him overqualified for what would be available. They may have been reluctant to ask him to do something not up to the high place he had more than earned for himself in the magazine world. He was out of work and in some financial straits when he died. It was a tragedy. He deserved much better.

At the outset, when I went with *McCall's*, Norton Simon was anything but partial to my appointment as editor, his conjecture fair enough that a man fifty-eight years old who had spent most of his working life in one shop would be too set in his ways and too much Hearst-oriented to be effective.

What was I planning to do with *McCall's*? It would have been a fair question but was asked by neither Simon nor Langlie. I had been hired, I was there, they were stuck with me. For all I knew, they may even then have been putting out feelers to find somebody else. I hadn't much time. The staff would be restive.

Should the magazine continue, perhaps a little better but with the same formula? Wouldn't *McCall's* then be just one more also-ran? From a personal standpoint, had I taken on something that was hopeless?

Those were questions to myself, they were the gist of my problem.

I thought of two possibilities, each calling for drastic changes. The first was to make *McCall's* more of a reading magazine, to deemphasize pictorial aspects, virtually do away with large illustrations; to substitute very small but very elegant color decorations. Home-service features would be handled only in short question-and-answer form. Even fashions, I felt, could be presented alluringly without the traditional photographic splash. The overall appeal would be to women who preferred good reading, and a great miscellany of it, to elaborate art.

I was pretty sure the approach would work. I was positive I couldn't make it work fast enough; that it would take a minimum of two years. In the meantime, several hundred thousand readers might and probably would become disaffected; they would miss the lovely pictures by Al Parker and Coby Whitmore; the familiar food and decorating layouts. We probably would have to reduce our circulation guaranty.

Advertisers, advised of the change, might and probably would decide to withhold their orders. They'd sit back and give me a chance to hang myself. Norton Simon and Arthur Langlie might be looking for the rope.

It would be a tremendous gamble. I had no right to risk it.

The other possibility was to go all out in the opposite direction.

Advertisers and agency media executives almost never read women's magazines. They flipped through the pages for a cursory glance at their own and their competitors' advertising. Fashion and food and other home-service editorial material rarely interested them. There had to be a way of compelling their interest. The editorial budget was to be the equivalent of *Good Housekeeping*'s, but for what I had in mind that wouldn't be nearly enough. But maybe—just maybe if we got enough attention from the early efforts, maybe Simon and Langlie would be willing to stretch the limits. Simon, I had heard, was a man willing to take chances. I decided to go ahead.

It was no stroke of genius to conclude that the transcending thrust had to be visual, certainly in the initial stages—a grand, radiant, opulent, smashing look. Perhaps advertisers would then stop and look. I was certain that readers would.

I was convinced the 10″ × 13″ size of *McCall's* pages opened vistas for illustration and creative use of white space not possible in *Good Housekeeping*'s smaller-size pages. In the service pages it must be possible to present what had not been seen before in any magazine, not even in *Life* at its best.

There was no doubt about the man I intended to bring in as art director—I had worked with him before. But there was to be no need for a new art director; I found the ideal person—Otto Storch—already in the shop. Not then especially well regarded in the trade because of the prosaic pictorial aspect of *McCall's*, Storch and his assistant Bill Cadge proved to be an art team unsurpassed in imagination and taste. All the two men were waiting for were the challenge and the opportunity to show how good they could be.

Having chosen the course, it seemed appropriate the staff should have before it a resolution of intent, of what I hoped for, which was summed up in four sentences: "We have a tough road ahead, but if we can get the articles and fiction I have in mind, and make the magazine the most beautiful anybody ever saw, if we do the best we can, we may be surprised by how many people will like it. If you will work as hard for me as I will work for you, we'll come out fine. If you fail me, you'll be out of jobs. If I fail you, I'll be out of a job."

One of my first approaches was to the heads of our printing plant in Dayton, Ohio, where I said we must have full color on every page, and every page with bleed—meaning color right to the edge of the page. George Sheer, long-time manager of the plant, was derisive. Our presses weren't equipped for that, he said, so it couldn't be done. Within two months he had done it.

Long before our first year was at an end, the magazine became something of a conversation piece. Our first issue— March 1959—was perfectly ordinary but was a newsstand success. Governor Langlie was exuberant, unwilling to concede it might only be beginner's luck. In August of that year a series of children's fashion pages, with photographs taken by Bert Stern, brought a sensational reaction. They were and still are unbelievably beautiful. Circulation began to soar. Like *Life* a quarter of a century before, *McCall's* was on the way to making publishing history. News of its activities dominated the newspaper ad press columns. It was awarded medals galore, became the pet of advertising agency art departments because this was the kind of art treatment all good art departments dreamed of having a chance to use. To no small extent it changed the face of advertising. Even now, after twenty years, there are editors and advertisers who study those old issues and fret because the likes of them are no more to be seen. Nobody looking at the pedestrian *McCall's* of today would believe what it once was. Charles Revson, the dynamo who led Revlon, whose advertising pages were every other advertiser's envy, said of *McCall's,* "It's about time a magazine began to show some kind of leadership." Fairfax Cone, who built the Chicago agency of Foote, Cone & Belding, said, "I didn't think it could be done. You fellows have come through." The most welcome comment of all came from a top Hearst executive, and I promised not to identify him. "The guy we fired," he was quoted as saying, "is making us look stupid."

Norton Simon's support was limitless. When on first arriving I found almost a half million dollars of editorial inventory that seemed wrong and I decided to write it off, Simon said, "Why not? You can't make progress on old mistakes." Then, noting the favorable reaction of readers and advertisers, he said, "Forget about budgets, spend what you need, don't be afraid to spend." Three or four times during the first year, Arthur Winston, one of Simon's chief associates, came to see me. "Norton wants you to know he's backing you all the way. He wants to be sure you don't give any thought to money."

The December issue the first year established a circulation record for the field of which *McCall's* was a part. Just under two million copies were bought at the newsstands. Those who remember the issue hold it to be the finest Christmas issue of a women's magazine ever published. Many libraries, especially in metropolitan areas, have the old files. Skeptics can form their own judgment.

When I went to *McCall's,* the monthly circulation was five and a half million. In two years it went to eight and a half million; in advertising it became the "hot" magazine. Henry Luce declared publicly, "What is this *McCall's*—something to read or something to eat? It is both—it feeds the mind and feasts the eye."

When told I had flown to England to see Anthony Eden, that Eden agreed to let us have his version of the Suez Canal crisis but was demanding $300,000, Simon was curious about the possible benefit. I explained that if the feature was blurbed on the magazine's cover we might gain

a few sales in Canada but probably would experience a
fall-off in newsstand circulation in the United States, because American readers were not that interested any more
in Eden. "What's positive about it?" Simon asked, and I
had to say nothing but prestige, and publicity most of all;
that it was likely every leading newspaper in the country
would carry a story about it. "What's your feeling about
the price?" Simon inquired. I said if it were my money I'd
be reluctant to spend it. "It's not your money," Simon said,
"we need the awareness, you ought to go ahead and spend
it."

When I suggested we might create a stir in advertising
and publishing circles by eliminating the advertising sur-
charge for bleed pages, Simon urged we do it immediately.
It so happened that *McCall's* presses, because of Sheer's in-
genuity, were unusual in the industry—it was possible for
us to produce the bleed pages at insignificant extra cost.
The move infuriated other publishers, who saw some of
their income being whittled away. But it was welcomed by
advertisers. Subsequently, other magazines followed suit,
though it cost them much more than *McCall's* to do so.

When I suggested we could really impress the industry
by eliminating the extra advertising charge not merely for
bleed but also for full color—making it possible for advertisers to run their color advertising in *McCall's* at the much
lower black-and-white rate—Simon had doubts but urged
me to do what I pleased. Promptly advertisers who normally used only black and white demanded a reduction in
their rates. It was a ghastly miscalculation and there was
little choice but to announce restoration of the original
color rates. Without a word of criticism from Simon or, for
that matter, from the trade, which seemed willing to let me
make one gigantic blooper.

When I announced I was dropping "The Magazine of
Togetherness" slogan the company had spent a fortune in
promoting over several years, Simon merely said, "Well, I
guess your reasoning makes sense and that's your business

anyway." When told that Kenneth McCormick, the Doubleday editor, and I had agreed to split the payment of a million dollars to J. Edgar Hoover for his autobiography, he beamed. Maxwell Rabb, who had been President Eisenhower's secretary to the cabinet, made the approach for us. Hoover was receptive but said he could not begin until he retired from office. He did not live long enough to begin it.

Richard Avedon had taken some pictures of Twiggy. For two of them he asked ten thousand dollars. I paid. I was learning how to spend money.

David Douglas Duncan walked into the office with a portfolio of some two dozen photographs he had taken in Paris. He had submitted them to *Life* he said, but his demand for fifty thousand dollars was refused. Now he was suggesting I buy them for the same price.

The photographs were spectacular. I chose twelve. "How much for these?" I asked. "Same price," Duncan said, "all of them or just one of them—the price is the same."

We paid the fifty thousand dollars. Later I wrote to Duncan to say we had gotten our money's worth. At the conclusion of *Yankee Nomad,* his autobiography, Duncan reproduced the letter. Simon grinned. "If I could have you for a customer," he said, "I'd take up photography myself."

The idea of spending money that way wasn't painful but it took getting used to. After a while I found comfort in knowing it was there, to be spent as needed.

In becoming associated with Norton Simon nobody could have had greater good fortune. A self-made man, daring, sentient, imaginative, his gray eyes deep-set in a craggy face with deep-set lines that could crinkle quickly into a smile, I knew him as restless, mercurial, impatient, sometimes moody. Not especially articulate—participles left dangling, sentences ending in mid-air—no one could be in doubt about what he was intending to convey. Flashes of anger now and then, few but fierce. He had an occasional peculiar enthusiasm, such as for Kierkegaard. "You familiar

with him?" he asked. I said I'd done my duty by ample
sampling of Aristotle and Plato and their fellow Greeks,
that as far as Danes were concerned I'd settle for pastry.
Simon had humor. He laughed with me; times enough
laughed *at* me.

He could do a card trick. He drove his own car.

His joy on beholding each issue of *McCall's* was heart-
warming. "Might have been even better if you'd spent a little more," he would say.

On a May day in 1960 he was inquiring about the size
of the editorial budget. I reminded him I had forgotten
about budgets, as he himself had suggested; wasn't giving a
thought to them.

"The same with promotion?" he asked. I said we were
using full-page ads every week in metropolitan newspapers,
were sponsoring exhibits, an endless assortment of projects.

"I'm going to give you an order," Simon said, but before
he could go on I interrupted. "You know I have a reputation for not taking kindly to orders."

"You won't mind this one," Simon said, and went on
quickly. "Between now and the end of the year I want you
to spend an additional two million dollars on editorial stuff
—I don't know what it would be, maybe more pages,
maybe higher prices to get better features, maybe more
staff. Anything you feel will help the magazine."

"That all?" I asked.

"No," Simon said. "Before the end of the year I'd like
you to put an additional million into promotion. Take more
full-page ads. Use the newspapers *twice* a week. Think
things up—*you* know."

"Is that all?" I asked again.

"No," Simon said. "I want you to know you have another million—a sort of personal editorial fund. You'll be
coming up with some nutty ideas and I don't want you to
worry about them. Go ahead on your own and don't bother
me. So altogether that's four million extra dollars you're to
use before the year is up. Is it such a tough order?"

I didn't find it unpalatable. By the end of the year, because of the enormous expenditures we already were making, it proved difficult to spend more than a fifth of the extra allotment. From a personal standpoint I lived well, but to spend a company's money, other people's money, was not in my nature and Simon assumed I'd use reasonable judgment. Like any other business, publishing has one goal—to show a profit. Not necessarily the immediate goal but always the ultimate one. To be in charge of a magazine receiving great acclaim but staying in the red was not my cup of tea. It never was Simon's. A man who has amassed his kind of fortune could not be accused of rash extravagance. He was willing to spend lavishly, there had to be reasonable prospect of profitable return.

One way or another I did manage to get rid of some money senselessly. It was during a spell when I was infatuated with bridge. Though the world's worst player, I was disinclined to sit down to a game except with the celebrated experts, including Richard Frey, Lee Hazen, Charles Goren, Harold Ogust, Sam Fry, Jay Becker, Sonny Moyse. Those unfortunate souls had little choice—all of them on and off had assignments to write bridge articles for me. Their consolation was that in the course of an evening each would be stuck with me as a partner. But they had patience with my weird bidding and loopy play of the hand.

Founded by Ely Culbertson, *The Bridge World* was— perhaps may still be—a magazine produced for championship-caliber players. I became obsessed with the desire to own it, to have it part of the McCall Corporation. When I confided in Simon my intention to acquire it, he advised against it. "It's picayune," he warned, "and will take up as much of your time as *Redbook* or *McCall's*. But if you want to make yourself ridiculous, go right ahead." I was not disposed to give in quickly to a man so dense he could not see what a miraculous property *The Bridge World* would be for the company, so I bought it, moved the editor and his small staff from their basement quarters in a run-down building, set them up in handsome quarters in the McCall building, promptly raised the salary of the editor. Before the end of the first year the magazine had become such a headache to me that I had to get rid of it. There was no buyer in sight. It was necessary to pay somebody to take it off my hands. When I told Simon, he laughed. "Those things happen," he said, "but I hear your game is as terrible as ever." It was. I quit it, and haven't played since.

Simon was eager for us to install more and larger presses though already in our Dayton plant* alone we were producing every year millions on millions of pages for other publishers—magazines, complete from front cover to back, including *Reader's Digest, Newsweek,* the *Journal of the American Medical Association, Harvard Business Review, Mademoiselle, Glamour, U. S. News and World Report, Progressive Farmer,* a portion of *TV Guide*—all in addition to our own *McCall's, Redbook, Saturday Review,* and trade magazines. *McCall's* was the company's flagship; the excitement it generated brought in more and more advertising and more printing customers. The more we spent on the flagship, was Simon's philosophy, the more we'd make. Printing and advertising were then the source of the company's prime profit.

Our Dayton printing plant was the country's largest under one roof. With George Sheer in charge, it functioned wondrously well. A weekly magazine like *Newsweek* was by itself a gigantic problem. Because the magazine had to be on every newsstand in the country on Tuesday morning, last minute changes of cover and content presented almost insuperable difficulties. Yet our Dayton unions, for all their cussedness, never failed us. They did what was needed to be done.

"I think we can plan on going to fourteen million circu-

* The company had subsidiaries that printed books and catalogues and almost all the telephone directories in use from Maine to New York.

lation on *McCall's*," Simon said, having more faith in me than I had in myself. He disdained the announcement by *Ladies' Home Journal* that we were playing a numbers game, initiating a circulation race to the poorhouse.

On his own, Mr. Simon had arranged to have the Bowater Company in London build a paper mill for us in Catawba, South Carolina, in order to free us from the price bind we were in with such domestic companies as International Paper and Kimberly-Clark. The Catawba mill meant that for fifteen years we would have all the paper needed for ourselves, with a supply left over that we could sell to our printing customers and at a lower price than market. The agreement conceived by Simon made it possible for us to break the monopoly the American suppliers had held for so long. It was a visionary concept. For the McCall Corporation it saved millions of dollars a year. It was money saved that I could spend.

There was one brief difficulty. The quality of paper being supplied by Bowater ceased being up to standard and we refused to accept any more until improvements were made. A process server entered my office; handed over a summons. The McCall Corporation and I were named as defendants in a suit for fifty million dollars damages. Before then I had not been sued for fifty dollars and did not appreciate seeing my name in the document. I phoned Simon. "Take it easy," he cautioned, "and just see we have the right lawyer." I engaged one law firm, and then another. During conferences with Bowater emissaries prior to court proceedings I suspected we were making progress backwards. At length I called on a man known to be supreme in legal matters of this kind, and in that way Milton Pollack came into my life and has stayed in it. His arguments not merely caused the suit to be withdrawn but obliged the Bowater outfit to pay us damages in the amount of $100,000. Milton Pollack is now a distinguished federal judge.

In nothing that had to do with me did Simon interfere,

intrude, tamper or tinker, though he would say occasionally, "People are more interested in great art than most of us believe—why don't you make reproductions of the masterpieces, send complimentary copies regularly to all subscribers? Let's make the country art-conscious. We'll get our money back in goodwill and renewed subscriptions." The editorial control promised at the beginning was never modified. Simon was as quick with praise of my small successes as of my fewer larger ones. He was affectionate, challenging, encouraging. He had the daring of Henry Luce, who had poured more than thirty million dollars into *Sports Illustrated* before seeing it turn the corner.

39

I have known successful editors who managed to keep regular hours; who could adjust to a nine-to-five routine, no attaché cases to take home bulging with manuscripts for night and weekend reading. They were better delegators. Whatever flair a person has for editing, his work habits and life style may be different. I think mine were. I could read and edit, play cards, go reasonably often to the theater and concerts, travel abroad. I arrived at the office at eight in the morning, never later; was home for dinner at seven-thirty. Three nights a week I worked at home, at least until midnight. Saturdays and Sundays, though usually at home, were almost always workdays. My workweek averaged eighty hours.

One morning in New York in 1961 I was given an award. Norman Cousins, editor of *Saturday Review,* made the presentation. When the affair was over we went to the hotel coffee shop. I said to Cousins, not having it in mind before, "Have you ever thought of selling your magazine? If so, the McCall shop might be interested." The idea of selling, Cousins said, had not entered his head. "But I can't think of any outfit I would be willing to sell to," he said, "other than yours." I asked if he was serious.

We took a plane to Los Angeles. There was prolonged discussion, Cousins staying with an asking price of $3,300,000, Simon with a buying price of $2,700,000. No decision was reached.

On the plane returning to New York I suggested to Cousins that we split the difference and on landing at Kennedy call Simon to say we had a deal. Cousins wanted time to think about it. Several weeks later everything was settled. There would be a pooling of interest, with *Saturday Review* exchanging all of its stock for shares of McCall stock worth $3,000,000. *Saturday Review* would be continued as an autonomous corporation, with its own board of directors, Cousins to have a seat on the McCall board, I on the *Saturday Review* board. Later, in a statement published in the magazine, Mr. Cousins was able to report: "During the past three years *Saturday Review* has enjoyed the greatest growth in its history."

Two days after our acquisition of the magazine, S. I. Newhouse, probably the country's largest owner of newspapers as well as of Condé Nast Publications, offered to buy it from us for a million dollars more than we had paid for it.

Those few years of association with the McCall Corporation were, as Cousins has said, the golden years of his magazine's existence. Sometime later, after I had gone, the McCall Corporation sold the magazine to John Veronis and Nicholas Charney. Those two men changed course radically, the golden years were followed by leaden ones, more than ten million dollars being quickly lost by the new owners.

Sam Newhouse, my long-time friend, phoned one day to say several television and radio stations in the South might be available, though not to him because he already had the quota permitted by the Federal Communications Commission. I studied the figures, felt the purchase would be a desirable one, then consulted Simon. He heard me out. "Too small," he said, "much too small. I think we ought to buy a stock position in a network."

"Great," I said mockingly, "we'll buy NBC."

"No," Simon said.

"O.K., we'll buy CBS."

"Just goes to show," Simon said, "how sometimes a smart fellow can be very stupid. It's the one you haven't mentioned—ABC."

I wanted to know how the devil we or anybody else would be able to get control of a broadcasting network.

"Don't know," Simon said, "but let's explore. Why don't we begin by buying some ABC shares for McCall? Maybe a million dollars' worth. In street names."

It sounded harebrained, but I asked Simon's friend Gus Levy of Goldman, Sachs to buy the shares for us.

Within a matter of weeks we had them. And I said to Simon, "So?" And he said, "Let's spend another million."

In the meantime my task was to develop a program that, if we were to become involved, would be viewed favorably by ABC. The broadcasting company had several agricultural magazines that could be comfortably integrated with the McCall group. I worked hard on plans that would make sense to everybody, and they included construction of an ABC laboratory that would dwarf any in the country, to be used for testing products of ABC advertisers. There was to be an ABC guaranty tag. It was not unreasonable to suppose that films of the laboratory in action, shown often in brief TV spots, would quickly enable us to eclipse the reputation of the Good Housekeeping Seal. Most important, I thought, was a digest-size magazine to be called *ABC Reports* that would be prepared monthly by McCall editors and issued under the auspices of ABC. I put together a comprehensive dummy. Advertising was to be made available primarily to companies using time on ABC radio and television. The effort put into all of the foregoing was considerable. We wanted ABC executives to be impressed with our homework.

Though McCall's acquisition of ABC stock was in street names, ABC executives were soon enough aware that Norton Simon and the McCall Corporation were the owners, prompting Leonard Goldenson, ABC's chief executive, to visit with Mr. Simon and suggest Gus Levy become a member of the ABC board.

Meanwhile, continuing to buy only gradually so that the price of ABC shares rose in price only gradually in Wall Street, McCall became owner of enough stock to enable it, under ABC's cumulative voting rule, to acquire a board position. To make matters official, McCall made a public declaration of its holdings. I called on Everett H. Erlick, ABC's general counsel, to so advise him, and stated that though Mr. Simon was interested in being represented on the board, he hoped the relationship would be a pleasant one, wanted us to be accepted in friendly fashion.

Erlick agreed to notify his ABC colleagues, a meeting was held in the Pierre Hotel, with Mr. Simon present, Mr. Levy, myself, Leonard Goldenson, and John Coleman, the financial wizard on the ABC board and formerly chairman of the Board of Governors of the New York Stock Exchange.

It was not what one would call an unpleasant meeting, just a short one. By then, Goldenson and Coleman had concluded they wanted to be free of any relationship with us and did not, after all, care to have Gus Levy in the picture. Or anybody else representing McCall. "Mr. Simon," Coleman said, "we really don't like the idea of having Levy on our board. Or you. Or Mayes. Let me be clear—we prefer not to have anything to do with your company or any other. We are not interested in a merger or consolidation with anybody."

Coleman was firm.

Simon listened, smiled pleasantly. "Have a good day," he said to Coleman, and the meeting was over.

Coming up was an ABC stockholders' meeting and introduced at it was a resolution to eliminate cumulative voting. It was approved, which meant that McCall would now have small chance of being represented. According to a recently published book there were "vigorous protests from McCall-Simon forces." In point of fact, there was no such protest. In point of fact, the McCall-Simon "forces" did not bother to vote their stock. In further point of fact, nobody representing McCall-Simon forces bothered to attend the meeting.

After word of ABC's maneuver came to us, I said to Mr. Simon, "So now? What's next on your great program?"

"We wait," Simon said, "and no need to be sarcastic."

There followed an attempt by International Telephone & Telegraph to acquire control of ABC. The pot, one might say, had been stirred.

Rumor of an ITT takeover caused ABC stock to rise more rapidly in value.

The ITT takeover attempt failed.

But by then we had sold all our ABC shares, netting McCall a profit so enormous that I am overwhelmed even now by the recollection. We won a lot. By not bothering to listen to or look at the program so conscientiously prepared for it, ABC may have lost something. It did fine, however, even without us.

40

The resurgence of *McCall's* was creating havoc at *Ladies' Home Journal*. Worse, Curtis's *Saturday Evening Post* was being badgered by competition from *Life* and *Look*, even more by television. Matthew "Joe" Culligan was brought in as president of Curtis. He went in with a flourish, ebullient, effervescent, his black eye patch his perpetual personal trademark. He swept across the country, using his every skill as a salesman to restore the confidence of advertisers. He had a little of the madman in him, a plethora of drama and melodrama that was infectious. But his long absences on the road made it possible for subordinates in his organization to form a cabal, led by one Clay Blair, intent on removing him. Disaffection became rampant. Ted Patrick, the distinguished and disillusioned editor of *Holiday*, visited me, offering to bring that Curtis magazine to us, complete with staff, but I didn't feel it belonged. Doubleday & Company became interested in acquiring Curtis, finally withdrew from negotiation. In the meantime, Serge Semenenko, the Boston banker, had entered the Curtis picture, in an effort to salvage it.

Also into the picture came Newton Minow, who as chairman of the Federal Communications Commission had made his famous reference to television as a vast intellectual wasteland. Recognizing the plight of Curtis, Minow, though aware of possible objections from the Federal Trade Commission, induced Culligan to discuss possible affiliation or merger of the *Journal* with *McCall's*. Culligan and I got together. He joined me on a visit to Mr. Simon in Los Angeles; offered to sell the *Journal* to us. In between, in desperation, he sought ineffectually to arrange a merger of the *Post* with *Look*.

At five o'clock one afternoon Culligan sent a message to ask if on my way home I would stop in to talk with him at the Regency Hotel. Invariably, wherever he was, he had several telephones on his desk; when I entered his Regency suite he was using two of them. He seemed harried and harassed but came quickly to the point: Could we decide then and there on a merger of the *Journal* and *McCall's* and make an immediate announcement? I said I would not again go to Mr. Simon unless Culligan had written approval of a merger from his board. He promised it would be available in the morning.

But in the morning, on the front page of the New York *Times,* was a staggering report. Top members of the Curtis shop had staged a palace revolution, issued a "Manifesto." Culligan was being charged with mismanagement, his ouster demanded. For all his backbreaking effort in the undertaking of an impossible task, confounded by an overambitious and rebellious staff, he was obliged to resign. Mr. Semenenko asked for a meeting with me; wanted me to release A. Edward Miller, publisher of *McCall's*, so that he could become president of Curtis. I refused.

The Saturday Evening Post, once the five-cent staple beloved in America's households, floundered, collapsed ignominiously. Nothing recedes like success is an ancient but sometimes forgotten adage.

My association with *McCall's* and Mr. Simon was elysian. In retrospect, even probes that ended in deadlock or failure had glorious moments; negotiations that almost brought Simon & Schuster into our fold, discussions that almost brought us G. P. Putnam's & Sons, talks with Bennett Cerf . . .

An old friend, Cerf did not challenge my statement that someday, perhaps because of inheritance-tax problems, he might be under compulsion to sell Random House; but he could not abide the notion of being part of a conglomerate. "Anyway, what do you think you'd be willing to pay?" he asked. I plucked a number out of the air and mentioned twelve million dollars. "No," Cerf argued, "it would have to be fourteen million." At least it was a beginning. Several times thereafter Cerf talked with us; he and Simon took to each other on sight. "Tell you what," Simon said at our final meeting, "whether it's twelve million or fourteen million, or more or less, all that can be fixed up when you're ready. In the meantime, why don't you buy a few shares of our stock, and we'll buy a few shares of yours, just as a token of each other's interest?" Cerf called it a capital idea.

Two years later Cerf sold his company to the Radio Corporation of America for something over thirty million dollars.

Mr. Simon thought we might consider trying to acquire *The New Yorker*. "What do you guess it would take?" he asked. I made another guess. "Go ahead and try," Simon said.

I met with a *New Yorker* official. "This isn't the right time," he said, "but possibly later. All would depend on Raoul Fleischmann. Just don't breathe a word of this conversation or I'll deny ever having talked with you." So, until now, except from Mr. Simon, it's been kept confidential.

One day in California I brought together Mr. Simon and Joyce Hall, founder of Hallmark, the world's largest greeting card company. There was nothing in my mind but a name for a possible merger: McCallmark. It intrigued me. More I cannot say for the idea.

We had dinner at the Bel Air. Shortly Mr. Hall said, softly but tartly, "You know, Mr. Simon, I've never cottoned to the idea of having partners, don't think I would now." "You know," said Mr. Simon, "I'm glad you said it first. I feel the same way. I'm glad we've met, but you must understand that our friend Mayes here is sometimes out of his mind."

On another occasion, after pressure on Alfred Fuller, whose Fuller Brush Company I felt would be a cozy acquisition, I was able to get Mr. Fuller to agree to go to Los Angeles to meet with Mr. Simon. But before Fuller was to leave for the West Coast, Simon phoned me. "Forget it," he said, "I know nothing about door-to-door merchandising and you know less. You're still balmy." There were times when I thought he meant it, and times when he may have been right.

"You know," Simon said to me one day, "you'd better get over to see the Canada Dry people and tell them we now pretty much have control."

"Have we?" I asked.

"You ought to know," Simon reminded me, "we've been buying it."

No doubt of it. We'd been adding Canada Dry shares to our portfolio, but who on a champagne honeymoon with *McCall's* would pay much attention to a soda pop?

The work on *McCall's* was hard. Except for my family, it would be impossible for anyone to know how hard I worked and how much of my body and soul went into it. An initial experience was shattering. Soon after my first appearance there I asked members of the advertising staff to join me for a meeting and hear the few words I had to say. The food department set an inviting table, with canapés and wine ready to be served. Of the two dozen salesmen, only nine were interested enough to show up, the others out scouting for new jobs. I looked at the festive board and the few souls there to feast on it, and my spirits drooped to as low an ebb as I have ever known. I went home and sat on the edge of my bed, with my wife to comfort me, and wept. I don't think I ever felt so bereft.

The despondency that set in that evening was almost too much to bear, but by morning it was gone, my readiness for the job, the determination to lick it, never greater. What I had to keep in mind was Mr. Deems. What I had to have was revenge.

The editorial staff was outwardly cheerful but I had no doubts about underlying reservations. When I added to my brief resolution of intent the details of what I proposed we should do, and described to the editors the kind of program I had formulated in my mind, there was some uplifting of courage and there were occasional gleams of hope. Most of the staff began to feel maybe we could pull it through. Advertisers too had been in a wait-and-see mood. *Good Housekeeping* had been one thing, I had been with it so long, its position had been so secure. What was I, now more than twenty years older than when I began with *Good Housekeeping*, likely to be able to do with an ailing property?

Whatever was needed to be done, the staff, with Maggie Cousins there as solid anchor, did.

Simon's enthusiasm was infectious, his decisions instantaneous. Occasionally I accompanied him to art galleries. One day he asked Mrs. Mayes and me to go with him to look at the Duveen collection, which had been rumored up for sale. Then and there he decided to buy all the paintings, antique furniture, tapestries and porcelains, and the building in which they were housed. Art dealers and museum curators have called Simon's feeling for art intuitive. The museum he acquired in Pasadena and did over from top to bottom is a monument to his genius. His collections are among the most remarkable in the world.

I thought it would please our readers if *McCall's* could get permission to photograph and reproduce the paintings in the Hotel Plaza apartment of Chester Dale; paintings that had not before been available for public viewing.* Dale said he would grant permission if I paid a friend of his $50,000 to write the captions! The captions were terri-

* All of Mr. Dale's art is now housed in the National Gallery in Washington.

ble; they had to be rewritten in the office. When the feature appeared, the reception was quite wonderful. Equally gratifying was Simon's delight. When told the cost of the captions not used, he said, "Well, that's part of the risk, isn't it?"

On another day, as he sat alongside my desk, Simon's eyes kept turning to several small pictures on the wall behind it. "What are those?" he wanted to know. I tried to look abashed. "Oh, just some silly stuff—now and then I make believe I'm a Sunday painter and dash off a couple of things." Simon stood up, peered closer. "You lunatic!" he laughed.

For the occasion I had borrowed several miniature paintings done by Chagall. When Mr. Simon next went to Paris he met Chagall, which was the beginning of a happy new acquaintance.

The foregoing reminds me of an evening when my wife and I were having dinner at the Voisin restaurant with Mr. Chagall, and Mr. and Mrs. Leonard Lyons. During the course of the meal I drew a picture on the tablecloth, asked Chagall to add something to it, which he did. Then, my wife translating in French and Mrs. Lyons helping out in Yiddish, I asked him to add his signature, because I wanted to buy the tablecloth. Mr. Chagall refused.

For all the intimate alliance with Norton Simon during my editorship, my nominal superior was Governor Langlie, as considerate and gentle a man as anyone could know. Rabidly patriotic, there was always an American flag displayed in his office and a photograph of Lincoln on the wall by his desk. Devoutly religious, there also was a portrait of Jesus. No person could have been more scrupulously honest and sentimental. Only long, long after the event did anybody know that President Eisenhower had offered him a cabinet post, as Secretary of the Interior. Langlie did not want the man finally appointed to feel he hadn't been the President's first choice.

It was no idle gesture that made me ask every company

official who came to my office to present the same information or problem to the Governor. I had a strong attachment to the man, who stated often he knew little about publishing. "I'm just lucky we found you," was the generous comment he made more than once.

Suddenly he began to seem tired. His walk slowed. He was stricken with a heart attack. The world changed for all of us.

Though Langlie was able to return, it was in the undemanding position as chairman of the board. Simon asked me to take over as president and chief executive officer. For so long an editor, I knew how to build and manage an editorial staff. But full responsibility for company administration had never been mine, nor did I seek it. *McCall's, Redbook, Saturday Review,* the dress pattern division, the engraving plant, the several printing plants—altogether some 5,700 employees—an enterprise of that magnitude held no allure for me.

Respectfully I told Simon I had no desire to be president; that I was an editor with no ambition to be anything else. I named others who were better qualified. My refusal to accept the presidency was positive. Then Simon brought my wife into the act. The three of us spent an hour together. "*You* know, Grace," Simon said, "that Herb can handle the job. *I* think you're the boss in the family, so you tell him he must." Being—I think—a well-trained wife, she would make no comment. But Simon had made up his mind. "Herb is president," he said, "and let's have no more debate." There was no more debate. In the end there was no choice.

To give up editing was not a welcome prospect. I vacillated by bringing in John Mack Carter from *American Home,* giving him the title of executive editor of *McCall's* with the understanding that soon he would have the top editorial title. But for well over a year I served as both editor and president.

Among members of the McCall Corporation board of directors was Harold Williams of Hunt Foods, later dean of the University of California's Graduate School of Management, currently chairman of the Securities and Exchange Commission. For a while former Governor Scranton of Pennsylvania was a member, in attendance regularly but not very voluble. Another sometime member was Dr. Franklin Murphy, once chancellor of the University of Kansas, later chancellor of the University of California at Los Angeles.

Dr. Murphy has an inquiring turn of mind; enjoys investigating what he doesn't fully understand. When he and Mr. Simon and I were looking over our printing plant in Dayton, Murphy removed his jacket and on his back slid himself under one of the gargantuan presses. It wasn't easy. What Murphy expected to see, no one could fathom; and to this day I assume he is the only doctor-educator on familiar terms with a press from the underside up.

In the course of a board meeting, when problems arose that could not instantly be resolved, Murphy seldom failed to move we appoint an ad hoc committee. We had ad hoc committees up to our ears. I became despondent whenever Murphy proposed another one. I became more despondent when a fellow board member whispered to me that Murphy was being talked of as a potential candidate for the presidency. I do not mean presidency of the McCall Corporation but of the United States. Another board member, who overheard, whispered he thought Mortimer Snerd would be a better candidate. Given a choice between the two, I am positive I would have voted for Murphy. I suppose I always underestimated that man; now he is chairman of the board of the Times-Mirror Company.

I have said my habit had been to be at my desk at 8 A.M. Two hours later Simon would be on the phone when for him it was 7 A.M. in California. All he ever wanted was to know what exploit was being contemplated for that day, what mischief I might be up to. Although eight years younger, he seemed to look on me as half his own age. He worried about me. "You're trying to do too much," he would say; "why don't you relax and just listen to some music?" He had an elaborate hi-fi system installed in my home.

Simon's interests were diverse; along the way, Hunt Foods & Industries, Wesson Oil, Harbor Plywood Corporation, Northern Pacific Railway Company, Wheeling Steel, Crucible Steel, Ohio Match Company; but it seemed to me, except for his passion for art, he had no deeper devotion than to *McCall's;* that he was somehow bewitched by it.

Now, as chief executive of the McCall Corporation it was I who would do all the calling. The company had gotten to be very big. There were more and more shareholders. Every hundred thousand dollars saved or spent meant a difference in the value of the shares. I wanted to make no mistakes. With Simon's availability and advice I could feel on safe ground, but I had little ardor for negotiations with bankers and was impatient in sitting around tables with fund managers who held large blocks of McCall stock, was ill at ease when appearing before the New York Society of Security Analysts. Despite the incomparable assistance of Bernard Rowe, who was in charge of our in-company legal staff, I was apprehensive when involved with registration statements, sinking funds, offerings of convertible subordinate debentures. Balance sheets and profit and loss statements were no problem but they too were numbers, not words. My hankering was for manuscripts and illustrations and photographs and talking with writers and stirring up the staff and conjuring up projects for magazines. But the time came when I knew that full responsibility for McCall's editorial program should be transferred to John Mack Carter. After all, I had promised him.

On the first morning that Carter showed up for work, I said something like, "Jack, let's first of all take a look at these schedules." He said, "My name is John and I don't like to be called Jack." The impudence of the grits-nourished Kentucky squirt, telling me what to call him! Whatever he had been nourished on, John Mack Carter had guts. For all his ingratiating grin, he was tough. A curly head bursting with brains. Smart as hell.

Alas and alack for courageous, brilliant Carter. Nominally he was editor, but I restricted authority, stuck my nose in his plans, upset them, criticized too much, complimented too little. How the man took it, had the fortitude to withstand my ceaseless probing, has been, ever since, a matter of wonder. He accepted, without complaint, all my petty puttering around his desk. He should have socked me. He could have.

Of all the editors I knew anything about, I believe I had (and had earned) the reputation for being my own boss; for not taking instructions, to say nothing of orders, from anybody. From the time I had my first magazine, in the far-back year of 1920, I wanted to edit as I saw fit, with nobody looking over my shoulder. And yet, with Carter, I lost all sense of proportion, because my wish was to be editor of *McCall's*, not president of the McCall Corporation.

I learned that the Curtis company would be interested in having Carter† as editor of *Ladies' Home Journal* and I encouraged him to move over. In his place I put Robert Stein, who had been editor of *Redbook*. I have made more scintillating appointments. I sure have.

The presidential years rolled on and we had come to the summer of 1964. By then I had had enough of managing, and not least of our printing plant unions, whose demands were increasingly untenable. I felt then, and feel more strongly now, that as printing technology improves, with labor saving devices invented whose introduction the unions will protest more than ever, all publishing will suffer greatly, and the reading public most of all. Differences

† He became editor of the *Journal,* now is editor of *Good House-keeping.*

with our own unions seemed irreconcilable but I had no stomach for taking a strike. Whatever small satisfactions had been in the job had been drained out of it. In anything but editing I would not have protested being called a dimwit, halfwit, nitwit. As an editor I was moderately prepared to acknowledge peers, though not likely a superior. As company chief executive I pretended no modesty in assessing myself as precisely half qualified. Though the stock of the McCall Corporation rose from a low of 7⅝ when I joined it to a high of 38½, the jump was due altogether to Mr. Simon. Except that the *Wall Street Journal* had announced my appointment, the investing community would not have known I was there. What it did know was that Simon was there. Without his counseling I could not have survived as president. I had a mounting desire to be away from it all. My employment contract still had several years to go but I was longing for time for myself, more time for my family. I so notified Mr. Simon, my friend, patron, and sponsor.

Twelve months passed, they seemed like long months, a successor finally was chosen; and at the end of July 1965 all was in order. Including an office for me in the McCall building, where I was to stay, "just in case."

But another alas. There was a rapid succession of presidents of the corporation, one after another. Nothing seemed to be going quite right with the magazine. And, it seemed to me, Simon had lost some of his zeal for it. It may have been my imagination, or wishful thinking, but I began to feel he missed the way we had worked together and complemented each other.

In October 1968 he came to the new McCall office I occupied occasionally. He was his old self, restive, excited, storming. "*McCall's* is awful," he said. "Why don't you get yourself into it again? You can do it if you really want to." A call came from David Mahoney, who by then was chief executive officer of what had been the McCall Corporation, Hunt Foods, and Canada Dry, and had become, after the consolidation, Norton Simon, Inc. "What would be needed to bring *McCall's* back to life?" The same question was asked by Harold Williams.

Later I reported that over and above the magazine's then princely budget another five or six million dollars would be needed for the following ten or twelve months. "I'll do a few issues," I said, "set up plans for several to follow, try to find the right editor, and then be on my way." Though I wasn't sure where to.

Mahoney phoned promptly. "All O.K. about the money," he said, "let's get moving."

I was quite ready to get moving but after Robert Stein's ineffectual efforts the magazine had come, unofficially, under the direction of Norman Cousins. Brilliant as editor of *Saturday Review,* Cousins was not the person to run a women's magazine; understandably had not enough interest in the indispensable service departments. It could be difficult for me to function with him in the picture.

Despite its small circulation, *Saturday Review* was a recognized power in the intellectual community and Cousins as its editor had long been a cult with several hundred thousand readers unwaveringly loyal and admiring. He was on comradely terms with many of the country's educational and political leaders. More than a few executives in the Simon domain were timid in his presence.

Mr. Mahoney wasn't. When I suggested I would prefer to work alone, he went to Cousins' office and cleared the way.

It was in mid-November of 1968 that I began on the March 1969 issue—the first of the several issues that were intended to restore *McCall's* position in the publishing world. Otto Storch had departed to open a photographic studio. To be art director I chose Robert Cato. It was my good fortune always to have talented art directors—Gene Davis, John Zwinak, Budd Hemmick, Frank Eltonhead, Suren Ermoyan, Otto Storch; Cato was equal to the best. Because of the brief tenure agreed on, I had not wanted my name to appear in the magazine, and it didn't. But responsibility for what appeared in it was to be, and was, mine.

Instead of three or four issues I produced only two, for March and April of 1969. They were—I have no reservation about saying so—splendid. More than splendid. *Stunning*. Interested students can find copies in libraries.

A year prior to my renewed romance with *McCall's*, I had at Mr. Simon's request introduced him to Edward E. Fitzgerald, who was the executive in charge of the Literary Guild. Simon had heard Fitzgerald might be an excellent president of the publishing company but at that moment Fitzgerald proved not to be interested. Then, as I was beginning again with *McCall's*, it was Mr. Mahoney who asked to meet with Fitzgerald. The three of us got together, I sensed that Mahoney quickly would have his man in tow, left, and left them alone. In December 1968, Fitzgerald assumed his new post as president of what had been renamed the McCall Publishing Company and made a subsidiary of Norton Simon, Inc. On the day of his arrival I said he might well wish to take for himself the authority I had assumed for the magazine; that I would gratefully hand everything over to him immediately.

Fitzgerald said it was vital for his peace of mind that I fulfill my commitment, he would not wish me to do otherwise. I agreed to stay on for four months but no longer. A week later, Fitzgerald had changed his mind. I received from him a memorandum in which he stressed his desire for the gift of independence; declared his intention to rely on the editors "to electrify the magazine and make it exciting and successful with their ideas and their imagination and their energies"—but without the additional budget that had been approved.

"I hope you are successful," I said in my response, "but in this valedictory must say I think you have an impossible dream and are expecting an unrealizable miracle. Without the kind of thinking, encouragement, stimulation, and willingness to invest that we used to get from Norton Simon, I don't believe the job can be done. Returning to the former formula, as you propose, won't do the trick. Over a long period there could be some improvement. But there isn't time enough. In view of the current circulation problems and the diminishing advertising volume, there simply isn't time. There isn't time for anything but the drastically dramatic."

In any enterprise there is a charisma in being first, but there is no disgrace in being second or even third. Some magazines not in the forefront of their field are the most successful financially. It is no dark secret that circulation is a commodity, that it can be bought. If a magazine is superior editorially, its owners can be right in believing greater circulation, even if acquired uneconomically, will invite greater volume of advertising at a higher rate that justifies the drive for numbers. If a magazine is not superior in quality, the cost of added circulation is beyond recapture. Unlike *McCall's*, whose editorial package made possible by Mr. Simon took it to a pinnacle, less qualified magazines sometimes put fortunes into circulation drives for no reason other than to keep up with the competitive magazine Joneses.

Sometimes it is easier to reach the top than to stay there. A change of editors or of editorial program that misfires can result in near catastrophe. Circulation guaranties must be reduced. No magazine stays on top forever. To know when to retreat and to dare to retreat is publishing virtue. To retrench for the single purpose of saving money is publishing vice.

Except for the disenchanting prospect of less often seeing Simon and Mahoney, my final departure from *McCall's* seemed like heaven. My wife and I thought it might be exhilarating to live in London for six months. We packed and went off.

When word came to me that Fitzgerald had selected Shana Alexander to edit *McCall's*, I sent him a congratulatory cable saying it seemed a most imaginative appointment. When he forwarded a copy of her first issue, saying it apparently was on the right track but undoubtedly would be improved, I wrote promptly to go on record; said I did not have to wait for a second issue, or a twenty-second, that one could tell already that Shana Alexander, whatever her other virtues, was without qualification to be editor.

I could easily have been wrong, but Shana Alexander didn't last long. Neither did her able successor, Pat Carbine, who resigned. Nor did Fitzgerald. Miss Alexander went back to her wonderful professional writing, Miss Carbine became successful head of the magazine *Ms.*, Fitzgerald returned to the field in which he is preeminently the expert, as president of the Book-of-the-Month Club.

By then Mr. Simon had gotten deep into other interests; had sold his NSI holdings. David Mahoney, endorsed by Norton Simon in his meteoric rise to the top of the conglomerate, came to the best of all possible conclusions, that magazines with their idiosyncratic problems no longer had a natural place in the kind of international structure he was envisioning and that soon was to embrace Avis, Max Factor, Halston, Orlane, and Somerset Imports with its wines, Johnnie Walker scotch, Hine cognac, and Tanqueray gin. On favorable terms he sold *Saturday Review* to John Veronis and Nicholas Charney. Similarly he sold *McCall's* and *Redbook* and the several printing facilities to others. He washed his hands of publishing. In many ways it was the end of an era.

It was the end of an era, and I knew there could be no inducement attractive enough to make me work again at a regular job. I had done as well as I could and know clearly what I wish I'd been able to do better. I have enough friends, a few new ones but mostly those from far, far back. Between the McCall era end and now, more than ten years have gone by, and I have passed into the halting pilgrimage known as old age without feeling old. Except when my children were very young, I have had no fear of death. Without being devout, I have been in my way religious, still saying at bedtime prayers taught me in childhood. I am writing this page on December 24, 1979; thus my Grace and I have been married for forty-nine years and eighteen days. I've been lucky.

When I was a young man and vainly ambitious to meet at least once all the editors still around, one of those I called on was Benjamin Hampton, who for some years had run his own *Hampton's Magazine* and done handsomely with it. When I saw him he had been dawdling with his autobiography, for more than two years he said, and now was about to give up on it. "Too much 'I,' 'Me,' and 'Mine,'" he said. Right now I could say the same. However . . .

Somewhere I mentioned A. A. Milne but did not say his first literary effort, *Lovers in London,* was done in by a leading critic with the line "The only readable part of this book is the title." I wondered how Milne was able to go on to create a Christopher Robin and I was planning to talk about discouragements overcome by other authors. Certainly could have been more interesting than listing authors' pseudonyms!

Tom Jones and *Tristram Shandy* put me to sleep. I wanted to dare say that. Now I've said it.

Henry James's *Turn of the Screw*, often championed as the best of all ghost stories, struck me as an interminable bore. I wanted to dare say that and now I've said it.

Willa Cather's *A Lost Lady* is one of the greatest of short novels, along with Richard Hughes's *High Wind in Jamaica,* Thornton Wilder's *Bridge of San Luis Rey,* Edith

Wharton's *Ethan Frome*, and, yes, Henry James's "Aspern Papers." I wanted to say that.

There was a time when people tried to name the one book—if they could have only one—they'd care to take along to the proverbial desert island. My choice was William Walsh's *Handy-Book of Literary Curiosities*. I was planning to say how frequently I became the life of the party by quoting copiously from that book. I should have given credit more often to Mr. Walsh.

There was another time when, with a psychoanalyst present, a group of us was asked to write down the titles of the first six books that came to mind. My list said *Count of Monte Cristo, Robinson Crusoe, Don Quixote, Lord Jim, Last of the Mohicans,* and *Adam Bede*. The analyst said the main characters in all those books were men and that it showed I hated being editor of women's magazines. He was crazy.

Several times I thought of *The Little Review*, celebrated as something of a milestone in literary circles in its day, which was between World War I and the market crash of 1929; thought of it not because I read it, I didn't, but because of what was said about it, that it never paid its contributors, discovered authors but only a minuscule audience.

When I mentioned Frances Parkinson Keyes, I intended to note that she invented the idea of the little flag with the gold star in it as a symbol of remembrance for a loved one lost in war; and that I published her *Joy Street*, a good novel. In mentioning the editor of *Godey's Lady's Book* I forgot to say that because of her propaganda we have Thanksgiving as a national holiday.

I was to talk of the Magazine Publishers' Association and the annual Henry Johnson Fisher Award. It will hold to another time, and I will only say here that half a dozen women editors were around who deserved the award more than half a dozen of the men who received it. No woman has ever received it, which I think is ridiculous.

I hoped to write a chapter about William Holmes McGuffey and his *Eclectic Readers* and explain why I made a study of the books and the influence they wielded on several generations of Americans; and another about *Ken* and *Coronet,* the *Golden Book* and *Encore,* four magazines I hoped would have a longer life; of my attempt that failed to have "God Bless America" replace "The Star-Spangled Banner" as our national anthem; of the terrifying account by General Leslie Groves that we published in *Good Housekeeping* of what New York would look like if struck by a single atomic bomb.

I talked too much of stories Maggie Cousins and I published and said nothing or not enough of the memorable ones that once upon a time ran in *Mademoiselle, Kenyon Review, Esquire, Harper's Bazaar,* and a dozen others. Those magazines called for more attention than I have accorded them.

I intended to talk about currently excellent magazines that got their start by being given away free, one of them *Woman's Day,* originally a single-page bulletin called *A & P Menus,* distributed to customers of the A & P stores. Another of the same genre, *Family Circle,* was originally distributed to customers of the Piggly Wiggly stores. Both magazines sell more than eight million copies per issue, all of which are bought for full price from supermarket racks. Other magazines I intended to talk about were those created by department stores; *Charm,* for example, by Bamberger's (it was later incorporated into *Glamour*), and *Everybody's,* by Wanamaker's.

As much or more has been omitted in these pages as has been put in. Either way, I don't suppose it matters, memory never stops feeding on itself, there is a great deal gone by that comes back to mind, and time and space are running short.

42

"Have you ever thought of living in London?" The hasty negative response given to John Bainbridge, who had asked the question only a few months earlier, proved to be somewhat wrong. For suddenly, after having been only an occasional visitor, and then always in connection with editorial errands, a longer London sojourn seemed a not melancholy prospect. "What would you think of spending six months there?" I asked my wife. "Couldn't hurt," she said.

We stayed on not for six months but for more than six years, for Americans the most auspicious six years England had known since the end of the war in 1945. Nothing was expensive. Everybody was courteous. The Labour government gave way to the Conservative, and nothing was different. If a visitor murmured a word about lessened amenities, it was more in humor than anger: on winter nights maids no longer placed hot stones under the covers of a bed to warm the sheets! One could get by.

Late on the evening before my departure for London, David Mahoney had come to have supper with me, a very special Irish sentimental gesture. On no visit to London did he or Mr. Simon fail to send word so that we could have breakfast or dinner together.

On the morning of sailing—our younger daughter along to help us get settled abroad—members of our little family, and friends, were at the pier to see us off. As the ship passed the Statue of Liberty, I gave a military salute. "Be

back before you know it," I thought. After debarking at
Southampton, then taking the train to Waterloo Station,
Mark Goulden and his wife, Jane, old friends, waiting to
greet us, we were there.

A new kind of life lay straight ahead. Leisure. Total
freedom. I would be an editor at large, in the clear, on the
loose.

London is a city to get cheerfully lost in; to take a bus,
any bus, sit on the upper deck and puff at a pipe, ride to
the end of the line, get off, begin to amble, take hours to
find the way back. It was London with everything intact,
better than as advertised in the guide books. All the pan-
oply and pageantry, which I loved. Our home became a
kind of auxiliary embassy, so many of the people we had
known at home, publishing and advertising friends, and
many strangers, stopping in to talk and have tea. I began to
like tea.

"Mayes is living in the most magnificent flat in London,
like a goddamned lord," a newspaperman wrote. It was a
long way from being true but also a long way from being
altogether wrong. I had purchased the expansive flat—four
bathrooms, in *England,* where almost a third of the homes
had no bathroom at all!—for a preposterously low price,
with monthly charges for maintenance, real estate taxes,
electricity and water also preposterously low. We had the
most efficient Portuguese couple for household help, full-
time, breakfast through dinner, to whom we paid less
a month than we now pay for a part-time maid.

The British were attentive and hospitable, invitations
to their homes frequent. Nobody could have been kinder
than Ben McPeake, the doughty Irish head of Hearst properties in England. Within hours after Neil Armstrong and
Edwin Aldrin set foot on the moon—"One small step for
man, one giant leap for mankind"—Americans were being
hailed on the streets, congratulations pouring forth, as
though we had been part of the exploit. Of the magazines I
had edited, *McCall's,* because of the publicity given it at

home, was the one with which I was usually identified.
Local magazine and newspaper editors became hosts.
There were invitations to take part in radio and television
broadcasts. The Australian Rupert Murdoch, most dynamic
of publishers in England, came to call: "Just want to pick
your brains a little, if you don't mind." The Bank of England permitted me to "come in and have a look around,
we're sure you won't steal anything."

To the Society of Authors—founded by Walter Besant,
Tennyson the first president,* Oscar Wilde, after he went
to prison in 1895, expelled, "a piece of administrative
panic," the Society says now, "and best forgotten"—I made
regular visits. In no small part because I never accepted a
fee, I was a frequent speaker at clubs in the city, in Zurich,
Brussels, Paris. I found pleasure in writing the monthly
"London Letter" for *Saturday Review*. In Bath, where
Mrs. Mayes suffered a serious accident, an ambulance arrived speedily, there was professional attention from doctors and nurses. "I'd like to pay for these services," I said,
"I should, and I'm able to." "Thanks," the hospital adminis-
trator said, "but we don't do things that way here." There
was no charge, as there isn't—or then wasn't—for any for-
eigner visiting England.

It was not the London of Addison and Steele, of Swift
and Congreve, but I could pay my respects to them in
Westminster Abbey, as to Spenser and Browning in Poets'
Corner there. Not then Samuel Johnson's kind of city but I
could go to his home in Gough Square, where he had compiled his dictionary. No longer the land of William Pitt and
Gladstone, I had access to the home they occupied in St.
James's Square when prime ministers. It was hardly the
London of Disraeli but I could wander through Hughen-
den Manor, his home in Beaconsfield. In Downing Street I
could stand before No. 10 and marvel that in so small a
place so much history had been made. In Highgate Ceme-

---

* Later presidents included Thomas Hardy, James Barrie, John
Masefield, George Meredith.

tery I could see the graves of men and women on whose
books my mind had been fed, and the hundreds of stones
saying "Lost at sea" and "Safe anchorage at last," because
England was always big on sailors; the resting place of
Ellen Wood, whose *East Lynne* I had once cried over, and
at the top of the steep hill there I saw the catacombs, one
crypt holding the remains of Radclyffe Hall, who had covered the once-startling lesbian theme in her *Well of Loneliness*. Conan Doyle also was long dead but I could become
a member of the Sherlock Holmes Society. For days on end
I sat in Old Bailey, the great criminal court, and in the
Royal Courts of Justice, the judges and lawyers in traditional wigs and robes. I could not walk in Curzon Street
without thinking how Becky Sharp had lived there. I came
to know the ins and outs of St. Paul's Cathedral, where
Wren and Nelson and Wellington are buried. I found proceedings in both houses of Parliament absorbing. At each
summer's end I went to the Prom in Royal Albert Hall to
hear the younger generation, despite empire and glory departed, cheer wildly the playing of "Rule, Britannia." I
joined the London Library, founded by Thomas Macaulay,
and the Reform Club, where I had to swear to uphold the
Reform Act of 1832, though my friend and sponsor Herbert Van Thal could not remember the meaning of the law.
I sat at the table-desk in the library where Karl Marx, so
they told me, wrote *Das Kapital*. That library, in the British
Museum, with its round reading room and glorious dome
("readers may not chew gum, or lay any book face down-
ward when open")—with the necessary pass I could enter at
will and while waiting for books to be delivered, roam
around and be dizzied by the Magna Carta and the Rosetta
stone, the Elgin Marbles from Greece that the British had
"bought and paid for," the original letters of the famous,
the signature of Shakespeare, the diaries of Samuel Pepys
in shorthand, the manuscript of *Alice's Adventures in Wonderland*, the work of Shelley and Milton and Burns. I came
to know every art gallery, the place where Florence Night-

ingale had lived, and Charles Dickens' house on Doughty Street, where he had written *Oliver Twist*. More than most natives I attended performances at the Royal Festival Hall, Royal Albert Hall, the Royal Opera House, the theaters. Walked along the Thames, mingled with Arabs, Chinese, Indians, Pakistanis. Like tourists, but more often, I rambled on Saturdays around the stalls and pushcarts in Portobello Road, sometimes on a Sunday watched the baseball game played in the area in Hyde Park "liberated" by Americans for themselves.

———— Six years, plus! Never once feeling blasé by the sight of the Changing of the Guard at Buckingham Palace, the resplendent Horse Guards in Whitehall, the handsomely accoutered soldiers straight and stern and uncommunicative in their sentry boxes, the Ceremony of the Keys at the Tower of London at night—the Tower, where Henry VIII had two of his wives beheaded and where the two little princes, Edward V, thirteen, and Richard Plantagenet, eleven, had been murdered by order of Richard III in 1483; every June the Trooping the Colour on the Queen's official birthday, every November the Lord Mayor's Parade, every day the striking of the hour by Big Ben. On a January 30 I was at Charing Cross, where prayers were said for Charles I who on that date in 1649 had been sent to the gallows by the forebears of the very people now on hand to honor his memory. The arrival of foreign dignitaries was signaled by the booming of cannon in Hyde Park; the cannons boomed on birthdays of members of the Royal Family. Headed by the Queen riding in the gilded State Coach, escorted by the Household Cavalry and Yeomen of the Guard, a grand procession starting at the Palace would march its way to the House of Commons for the reconvening of Parliament. It was inspiring to motor along country roads and see the scenery unobstructed. "Do not declare too passionately how much Americans love their landscape," Alistair Cooke chided in an address to American students some thirty years ago, "until you have looked at a bill passed with little fanfare by Parliament and which makes it an illegal act to put up an advertising sign or billboard anywhere in the open countryside of Britain. You are going to know a generation of Britons who will soon look on billboard advertising outside towns as a rude obscenity, like spitting in church."

Thanks to press attaché Gene Rosenfeld I could visit with Walter Annenberg, old magazine business acquaintance, newly appointed U.S. ambassador; with John Minnock, passing as embassy Legal Adviser, in fact head of FBI operations there. When I lost some valuable papers in Paris it was Peter Skoufis, Counselor of the Embassy, who through one phone call to the Paris police had them found and returned.

Like all Americans who go there, I was smitten by the roomy taxis, the friendly pubs and spacious parks—St. James's in particular—by the Loyal Toast proposed at almost every luncheon and dinner, after which, with the chair declaring, "My lords and ladies, ladies and gentlemen, you may now smoke," I could light my pipe.

Brighton, Oxford, Cambridge—I hadn't known Cambridge was named after the river Cam that runs along it— and Stratford-on-Avon, other little towns, Coventry, whose people and cathedral were destroyed by the German Luftwaffe, I went to see them all. I remembered some of Mencken's *American Language,* and learned to pronounce Beauchamp as *Beetcham,* Magdalen as *Maudlen,* Cholmondelay as *Chumli;* soon enough knew our cop was their *constable,* our trailer truck their *articulated lorry,* our newsstand their *kiosk,* our flashlight their *torch,* our fruit and vegetable dealer their *costermonger.* A friend and lawyer, Norman Schur, Anglophile but strictly American-born and -bred, wrote the most intriguing of books, *British Self-Taught: With Comments in American,* defining some two thousand differences.

I was charmed by the grocery department in Fortnum & Mason's, the salesclerks (*clarks*) in morning coats and striped trousers; by the splendor of the food hall in Harrod's; on Sunday mornings bewildered by the freakish men and women at Speaker's Corner spouting from soapboxes their theories and venting their spleen about everything. There were surprises every day and at every corner. I had walked the same path in Kensington Gardens a hundred times before stopping to glance at a slab of stone lying in the ground: "In memory of William Forsyth, long the keeper of these gardens, after whom the shrub Forsythia is named." Of course—as though I didn't know! Which indeed I didn't. I made my presence known in two dozen different libraries, including those maintained by the Bee Keepers' Association and the Cremation Society, but not the Madrigal Society because madrigals are not for me.

Enough Americans were in residence—businessmen, authors, reporters—so that one never felt alien: Henry Pleasants and Alexander Colt, both with the *International Herald Tribune;* John Crosby, once television critic for the New York *Herald Tribune;* Arthur Schwartz, composer; Richard Asher, of Columbia Records; Stanley Kapner, in charge of public relations abroad for Time-Life; Russell Anderson, in charge of McGraw-Hill overseas publications; Frank Cornwell, of Monsanto; Howard Goodkind, of the *Encyclopaedia Britannica;* Sam Jaffee, once famous Hollywood agent; Willa Petschek, writer; Allan Hurlburt, once art director of *Look;* Nunnally Johnson, Chester Erskine, and Walter Shensen, film writers and producers; Mort Nasitir of Billboard Publications; William Yelverton of the Kiplinger organization; Victor Lownes, who ran the local Playboy Club; Max Wilk, author; Phil Kaiser, second in command at our embassy; Gordon Riess, handling Ford Motor Company matters in Europe; Burt Shevelove, playwright and producer; Roland Gelatt, foreign editor of *Saturday Review;* and of course John Bainbridge of *The New Yorker.*

It is different now, I know, and the regrets are universal; but I have been talking about the London I lived in, London at its loveliest and most gracious.

43

The British are a private people, want to be left alone, resent any intrusion in their lives. The imminence of the Census in 1971 posed problems for the government. Not that the citizens didn't recognize the need for a census at regular intervals, but their backs were up anyway. Even something as innocuous as "Do you go to your place of business by bus or underground?" provoked arguments. "Whose bloody business is it but mine? Next thing you know, they'll be asking if I take a nip at night." The approach to the populace was timid, kindly, paternal, only slightly menacing. "We apologize for the chore we are inflicting on you. But we can't guess our way into the future, can we, by assuming we are this and that when, for all we know, we may be nothing of the sort?" At the end a gentle "For your help, we thank you." And then a postscript: "There are penalties of up to £50 for failing to comply."

On Friday, April 16 of that year, 105,000 enumerators personally delivered to the millions of households the questionnaires that had to be filled out on Sunday, April 25, for the seventeenth British census in 170 years. "We dislike the word 'enumerators,' it's long and ungainly, but tradition has saddled us with it."

For several prior months a folksy but vigorous campaign had been conducted by the government, via press, radio, and television, to persuade the country the questions were essential. Stressed especially was the absolute confidence in which the accumulated information would be held. "Your answers are strictly private. They go into computers and simply become statistics that will help us determine future housing, education, health, and traffic needs. Nobody will know your name or address."

"Who is the head of your household?" Not a frightening question; but, damn it, it was *prying*. Whether or not there was an inside toilet in their home they considered nobody's business but their own. Immigrants in particular were chary about questions having to do with their date of arrival and the birthplaces of their parents. "But we want to be sure," said the government, "that our immigrant communities get their future share of homes and jobs. Britain is a melting-pot nation—we want to be fair to everybody."

All households were provided with copies of the questions in English, Italian, and Greek; and also in Urdu, Bengali, Gujarati, and Punjabi. It was mandatory, however, for answers to be in English, only the finicky Welsh being permitted, if they preferred, to use their own language.

What intrigued me most about the census was a letter directed to education authorities throughout the country. "Children are being invited, for the first time," it began, "to take part in a census—to make Census Day the most recorded day in British history. Pupils are invited to write about *their* day and their lives on April 25th, so that future historians will know what it was like being young in Britain in 1971. We do not want essays—just first-person records of local life, like diaries, telling about the things that happened to them on Census Day, the people they met, the clothes they wore, who came to dinner, how their fathers grumbled filling in their forms, and their mothers couldn't remember the dates they were born."

For a hundred years the best entries would be stored in vaults beneath Somerset House, the children were told, and there would be no prizes—except that the writers of the most interesting diaries would become, in effect, "a part of history." Each school head was asked to select up to four submissions. "There is only one rule, the rule of Census Day: secrecy. Children must show their diaries to parents before submitting them to teachers. This is to ensure that children do not commit to history information which is none of the business of historians anyway."

After persistent pleading and crossing my heart and pledging Scout's Honor, after conferences of the top officials among themselves and references to courts and ethics committees, permission was granted me to read the five hundred entries that would be hidden away until January 1, 2071. "You must remember the utmost confidentiality of this material" was the warning dinned into my ears. *What* confidentiality? Xeroxes had been made, on the entries given me all names and addresses of children had been carefully removed!

I read through almost four hundred. If one fact impressed me above any other it was the evidence of close family relationships. On Census Day 80 percent of the children and their parents visited briefly or were visited by grandparents, uncles, aunts, and cousins. There was an occasional sad note, such as "When we got home, Alistair and I found that our daddy was there. You see, mummy and daddy are separated, and daddy comes up every Sunday. He comes up and we have tea, and then he goes away again."

On Census Day the overwhelming majority of children went to church, though not all of them with enthusiasm. "Helen and I sat in our usual place and exchanged our weekly news of dances, discotheques, youth clubs, and new films. Sometimes, like many people today, I doubted the existence of God." "Went to our little Methodist Chapel and sang my favorite hymn which is jesus wants me for a sunbeam and I put 2½p on the plate. The rest is boring."

Almost a third of the children that Sunday were giving some attention to books. "I read another 40 pages of Sense & Sensibility and noticed that in the book there are three sisters but in the telly series there are only two sisters and I shouldn't have thought BBC would have allowed such a drastic change." "I read wind in the willows again but I don't know what for."

I learned they received more of their news from radio and television than from newspapers. "BOAC's jumbo jet, only ¼ full, took off this afternoon." "The funeral of Papa Doc, dictator of Haiti, was held today. His coffin was solid bronze and bullet-proof, though why anyone should try and shoot a dead man is beyond me." "More trouble in Ireland. Nothing but trouble." Quite a few children were impressed by Princess Anne, "who came fifth in the Badminton Horse Trials today."

Here and there was a depressing line: "Dad was made redundant a week ago. He is worrying when he will find some other work. Mum is worried and I am too. I made him a cup of tea." Here and there was a personal problem: "Andrew came to spend the evening with me. Mum and Dad went visiting somewhere. My sister Fran kept coming in. Dad had told me he told her to. I said didn't he trust me, and he said no." Here and there appeared a glimpse into the future: "I think all countries will talk the same language, no colour discrimination, eat a week's meal in a pill. I live in Kirby. Our population is 375. Expected to rise to 470 by 1981."

From the youngest child of seven who wrote "I had sugarpuffs for breakfast, we played hideandseek" to the oldest child of fifteen, there emanated a naïveté and sense of awareness that must be common to every land. "I went to the toilet and took care of myself." "I made tea and Daddy came down in his old gown. I was relieved to see he had his pyjama trousers on. Sometimes he forgets them and the sight of two hairy legs at breakfast is quite repellant."

In the diaries was material for future archivists that will reveal in guileless detail the haunts and habits of a nation: what kinds of food the people ate and what it cost, the brands of soap and dentifrices they used, and the kitchen utensils; the size and color of coaches and buses; the names of periodicals read; descriptions of supermarkets and the variegated stalls in Petticoat Lane; the games played, the football teams cheered for, the fashions worn, with uninhibited comments on minis, midis, and maxis, and on hot pants in particular.

Attached to some of the diaries were bus tickets, car-park tickets, playing cards, clippings from newspapers listing television and wireless programs, theater and musical events, sports, weather reports, horoscopes, and advertisements. Many children, some with commendable skill, made drawings and paintings of themselves and their parents, of their homes and pets and gardens. Four children spent pocket money to buy and attach postage stamps for their descendants to observe.

Thus in Somerset House, the repository for all records of births and deaths and marriages, at the beginning of the year 2071 there will be found an encyclopedia of childhood. It may represent the most authentic and comprehensive story ever told of the life of children in one country on a given day at a given point in time. If it contains no hint of Kipling and vanished empire, no rallying cry to God and King, there will be at least this unequivocal if only twice-mentioned reference to a people who have given so much of their law and culture to the world: "Nobody but the English know how to make a proper cup of tea."

My experience then, with the results of the children's contributions to Census Day, was one of the most rewarding I have known.

For all the frenzied gallivanting, there was one thing I began to miss: regular deadlines. Life had become snug and self-indulgent. I still had miscellaneous matters to look into for Norton Simon, Inc., but on the whole there were too few obligations. In the summer of 1973, when I was seventy-three, to the dismaying exclamations of friends who thought I was too old, I decided to publish a fortnightly newsletter for American citizens living in foreign countries. Called *The Overseas American,* I wanted it to be a professional product, one to be proud of, to report on taxes, schools, voting rights, homes, hotels, clubs, medical services, consulate services, residence permits, driving licenses, jobs, currencies, exchange rates, markets, passports, places to visit and others not to—even on how an American male wanting to get away from it all could join the French Foreign Legion and assume a new identity. The project would demand a substantial investment. Norton Simon, "Dear Abby" Van Buren, and another friend from California, Sheldon Wilson, volunteered to invest as much money as I. As editor and general overseer of operations was the brilliant Roland Gelatt, just recently resigned from *Saturday Review.* As managing editor there was David Walker, the most intelligent young American we could find in London. In addition to a local staff of six, we had correspondents—a few full-time, most of them from Associated Press and United Press part-time—in Japan and Italy, Thailand and Greece, Portugal and Polynesia, Belgium and Spain, Austria and Germany, Holland, Kenya and Lebanon. We covered the continents. It was a time-consuming venture. We worked day and night, inquired and learned. Told how to find a qualified doctor in the interior of Africa, where to get English-language newspapers in Egypt and kosher food in Ireland, why not to go to Algeria, what problems would be encountered in opening a bank account in Switzerland, where to engage a baby-sitter (called child-minder in England). When Britain proposed to introduce a tax penalty on resident foreigners, Mr. Gelatt prepared a questionnaire to learn how many would plan to leave the country. The response was amazing and made headlines in the local press. Still my favorite letter was from a woman in Norway: "My husband lost the issue in which you listed the good small hotels of Paris. Can you send another copy quick and help save a marriage?"

It was exciting, all of it. Gratifying, all of it, with nobody giving a thought to anything but having a newsletter that intrigued its readers and rendered a valuable service. It was also costly, the income from the $35 annual subscription price not remotely enough to meet expenses. Though my services and my wife's were contributed free, the first hundred thousand dollars was soon gone, the three silent but generous partners joining me in providing additional funds.

For all the labor, there was so much satisfaction. Now and then, however, a twinge of regret, concern about the distance between our new home and our old, a pang about being so long away. There was, also, a health problem. The heart that had served so long and so well was losing its regular rhythm. At the finish I wanted to be back where I had been born.

By the beginning of 1975 there were glowing reports about preparations for our country's Bicentennial. Our native land was getting ready for an unparalleled celebration. My wife and I began to long to be there for the observance, and to stay. The flights to New York to see our little family had not been frequent enough and we hadn't ever stayed long enough—we were yearning to be closer. We were becoming homesick.

Reluctantly, with misgivings, I transferred *The Overseas American* to a group of English publishers, depositing sufficient funds to ensure that subscribers would receive the copies to which their subscriptions entitled them.

We reached the inevitable decision; began to bid our adieus, take last looks at what had become so familiar and dear to us. We sold our flat. In the fall of 1975 we booked passage, boarded the *Queen Elizabeth*, and were on our way. As we approached the Statue of Liberty, I saluted again. We were home.

Over the years I had been around a fair part of the world; seen Buddhist temples and the Taj Mahal, the Acropolis and the Little Mermaid; walked among Japanese and Chinese, Viennese and Yugoslavs and French and Indians. I had seen their towns and their treasures. But for me all their sights and wonders weren't London, not a patch on London. London had become my other city, England my other country.

44

At midnight we sat by the window with our then five-year-old grandson and watched the fireworks in Central Park herald the 200th anniversary of the birth of our country.

Life resumed a familiar pattern, of sorts. The bookshelves were in, and stacked. We found new but uncaring domestic help. A different dentist. A doctor who would make house calls! Change-of-address cards had been signed and mailed.

In London I had met Edward R. Downe, Jr., there on a visit. Having disposed of the holdings acquired in the old Curtis company, then formed Downe Communications, which he sold to Mason-Charter, he now had some desire to return to publishing. We joined forces, set up a partnership, anticipated a little challenge and perhaps some fun. We furnished elaborate offices, then for a year studied magazine properties brought to us to buy; magazines dedicated to gourmets, working women, astrology, astronomy, computer technology, the breeding of horses—two dozen in all that were brought to us. All sought help; not any of our experience, only money—Mr. Downe's money, because it was mostly his that was our capital. Nothing that we examined was what we wanted. Everything we saw was what we didn't want. So we sold the partnership and came out, astonishingly, with a profit.

I returned to my reading, unlike Prospero began to find

my library a dukedom not quite large enough. I added to
my anthology files. Basically I was aimless, came down now
and then with a case of the fidgets. Thought of having another go at *War and Peace*, from start to finish, no interruptions. Well into his eightieth year, an editor, unlike a
certain general, is not necessarily ready to fade away. I
wasn't ready at all. If not with the same stride, at least I
could walk a far distance. I could devour three meals a
day, sometimes four, and still not gain weight. Inderal tablets kept heart beating in normal rhythm. I continued with
minor chores for Norton Simon. Here and there experienced a moment of frustration. A lifelong habit, the compulsion to be busy, was not likely to change. There had to
be a project. Take up tap dancing? Kathryn Murray might
have approved, my doctor wouldn't. Really try to be a Sunday painter? Mr. Simon would have chuckled. Perhaps I
could write a book. Everybody else writes a book. There!
But I was an editor, not a writer. And anyway, if a book,
about what, for whom, to what purpose? I had no great
message to give. I had no message at all. But maybe some
anecdotes, about how things were, as they had seemed to
me. "Go ahead," Kenneth McCormick of Doubleday said,
"take a whack at it." I began to make some notes, opened
old files, unearthed diaries, letters, memoranda. Suddenly it
was looking like an adventure. And at last, in shorthand, I
began:

*There wasn't any uncertainty about it, I never
wanted to be anything but an editor.*

Appendix

FIFTY BOOKS THAT OFFER AN OVERVIEW
OF THE MOST POPULAR FICTION
PUBLISHED FROM 1900 TO 1930

The Green Hat: Michael Arlen
Black Oxen: Gertrude Atherton
The Gay Cockade: Temple Bailey
The Barrier: Rex Beach
The Four Horsemen of the Apocalypse: V. Blasco-
    Ibáñez
The Woman Thou Gavest Me: Hall Caine
The Brimming Cup: Dorothy Canfield
The Common Law: Robert W. Chambers
Sorrell and Son: Warwick Deeping
Jalna: Mazo De La Roche
Bad Girl: Viña Delmar
The Private Life of Helen of Troy: John Erskine
Show Boat: Edna Ferber
The Great Gatsby: F. Scott Fitzgerald
The Little Shepherd of Kingdom Come: John Fox, Jr.
The Forsyte Saga: John Galsworthy
Riders of the Purple Sage: Zane Grey
Mamba's Daughters: DuBose Heyward
The Garden of Allah: Robert Hichens
The Shiek: Edith M. Hull
If Winter Comes: A. S. M. Hutchinson
The Constant Nymph: Margaret Kennedy
Main Street: Sinclair Lewis
The Call of the Wild: Jack London
Gentlemen Prefer Blondes: Anita Loos

When Knighthood Was in Flower: Charles Major
Of Human Bondage: W. Somerset Maugham
Graustark: George Barr McCutcheon
The House of a Thousand Candles: Meredith Nicholson
The Pit: Frank Norris
Mother: Kathleen Norris
The Great Impersonation: E. Phillips Oppenheim
All Kneeling: Anne Parish
All Quiet on the Western Front: Erich Maria Remarque
The Man in Lower Ten: Mary Roberts Rinehart
Scaramouche: Rafael Sabatini
The Tree of Heaven: May Sinclair
The Jungle: Upton Sinclair
Topper: Thorne Smith
The Girl of the Limberlost: Gene Stratton-Porter
Dere Mable: Edward Streeter
Penrod: Booth Tarkington
The Greene Murder Case: S. S. Van Dine
Mr. Britling Sees It Through: H. G. Wells
The Age of Innocence: Edith Wharton
Rebecca of Sunnybrook Farm: Kate Douglas Wiggin
The Bridge of San Luis Rey: Thornton Wilder
The Virginian: Owen Wister
Beau Geste: P. C. Wren
The Winning of Barbara Worth: Harold Bell Wright

BOSWELL WRITES A BOOK

The following is from his advertisement
for the First Edition of his *Life of Johnson.*

I at last deliver to the world a Work which I have long
promised, and of which, I am afraid, too high expectations
have been raised. The delay of its publication must be im-
puted, in a considerable degree, to the extraordinary zeal
which has been shown by distinguished persons in all quarters to supply me with additional information concerning its illustrious subject; resembling in this the grateful
tribes of ancient nations, of which every individual was
eager to throw a stone upon the grave of a departed Hero,
and thus to share in the pious office of erecting an honoura-
ble monument to his memory.

The labour and anxious attention with which I have
collected and arranged the materials of which these volumes are composed, will hardly be conceived by those
who read them with careless facility. The stretch of mind
and prompt assiduity by which so many conversations were
preserved, I myself at some distance of time, contemplate
with wonder; and I must be allowed to suggest, that the
nature of the work, in other respects, as it consists of innumerable detached particulars, all which, even the most
minute, I have spared no pains to ascertain with a scrupulous authenticity, has occasioned a degree of trouble far beyond that of any other species of composition. Were I to
detail the books which I have consulted, and the inquiries
which I have found it necessary to make by various chan-
nels, I should probably be thought ridiculously ostenta-

tious. Let me only observe, as a specimen of my trouble, that I have sometimes been obliged to run half over London, in order to fix a date correctly; which, when I had accomplished, I well knew would obtain me no praise, though a failure would have been to my discredit. And after all, perhaps, hard as it may be, I shall not be surprised if omissions or mistakes be pointed out with invidious severity.

TYPICAL REVIEWS OF THE ALGER BOOK

"It is thin, sorry stuff" (*The Nation*). "Mr. Mayes' book is interesting for the amount of material in it upon the times in America when Alger was writing his countless books" (*North American*). "Horatio Alger, while worth a good magazine essay, or a chapter in a history of popular literature, is not worth a $3.50 book. Nor is this in any sense a good biography" (*Saturday Review of Literature*). "One could not hope for a better biographer than Mr. Mayes. He has a delicate and whimsical humor which seems to be the best possible medium in which to introduce Alger to the public" (*The Outlook*). "Don't miss it" (New York *Morning World*). "The book is wholly modern in tone and approach, pursuing methods used by other successful biographers; it attempts to pierce through every aspect of Alger's life and takes what seems at times an unnecessary disparaging attitude toward the books which, with all their demerits, were relished as entertaining stuff by at least two generations of American boys" (New York *Times*). "Mr. Mayes' biography of Alger is a little better than the average of its class. Its subject is interesting, its style is undistinguished but vigorous, it summarizes a certain amount of original research and shows a certain feeling for the picturesque, but it is thin" (*The New Republic*). "Author Mayes writes with humor, insight, sympathy, economy and uncanny balance. His book should be welcomed by all" (*Time*).

IN RESPONSE TO A QUESTIONNAIRE SENT TO
CURRENTLY ACTIVE MAGAZINE EDITORS,
THE FOLLOWING LITERARY AGENTS
WERE UNANIMOUSLY MENTIONED
AS BEING RELIABLE

Maxwell Aley Associates
145 East 35th St.

Julian Bach Literary Agency, Inc.
747 Third Ave.

Bill Berger Associates, Inc.
535 East 72nd St.

Brandt & Brandt Literary Agents, Inc.
1501 Broadway

Curtis Brown, Ltd.
575 Madison Ave.

James Brown Associates, Inc.
25 West 43rd St.

Knox Burger Associates, Ltd.
39½ Washington Sq. S.

Collins-Knowlton-Wing, Inc.
575 Madison Ave.

Anita Diamant
51 East 42nd St.

Candida Donadio & Associates, Inc.
111 West 57th St.

Ann Elmo Agency, Inc.
60 East 42nd St.

Barthold Fles Literary Agency
507 Fifth Ave.

International Creative Management
40 West 57th St.

Bertha Klausner International Literary Agency, Inc.
71 Park Ave.

Lenniger Literary Agency, Inc.
437 Fifth Ave.

Robert Lescher
155 East 71st St.

The Sterling Lord Agency, Inc.
660 Madison Ave.

McIntosh & Otis, Inc.
475 Fifth Ave.

Harold Matson Co., Inc.
22 East 40th St.

Scott Meredith Literary Agency, Inc.
845 Third Ave.

William Morris Agency
1350 Ave. of the Americas

Harold Ober Associates, Inc.
40 East 49th St.

Arthur Pine Associates, Inc.
1780 Broadway

Paul R. Reynolds, Inc.
12 East 41st St.

Marie Rodell–Frances Collin Literary Agency
156 East 52nd St.

Russell & Volkening, Inc.
551 Fifth Ave.

John Schaffner Literary Agency
425 East 51st St.

Roslyn Targ Literary Agency, Inc.
250 West 57th St.

(All of the foregoing are
located in New York City)

GRAMMAR IN A NUTSHELL

Three little words you often see
Are articles—A, An and The.
A Noun's the name of anything,
As School, or Garden, Hoop or Swing.
Adjectives tell the kind of noun,
As Great, Small, Pretty, White or Brown.
Instead of nouns the Pronouns stand—
Her head, His face, Your arm, My hand.
Verbs tell of something being done—
To Read, Count, Laugh, Sing, Jump or Run.
How things are done the adverbs tell,
As Slowly, Quickly, Ill or Well.
Conjunctions join the words together,
As men And women, wind Or weather.
The Preposition stands before
A noun, as In or Through a door.
The Interjection shows surprise,
As Oh! how pretty! Ah! how wise!
The Whole are called Nine Parts of Speech,
Which reading, writing, speaking teach.

ENIGMA ON THE LETTER H

Catherine Maria Fanshawe

'Twas whispered in heaven, 'twas muttered in hell,
And echo caught faintly the sound as it fell;
On the confines of earth 'twas permitted to rest,
And the depths of the ocean its presence confessed;
'Twill be found in the sphere when 'tis riven asunder,
Be seen in the lightning, and heard in the thunder.
'Twas allotted to man with his earliest breath,
It assists at his birth and attends him in death,
Presides o'er his happiness, home, and health,
Is the prop of his house and the end of his wealth,
In the heaps of the miser is hoarded with care,
But is sure to be lost in his prodigal heir.
It begins every hope, every wish it must bound,
It prays with the hermit, with monarchs is crowned;
Without it the soldier, the sailor, may roam,
But woe to the wretch who expells it from home.
In the whisper of conscience 'tis sure to be found,
Nor e'en in the whirlwind of passion is drowned;
'Twill soften the heart, but though deaf to the ear,
It will make it acutely and instantly hear;
But, in short, let it rest like a delicate flower;
Oh, breathe on it softly, it dies in an hour.

COMMA CAUTION

Harold Willard Gleason

Be gentle to the comma with its curly little tail:
Though dainty and diminutive, its power turns one
    pale!
It causes much confusion when neglected or misplaced,
So slur it not through ignorance, nor hobble it through
    haste!
Expressions parenthetical (*however* or *said he*),
All nominatives of address, appositives *aussi*,
Inverted-order clauses, which come before the main,
The members of a series (Lizzie, Annabel, and Jane),
Long phrases introductory containing verbal parts,
All nonrestrictive elements (His hobby, *which is arts*),
Dates, addresses in detail (10 Broadway, Hartford,
    Conn.),
Or Saturday, June, '36, and, last to ponder on,
The parts of compound sentences ("Ike hops, but
    Willie flees")—
All these require commas tucked in their interstices.
One may not move a mountain, but one *may* preserve a
    state
By cultivating commas . . . And tomorrow is too late!

THE ASTERISK

Stoddard King

An author owned an asterisk,
    And kept it in his den,
Where he wrote tales, which had large sales,
    Of frail and erring men;
And always when he reached the point
    Where carping censors lurk,
He called upon the asterisk
    To do his dirty work.

THE VOWELS

Jonathan Swift

We are little airy creatures
All of different voice and features;
One of us in glass is set,
One of us you'll find in jet,
T'other you may see in tin,
And the fourth a box within.
If the fifth you should pursue,
It can never fly from you.

WHAT I SAW

A Verse with Semicolons Omitted

I saw a peacock with a fiery tail
I saw a blazing comet pour down hail
I saw a cloud with ivy circled round
I saw a sturdy oak creep on the ground
I saw a beetle swallow up a whale
I saw a raging sea brim full of ale
I saw a pewter cup sixteen feet deep
I saw a well full of men's tears that weep
I saw wet eyes all in a flame of fire
I saw a house as high as the moon and higher
I saw the sun even in the midst of night—
I saw the Man that saw this wondrous sight.

PLURISY

We'll begin with a box and the plural is boxes,
But the plural of ox should be oxen, not oxes;
Then one fowl is a goose but two are called geese,
Yet the plural of mouse should never be meese.
You may find a lone mouse or a whole set of mice,
Yet the plural of house is houses not hice.
If the plural of man is always called men,
Why shouldn't the plural of pan be called pen?
If I speak of a foot and you show me your feet,
And I give you a boot, would a pair be called beet?
Then one may be that, and three would be those,
Yet hat in the plural is hats and not hose.
We speak of a brother and also of brethren,
But though we say Mother, we never say Methren.
Then the masculine pronouns are he, his, and him,
But imagine the feminine she, shis, and shim.
So English, I fancy you all will agree,
Is the silliest language you ever did see.

Index